Books by James Finn

Protest: Pacifism and Politics

*A Conflict of Loyalties: The Case for Selective
Conscientious Objection* (Editor)

Conscience and Command

Conscience
and Command

Justice and Discipline
in the Military

Edited by James Finn

Random House · *New York*

To

Julia Stevenson

Marie Halloran

Theresa Hannon

John Finn

Acknowledgments

Clergy and Laymen Concerned About Vietnam bears the responsibility for a large share of what is valuable in this book. It was at the instigation of that organization—in the persons of its Director, the Rev. Richard R. Fernandez, of the Rev. Richard John Nuehaus and the Rev. Richard Killmer—that I focused long-standing interests of my own on the rights of conscience within the armed forces of the United States.

Several contributors to this volume have provided aid and counsel which only the editor can appreciate. In addition several other people offered encouragement and information when it was badly needed: Melvin Wulf, Chief Counsel, American Civil Liberties Union; Gordon Zahn, University of Massachusetts; Carl Rogers, *Serviceman's* LINK *to Peace;* Arlo Tatum and Michael Wittels, Central Committee on Conscientious Objection; William V. O'Brien, Georgetown University; Stacy Siegle, G.I. Civil Liberties Defense Committee; Clariss Ritter, Workers Defense League. None of these people is responsible for the final shape of *Conscience and Command* and more than one might take sharp exception to some aspects of the book.

I would, in addition, like to thank the editors of the

I would, in addition, like to thank the editors of the *Maine Law Review* in which Edward Sherman has published some material included in this volume. Finally, I would like to thank Susan Woolfson and Jane Johnson for preparing the typescript of this book under great pressure.

Contents

The Two Societies

The Two Societies

James Finn

When a person enters the Armed Forces of the United States, he leaves one society for another. When he enters military society, he leaves behind some of the Constitutional and due process rights which were his in the civil society he is now called upon to defend. This book is intended to pose and probe the question of whether the system of military justice to which he is subjected is necessary, desirable or adequate. Despite the differences among the contributors to this volume, it drives rather directly to a single, firm answer: No, our present system of military justice is not adequate, not desirable, not necessary. There are, of course, many people who dispute these conclusions head on. But, except by quotation, the supporters of the present system are not included here; they *have* their legions.

In his commencement address to the Air Force Academy in Colorado Springs on June 4, 1969, President Richard Nixon said: "I believe that every man in uniform is a citizen first and a serviceman second, and that we must resist any attempt to isolate or separate the defenders from the

defended." A consummation devoutly to be wished. But
unless substantial changes are made within present military
procedures, the President's belief will remain a pious hope
rather than a reality. For the basic freedoms of speech and
press and assembly do not apply to the men in the military
—particularly not to the enlisted man, the ordinary G.I.
That they do not is almost beyond dispute. When it is suggested that the soldier should enjoy the same rights as his
civilian counterpart, defenders of the present system frequently respond as if the suggestion were outlandish. "God
help us if we continue to worry about the interpretation of
the Constitution at the cost of losing our country." This
sentiment of Representative John Hunt (Rep.-N.J.) is
given a more relaxed and pungent expression by a sergeant
quoted in one of the G.I. underground papers: "The Constitution is not Army issue."

The present system of military justice is supported, however, by more than high emotion or complacency. It is also
supported by tradition and a sturdy rationale. When developed by a skilled and dedicated proponent, the rationale
for the present military system can be coherent and com-
pelling. In March of 1970, at a national conference devoted
to Human Rights of the Man in Uniform, a strong expression of the institutional view was presented by Colonel
Samuel H. Hays, a former professor in the Office of Military
Psychology and Leadership, United States Military Academy. "It must be understood," he said, "that the Armed
Forces are objective instruments of public policy whose ultimate duty is to respond to the direction of its political
leadership to impose the national will through the use of
force." For those instruments to be most effective the military must have special structures, operating procedures and
methods of training and discipline, a special doctrine and
a special mystique.

And military justice must also be special. As Colonel Hays explains it, "The primary objective of the system of military justice must always be to maintain discipline within the organization and to ensure prompt compliance with its dictates. With the other systems it must be focused more on producing organizational effectiveness than on punishing or protecting individual action. Unlike the legal systems of the larger society, it must cope with individuals who are subject to great stress, pressure and responsibility and enforce rules and regulations that have no counterpart in civil life. Any punishment meted out must be viewed more from its effect on the organization as a whole than in its effects on the individual. Hence military justice must act as a deterrent to undesirable behavior and an instrument to reinforce organizational standards and command control."

There are people who understand such reasoning to say that discipline takes precedence over justice. According to Colonel Hays, the demands of discipline and institutional effectiveness establish yet other limitations which distinguish civilian from military society. "Given the requirements of the institution and the society it supports, the values supported by the rights of freedom of speech and press simply do not apply in their entirety. Support for the military institution and its ability to defend society must take priority even if it requires some restrictions on those rights normally possessed by the citizens. In varying degrees the constraints against freedom of speech apply to other rights as well." And, one last quotation from Colonel Hays, "Today the soldier is required to give complete loyalty and obedience to his organization and service. Whatever it says he must do, go where it directs, fight whomever is indicated and suffer whatever must be suffered. If the institution is to be responsive to public needs it must be so."

We are, with these statements, some distance from President Nixon's statement of belief. The general weight of military opinion and procedure is, however, on the side of Colonel Hays. One could readily find historical and contemporary spokesmen who, in their own terms, support the Colonel. But both in and outside of the Armed Forces there are men who disagree and who oppose, in thought, word and deed, his version of the relations between the individual soldier, the military institution and the larger society of the United States. In different ways they argue first, that military justice falls far short of its claimed intentions; between theory and practice there falls the dark shadow of command influence, that is of the commander who unduly and improperly influences the outcome of courts-martial. Second, they argue that the levels of justice to which the military aspires are inadequate. Third, they argue that present methods of training and discipline encourage if they do not indeed provoke conflicts between the soldier who wishes to be autonomous and the military institution.

And some at least press on to make what is possibly the most difficult and delicate argument: that if proper modifications are made in the system of military justice, in the traditional military view of constitutional rights, and in the present disciplinary system, the result will be an armed force with no less strength, servicemen with higher morale, and a society with greater faith in its military institutions. If I myself did not believe this to be the case I would judge the present pressure to reform the military to be both frivolous and dangerous. For the United States is and for some time will continue to be a great power with great responsibilities. Whether it functions well or badly in international affairs, it will need and it will have formidable military might. Given a choice between an effective fighting force and the extension of human rights to the man in service, there are officials with high political office and many citizens with none who will unhesitatingly choose the former. My contention is that such a choice is not necessary, that there are significant changes that can be made now, changes which will not render our fighting forces less effective and which will enlarge the area of freedom for the serviceman. I do not expect most spokesmen for the military to agree that real modifications are necessary or desirable. They rarely have. The impetus must come, initially, from the servicemen who know first hand the conditions to which they are subjected, and then from an aroused citizenry who can appreciate some of the unwelcome and unwholesome consequences of those conditions.

As our military leaders would probably be the first to admit, however ruefully, dissenting servicemen are doing a disturbingly good job of calling attention to what they regard as inequities and injustices, degradation and cruelty in the armed services. Even as they have consented to the draft they have insisted upon its inequities and have expressed sympathy and sometimes support for the draft resisters and deserters who have fled to other countries (at least 40,000 of whom have emigrated to Canada). They are neither mollified nor persuaded by such observations as that made by Daniel P. Moynihan some years ago: "The world is unjust; most people know this and, perceiving the impartiality of the injustice meted out by the draft boards, accept the decision." [1] It is not that these servicemen disagree with that judgment; it is rather that they are determined not to be part of "most people."

Once inducted into the armed services they do not agree that their views and attitudes must be restructured to conform with those of their military superiors, up to and including the Commander-in-Chief. Nor do they understand why they should keep in suspended animation their very lively views on major moral and political issues, e.g., the war in Southeast Asia. They regard themselves not as professional soldiers with a life-long commitment and allegiance to military traditions and mores but rather as civilians in uniform who have the citizen's rights and obligations to engage in national debate on the crucial issues of the day, not the least of which is a military conflict in which they may be killed.

These dissenting servicemen have searched out means, traditional and innovative, to express their views and opinions. They have written letters to congressmen and editors; they have participated in anti-war demonstrations, on and off post, in uniform and in civilian clothes; they have boycotted mess halls and have gone on massive "sick-calls"; they have published, printed and distributed fliers, posters, pamphlets and underground newspapers that criticize, often in harsh and obscene terms, military personnel, military doctrine, military tradition—in short, everything military; they have formed united groups and unions in order to wield collective strength; they have held "war-crime trials" in which our highest military and political leaders are judged to be criminals; they have, in Army indoctrination courses, challenged the official version of the immediate history which has brought them to those very courses; they have refused to engage in activities which directly support a war effort they have come to regard as immoral and unjustified; they have united many of these activities in off-base coffee houses designed especially for the continuing education of dissenting G.I.'s; and when these activities have brought them into conflict with their superiors and they are subjected to harassment, disciplinary punishment or courts-martial they have done their best to see that their cases are brought to public attention. Radio, press and television, they have learned, are their allies.

And how has the military responded to these activities?

In the words of a *New York Times* editorial: "Army authorities have tended to respond to these signs of independent thought in the ranks with all the imagination of tradition-bound automatons. . . . The Army certainly has an overriding concern for the preservation of discipline, which can be a life-or-death matter for the soldiers themselves under battle conditions. But the employment of McCarthy-type inquisition tactics and the imposition of Neanderthal disciplinary practices from the 'theirs-not-to-reason why' days are not going to command the respect and obedience of the educated young men needed to man a modern army." [2] To which I would add only that there are a number of not-so-educated young men who are equally unimpressed with such tactics and practices.

But what are these tactics and practices? Are they really so harsh and unfair, or are we being taken in by the grievings of a generation whose permissive parents have failed to inculcate respect for authority, discipline, order? In the annals of G.I. dissent, the growing list of well-publicized cases argues against that thesis. For those who are familiar with these cases if only through reading the daily papers, whole clusters of issues are associated with names such as Levy, Noyd, Stapp, G.I.'s United, The Fort Hood Three, Daniel and Harvey, the Priest, the Presidio 27, Henry Howe, UFO, Stalte and Amick, Bruce Petersen. But as different as the cases are, what they have in common, in the minds of many people, is a miscarriage of justice.

Consider the case of Pfc. Bruce Petersen, founding editor of *Fatigue Press,* Fort Hood's on-base underground paper, and a participant in the Oleo Strut, a G.I. coffee house in nearby Kileen. With variations in detail his case was reported in a number of underground newspapers. The essentials on which they agree state that in the fall of 1968, Petersen was twice arrested by Kileen police on charges of possession of marijuana. Microscopic analysis of the lint in his pocket allegedly proved that he was in possession of marijuana although the evidence was destroyed in the process of the analysis. The possession of such minuscule amounts of marijuana, even if existent, is not grounds for conviction in a civilian court. But when Petersen was turned over to the Army he was immediately charged with two violations of Article 134 of the Uniform Code of Military Justice (UCMJ), held in pre-trial confinement in the post stockade for two months before going to court, subjected to a general court-martial in which all prosecution motions were sustained, all defense motions denied, and sentenced to eight years hard labor in Leavenworth and a dishonorable discharge.

When Petersen's case came to review, the Judge Advocate General's office declared that he had been subject to illegal search and seizure, that since the alleged offense had occurred off-base and was non-connected with duty the Fort Hood authorities lacked jurisdiction, that due process of law had been violated in trial procedure and that for such an offense the sentence was cruel and unusual. After fifteen or so months in confinement, Petersen was freed. Although Fort Hood officers denied any connection between Petersen's anti-war activities and his trial, G.I.'s remain skeptical. Their skepticism is reinforced by the harassment of other G.I. coffee houses and the sentencing of the three operators of the UFO, a coffee house at Fort Jackson, to six years in prison for maintaining a public nuisance. They are also skeptical of a system of justice which tries four G.I.'s who attempt to set up a "War Crimes Commission" while a captain actually charged with such crimes tours the country to substantial acclaim.

But aren't these admitted faults or failures in the application of military justice simply the mistakes that are inevitable in an organization that must cope with close to 3.5 million servicemen and women? Couldn't we find similar kinds and a proportionate number of failures in our system of civil justice? Isn't the Army simply the unfortunate whipping boy at a time of deep societal fears and frustrations?

The last question demands a developed response, but the answer to the other questions must be a firm No! The cases of justice miscarried, of men penalized, radicalized and brutalized, are not simply the fault of human weakness and frailty with which we must live. They are that, but they are more. They are also the result of a system to which the "judge" is as much a thrall as is the "judged." Nor do the reports on those cases simply represent journalistic enterprise in digging up isolated instances of injustice and brutality. The evidence is altogether too available, too abundant to allow us to rest on that happy, comfortable assumption. It would be more accurate to say that what is reported, what receives even minimal public attention in radio, press and television is the tip of the iceberg, the great mass remaining submerged and unexposed. Harris Tobias, a young G.I. who fought his way through to a successful CO claim at a great cost of time, money and spirit, stated one aspect of the problem quite accurately: "If I'd been a green kid, broke, just out of high school and basic training, I'd still be in jail." [3] Many who answer that description still are.

To return to an earlier question. Is not the Army our public whipping boy today, everybody's favorite scapegoat? There is some truth to that allegation. But even as we assert that the military is partly responsible that this is the case, we should also assert—and attempt to show—that there are deep underlying reasons for present criticism of the military, reasons over which the military has no control but to which it is subject.

We are tempted today to trace every discontent in our society back to the war in Vietnam, to see it as the cause of everything from student riots to irregular sunspots to in-grown toenails. We must recall ourselves to the certain knowledge that the fortunes of the United States and of the world do not turn wholly on the state of Vietnam. There are other vicissitudes in our domestic and foreign affairs and other reasons for them. Granting that, we are nevertheless right to insist that the war in Vietnam is a cause of severe dislocations in our society and that the military institution of the United States is one of the battlegrounds for conflicting views of how that war can best be resolved and how the policies which led to it and support it can best be either strengthened or overturned.

In attempting to confine and dampen down that conflict the Army places severe restrictions upon the extent to which soldiers are free to explore and express divergent views about the war and related issues. The official view is that the military man can entertain private views and opinions on the war but open prosyletizing, especially on base, is forbidden. Once the Commander-in-Chief has spoken, the soldier—as distinct from the citizen—ceases to speak and act against the established policies. His duty is now to fulfill them. There are two major things wrong with that proposition: first, it is, today, unrealistic; second, the military does not, in this instance, mean what it says, or, to put it more circumspectly, it applies its rules with high selectivity.

Unrealistic. Consider the young man faced with the draft today. It is possible that he has remained oblivious to the larger world around him and accepts unquestioningly his passage through the draft and the Armed Forces. Or he may support the U.S. venture in Vietnam and willingly accept a place in the military. Or he may go questioningly and reluctantly. Or—and this is the group that disturbs the

Armed Forces—he may have attended to our national debate over the years and be conscious of such facts as these:
that the war in Vietnam is opposed by most of our Western
allies, by leaders high in our government, by religious leaders and high councils of the major religious faiths in this
country; by an increasing number of those officials who
initiated or offered early support for U.S. military engagement in Vietnam; by a variety of people knowledgeable
about Southeast Asia, its people, its culture, its politics; by
the editorial policies of leading newspapers in this country;
by a number of retired military leaders; and possibly by
close friends, family, teachers and counsellors. And he may
have engaged in anti-war activities in comparison with
which the activities of these critics would be remarkably
pallid.

If this young man does not become a draft dodger, he
will enter the Armed Forces with ideas notably different from
those to which he will be exposed in military service. Is it
realistic to expect him to keep his views to himself, not to
attempt to counter what he regards as incorrect information
and bad judgment? Is it not more realistic to expect that he
will seek out others whose views coincide with his own, and
to support and strengthen his and their position by open
discussion and joint activities? And that if such activities
are met by what appears to be—and often are—harsh and
arbitrary measures, that his own critical views will not only
be strengthened but hardened? And if the young man cracks
under that system and learns to keep his views to himself,
can we realistically say that he has learned to be a better
citizen? To raise such questions is not to say that they can
be easily resolved. They cannot. Questions of free speech,
even in civil society, are often complex and tangled and
there is no reason to think that they are simplified because
they are militarized. But today, now, it is the military which

insists that these complicated questions have simple answers, that "military necessity" is the single overriding criterion. Given the unpopular character of the war in which we are engaged and the society from which our conscripted Army is drawn, it is the Army's response which is unrealistic. There is much to be said for the statement that the Army cannot allow political proselytizing, that its function is to fulfill the will of the civil authorities, not to determine it. But surely the danger of military control or influence— insofar as that is a danger in the United States—is located in the upper echelons of the military, not down among the enlisted men and the lower-ranking officers. As Leonard Boudin reminds us in his article, it was General Douglas C. MacArthur who posed his politico-military judgment against the President, not the men under him. But, of course, one of the reasons that we are generally unaware of the political aspects of addresses and speeches by high military leaders is that—most frequently and not surprisingly—they fortify what are the present government policies. On the whole, it is better that the military support rather than challenge government policy. But we should not blind ourselves to the fact that military leaders *do* have political positions and they *do* make them known publicly and at public expense. When General William C. Westmoreland, for example, appears before Congress to report on the war, and diverges to make an invidious comparison between the men who are fighting and the men and women who are protesting, he has strayed some distance from the area of military expertise which is expected to be his. When Colonel Frank Borman returns from outer space and urges us, on television, to support the President's plans for Vietnam, he, too, is engaging in political talk. When Major James N. Rowe prepares programs for radio and television in favor of U.S. policy in Vietnam and criticizes those who are distressed with that policy, he cannot be regarded as politically virgin. Nor do his public statements allow us to think he and his superiors are naive or unaware of what they are doing. He knows that his "military" statements are also political. "We are entering into an ideological conflict," says Major Rowe, "where the political and the military are married into one. If somebody says you can't speak and stay in the military, I would resign. . . . The thing is, you're going to have to choose sides." Now there is a speech that would bring the audience in any G.I. coffee house to its feet loudly applauding, particularly that bit about resigning. And that's what I and many others mean when we speak of selective application of some Army regulations. High Army officials *know* themselves to be dedicated, patriotic, honest men, and that their views openly expressed can only strengthen the sound policies of our government; it is those dissenters, mostly part-time soldiers, whose views are questionable who must be kept under control. In the attempt to establish such control the Army has, with erratic impartiality, clamped down on the expression of dissident views.

These dissident views, the military understands, go far beyond the question of Vietnam. As Westmoreland told the Senate Armed Services Committee, "There are disturbing indications that deliberate efforts are being made to introduce the divisiveness found in our society into the Army." Another but overlapping view was expressed by Lieutenant General A. O. Connor in an attempt to explain the large increase in the number of desertions: "Getting more kooks into the Army, for one thing. We are getting more men who are coming in undisciplined, the product of a society that trains them to resist authority." [4] Add to these comments Robert McNamara's remark when he was Secretary of Defense that drafting into the Army many well-educated young men would noticeably complicate the problems of that institution and we have the basis of a real insight undeveloped by any spokesmen for the Army. For the divisiveness noted by General Westmoreland is real; it extends throughout our society. The hope, implicit in his comment, that it can be kept out of the Army is not only baseless but dangerous. He may view himself as the heroic boy stopping the leak in the dike, holding back the forces of anarchy and disorder, but the person who wishes to keep divisive and dissenting views out of the Army is more like King Canute attempting to beat back the waves of the ocean. The Armed Forces are a separate society, but not that separate.

What is at work in society today is a renewed perception of the individual person, of what he may become in a true community, and what he can and has become under the pressures of our major institutions. This perception is not always clear to those who have it; it is often distorted and sometimes put in the service of ugly and destructive forces. This active perception is not the sudden and surprising discovery of youth and youth culture. It is the outcome of many decades of thought and perception by people who have striven for the more complete liberation of the human being. The fact that this perception has been distorted by some who would elevate the individual will into sovereign rule does not negate the real insight that our major institutions are failing us, that however necessary they are, today these institutions unnecessarily hobble the human mind and spirit. It is no accident that the institutions subjected to most severe attack today are the Church, the State and Education as they are presently incarnated. As an adjunct of the State, the military establishment cannot be immune from that attack.

General Connor correctly identified one large area of concern and dissension when he spoke of the resistance to authority. For authority as it has long been exercised is now a matter for real scrutiny and concern. Can we believe that the concepts of authority and obedience as they are understood in the military are beyond improvement, that they are adequate to our stated beliefs of the relation of the citizen to the state, of our society to the Armed Forces? The many examples and cases explored in this book provide some intellectual tools for examining this question. In brief compass, however, the Army's handling of the Son My incident dramatically highlights the problem.

The Son My story was, of course, buried for a long time before a soldier with a memory and a conscience and an enterprising reporter helped to uncover it. When it was uncovered, the Pentagon initiated a study under Lieutenant General William E. Peers in which fourteen officers of various rank, up to and including the commanding officer of the America division, were charged with various crimes. Within the Army, reactions to that study varied, but shock was the most common. Said one colonel, "This may be a virtue carried to a dangerous excess. First of all, it may give us a new breed of soldier, who will stop and ask why, and when that happens you're in trouble in combat. Second, it may shatter the individual soldier's faith in his professional leadership. That's equally fatal. Third, it makes a man feel pretty bad when he hears about his fellow career officers facing this kind of charge after distinguished service." [5]

But there is already a new breed of soldier who does not think authority is conferred simply by fiat. Though it cannot be divorced from office or rank, authority will nevertheless be strengthened or dissipated by the way in which it is employed. It is not well employed when it expects blind trust and attempts to stop soldiers from asking why, if it expects command always to take precedence over conscience. It is not well employed when it is used to protect career officers under the general principle of protecting the armed services. Yet these seem to have been the working principles in this particular incident. After a four-member panel of a House subcommittee pursued the investigation of the alleged massacre of March 16, 1968, Representative F. Edward Hébert of Louisiana said, "The committee was hampered by the Department of the Army in every conceivable manner." Another member of the committee, Representative Samuel Stratton of New York, added that they were "stymied at every step of the way by the Secretary of the Army and top Army brass." [6]

Our present method of recruiting armed forces, the nature of the present conflict in Southeast Asia and the deep self-questioning and self-investigation taking place in our society have their inevitable repercussions within the military establishment. We can ignore the questions of conscience and command, of constitutional and human rights, which are raised within the armed services today only if we refuse to see and hear the evidence mounting around us that our ignorance and indifference are purchased at a cost that is inhumanly high, far too high for a nation and society whose stated intent it is to extend and preserve the area of man's freedom. At a minimum we should support strongly and attempt to implement the statement of Senator Sam J. Ervin of North Carolina: "I can think of no more fitting expression of this country's appreciation for the sacrifices of our young servicemen than to grant them the same rights they are defending."

Notes:

1. Daniel P. Moynihan, "Who Gets in the Army?" *New Republic,* Nov. 5, 1966, p. 19.
2. *New York Times,* April 13, 1969.

3. Brian Donovan, "The Man Who Beat the Army," *New Republic,* Jan. 31, 1970, p. 19.

4. *Milwaukee Journal* (June 20, 1969). Quoted by Gordon Zahn in "Conscience and the Soldier," unpublished manuscript.

5. *New York Times,* March 19, 1970, p. 4.

6. *New York Times,* July 16, 1970, p. 15.

Justice in the Military

Edward F. Sherman

The system of law maintained by the American military for the control, discipline, and punishment of its personnel is something of an anomaly among modern legal institutions. Clemenceau's remark that "military justice is to justice what military music is to music" catches rather well the paradox in applying the term "justice" to the court-martial system. Historically, the court-martial has been primarily concerned with the discipline and control of troops, a function which is not always consistent with the objective of providing a fair and impartial legal system for the trial of persons charged with crimes. Despite reforms over the years which have removed many aspects of the old "drum-head" court-martial, military justice has retained some of its distinctly military aspects. "A court-martial," as the Supreme Court wrote in a 1969 decision, "is not yet an independent instrument of justice but remains to a significant degree a specialized part of the overall mechanism by which military discipline is preserved." [1]

Historical Development of American Military Justice

Military justice in the United States has always functioned as a system of jurisprudence independent of the civilian judiciary, with its own body of substantive laws and procedures. The first American Articles of War, enacted by the Continental Congress in 1775,[2] copied the eighteenth-century British Articles of War which had, in turn, evolved from the seventeenth-century rules adopted by Gustavus Adolphus for the discipline of his army. Despite subsequent alterations by Congress, the American military justice code still retains a number of substantive and procedural aspects of the eighteenth-century British code. Dissimilarity between military and civilian criminal law has been further encouraged by the isolation of the court-martial system. The federal courts have always been reluctant to interfere with the court-martial system; as explained by the Supreme Court in 1953 in *Burns* v. *Wilson:* "Military law, like state law, is a jurisprudence which exists separate and apart from the law which governs in our federal judicial establishment. This Court has played no role in its development; we have exerted no supervisory power over the courts which enforce it . . ."[3] As a result, the court-martial system still differs from the civilian court system in terminology and structure, as well as in procedural and substantive law.

The procedural framework of the court-martial evolved over the years as a practical means of formalizing punishment of soldiers and sailors. Its principal characteristic was control by the commander. Since military units were sometimes isolated from other units and the civilian population, it was necessary that court-martial authority be decentralized, with lower-echelon commanders having power to convene a court-martial and staff it with their own officers so that a verdict could be rendered quickly and the unit could get back to its main tasks. Thus, the court-martial had to be a relatively simple proceeding with few legal formalisms, sometimes conducted in the field with a drum as a desk, hence the term "drum-head justice." There was little pretense at providing an impartial and adversary "judicial" hearing. No one blushed in admitting that the court-martial was not a real trial, that the commander used it to enforce his disciplinary policies and inculcate military values in his men, that it was administered by officers alone, that there was no right to review, and that the penalties were calculated to set an example and not to provide equal justice.

Throughout the nineteenth century and well into the twentieth, the court-martial system remained relatively unaffected by civilian notions of criminal law and judicial due process. Perhaps the best example of the military's attitude is the statement of General William T. Sherman, Commanding General of the Army from 1869 to 1883, before a congressional committee in 1879:

> [I]t will be a grave error if by negligence we permit the military law to become emasculated by allowing lawyers to inject into it the principles derived from their practice in the civil courts, which belong to a totally different system of jurisprudence.
>
> The object of the civil law is to secure to every human being in a community all the liberty, security, and happiness possible, consistent with the safety of all. The object of military law is to govern armies composed of strong men, so as to be capable of exercising the largest measure of force at the will of the nation.
>
> These objects are as wide apart as the poles, and each requires its own separate system of laws, statute and common. An army is a collection of armed men obliged to obey one man. Every enactment, every change of rules which impairs the principle weakens the army, impairs its values, and defeats the very object of its existence. All the traditions of civil lawyers are antagonistic to

this vital principle, and military men must meet them on the threshold of discussion, else armies will become demoralized by even grafting on our code their deductions from civil practice.[4]

General Sherman's view of military justice was consistent with his emphasis upon professionalism in the small volunteer post-Civil War Army, and until World War I this view was generally accepted and rarely criticized. However, the nature of the issue changed dramatically with World War I. Court-martial abuses during World War I and outrageously severe sentences led to the first public movement for the civilianization of military law. For the first time the question was asked why members of the military had to be subjected to a system which failed to afford them the constitutional and due process rights to which they would be entitled in civilian courts.

The World War I movement for civilianization was led by General Samuel T. Ansell, the acting Judge Advocate General of the Army. In sharp contrast to the prevailing view as described by General Sherman, General Ansell argued that the military system itself was foreign to our American system of justice and was injuring the effectiveness of the Armed Forces:

> I contend—and I have gratifying evidence of support not only from the public generally but from the profession—that the existing system of Military Justice is un-American, having come to us by inheritance and rather witless adoption out of a system of government which we regard as fundamentally intolerable; that it is archaic, belonging as it does to an age when armies were but bodies of armed retainers and bands of mercenaries; that it is a system arising out of and regulated by the mere power of Military Command rather than Law; and that it has ever resulted, as it must ever result, in such injustice as to crush the spirit of the individual subjected to it, shock the public conscience and alienate public esteem and affection from the Army that insists on maintaining it.[5]

General Ansell called for major changes in the court-martial system which, had they been adopted, would have removed many of the traditional peculiarities of military law and embraced many of the modes of civilian law. Instead of vaguely defined crimes he called for the drafting of military crimes with definiteness. In place of a court-martial controlled by the commander through his powers to appoint the court members, oversee the administration of the court, and review the sentence, Ansell called for an independent military judge, a court chosen by the judge rather than the commander, and the right of the accused to have a portion of the court chosen from his own rank. Ansell further asked for definite limits of sentences, a mandatory and binding pre-trial investigation, right to lawyer counsel, and a civilian court of military appeals. In short, General Ansell urged the partial remaking of the military law system along civilian court lines and the reworking of military substantive laws and due process procedures in conformity with civilian standards.

Most of General Ansell's proposals were rejected by the Congress with only a few reforms reflected in the new Articles of War passed in 1920.[6] However, the movement for reform of military justice was renewed with increased vigor after World War II. "When Johnny came marching home again from World War II," wrote Robinson O. Everett, Commissioner of the Court of Military Appeals, "he brought with him numerous complaints about justice as then dispensed in the Army and the Navy. Many of these were prompted by a conviction that the administration of military justice had not always lived up to the goals of fairness and impartiality which were accepted as part of the American legal tradition." [7] More American servicemen than ever before had experienced military justice first hand,

and it was clear that they did not like it. There had been over 1.7 million courts-martial during the war (out of 16 million men on active duty), most of them resulting in convictions. There had been 100 capital executions, and 45,000 servicemen were still imprisoned when the war ended. Some 80 percent of the courts-martial were for acts which would not have been crimes in civilian life, with AWOL and desertion the most frequent charge.

Undue severity of sentences was once again a principal complaint. A Clemency Board appointed by the Secretary of War in the summer of 1945 to review all general court-martial cases where the accused was still in confinement, remitted or reduced the sentence in 85 percent of the 27,000 cases reviewed. Substantial numbers of servicemen who had never been in trouble with the law served time in military jails and came home from the war with military records showing court-martial convictions or less than honorable discharges. Senators and Congressmen were flooded with complaints. Rear Admiral Robert J. White described the ground swell of criticism against military justice: "The emotions suppressed during the long, tense period of global warfare were now released by peace, and erupted into a tornado-like explosion of violent feelings, abusive criticism of the military, and aggressive pressures on Congress for fundamental reforms in the court-martial system." [8]

A long and sometimes bitter battle for court-martial reform was waged from the end of the war until a compromise military justice bill was finally passed by Congress in 1950. Extensive reforms were urged by bar associations, special investigating committees, veterans' organizations, and large numbers of veterans who felt they had not been treated fairly by the military justice system. However, the military opposed those reforms which would remove commanders' control over court-martial machinery and appointments and which would introduce such civilian aspects as a trial conducted by an independent judge rather than the senior non-lawyer military officer, right to trial by a jury of peers, and broad civilian review of court-martial convictions. The military argued that the Armed Forces would be weakened if command control over courts-martial were removed, and a number of prominent generals, including Generals Bradley and Eisenhower, made strong pleas for preserving the traditional role of the commander. At a meeting of the New York Lawyer's Club on November 17, 1948, General Eisenhower stated:

> I know that groups of lawyers in examining the legal procedures in the Army have believed that it would be very wise to observe, in the Army and in the Armed Services in general, that great distinction that is made in our Governmental organization, of a division of power . . . But I should like to call your attention to one fact about the Army, about the Armed Services. It was never set up to insure justice. It is set up as your servant, a servant of the civilian population of this country to do a particular job, to perform a particular function; and that function, in its successful performance, demands within the Army somewhat, almost of a violation of the very concepts upon which our government is established . . . So this division of command responsibility and the responsibility for the adjudication of offenses and of accused offenders cannot be as separate as it is in our own democratic government.[9]

A committee which was appointed in 1948 by the Secretary of Defense to draft a Uniform Code of Military Justice (UCMJ) completed its work in early 1949. It offered a code which extended substantial new due process rights to servicemen (for example, servicemen would be entitled to a lawyer in a general court-martial and certain cases could now be appealed to a newly created civilian Court of Military Appeals), but which retained the basic structure of the court-martial system and preserved command control. Arthur E. Farmer, chairman of the War Veterans Bar Association committee, expressed the disappointment of many reformers:

> [t]he basic reform which the court-martial system requires and without which no real reform is possible—the elimination of command control from the courts—is conspicuously lacking [in the new Code]. Under the Uniform Code the commanding general will still appoint the members of the court, the trial counsel and the defense counsel from members of his command, and will review the findings and sentence. We will still have the same old story of a court and counsel, all of whom are dependent upon the appointing and reviewing authority for their efficiency ratings, their promotions, their duties, and their leaves.[10]

Hearings were held on the UCMJ in March and April, 1949, and the committee's draft was passed without substantial change. The UCMJ was signed into law by President Truman on May 5, 1950, and took effect on May 31, 1951.[11]

The period since the passage of the UCMJ in 1950 has brought continued improvements in the quality of military justice. Substantial expansions of servicemen's due process rights in courts-martial have resulted from the decisions of the United States Court of Military Appeals, a civilian tribunal which was created by the UCMJ. Expanded federal court review of military determinations has also furthered the process of applying civilian constitutional standards to the military. However, in a period in which there were immense legal changes in our society, reflected by such significant developments as—under Chief Justice Warren—the Supreme Court's revolution of criminal due process and acceptance of new broader concepts of civil rights and civil liberties, the developments in military justice were not remarkable. Attempts at further legislative reform of military justice since the UCMJ have been limited. Despite considerable support for introducing additional civilian law elements in the UCMJ (a number of groups proposed changes in the UCMJ in the 1950's, including a proposal by the American Legion that command control finally be removed), reform bills languished in Congress. The only major change in the UCMJ has been the Military Justice Act of 1968 [12] which, although it adopted further civilian court practices, did not make basic changes in the court-martial structure or the command control of court-martial machinery.

Military Justice in the Vietnam War Period

A recurring phenomenon in the history of military justice reform in this century has been the challenge which each new war has raised to the adequacy of the court-martial system. For example, the relatively non-judicial court-martial system which General Sherman found acceptable for the small volunteer army of the late nineteenth century was proven inadequate for dispensing justice to the large conscripted army of World War I. And likewise, the still heavily disciplinarian court-martial system which survived the limited post-World War I reforms proved inadequate in the prolonged global hostilities of World War II. Today, with the Vietnam war, we are witnessing another test of the adequacy of the court-martial system. Because the Korean War was relatively short and the UCMJ did not take effect until the middle of it, and because of the relatively low level of conscription throughout the 1950's, the UCMJ had never been put to a real test. But with the increase in the draft accompanying escalation of American involvement in Vietnam in the middle 1960's, the military justice system has been put to the test, once again, of dispensing justice to a huge conscripted armed force in time of war. Its record has not been favorable and it now appears, as many predicted, that the concessions made to the military in the UCMJ in 1950 have seriously compromised the quality of court-martial justice and limited the ability of the military justice system to provide fair and impartial justice to servicemen.

The unique nature of the Vietnam war has also brought special challenges to the traditional system of military justice. In addition to the particular strains on the military in attempting to prosecute a war to which a portion of the population is opposed, the intense national self-examination and social awareness loosed in America by the war have raised questions never before asked concerning many of the premises on which the present military justice system rests. Levels of militarism and authoritarianism which had been generally accepted in our society in the past have now been subjected to question. Traditional attitudes which accepted the premise that servicemen, whether volunteers or draftees, are not entitled to most of the basic rights of citizens, particularly First Amendment rights, are no longer accepted without dispute. And traditional notions of patriotism which, in past wars, have tended to accept certain individual injustices within the military as necessary for the successful conduct of the war, no longer satisfy many who see unnecessary injustice, brutality, and waste in the system of military justice and discipline. The result has been the growth in the late 1960's of an active and vocal reform movement calling for fundamental changes in the UCMJ.

Present Deficiencies in the Court-Martial System

Although there are differences between the procedural due process rights guaranteed in military and civilian courts, today they are quite similar, and this is not the principal area in which courts-martial are vulnerable to attack. Probably the most objective assessment of military and civilian due process rights (such as protection against unreasonable searches and seizures, self-incrimination, and double jeopardy and the right to a speedy and public trial, to discover evidence, and to subpoena witnesses) would find them roughly equal, with, perhaps, a slight edge for the civilian procedures because of the command control aspect which still detracts from certain military rights. However, as regards the manner in which crimes are defined and charged, the court-martial convened, the personnel chosen, the verdict arrived at, and appeal made, the military comes off less favorably.

1. *Crimes and Punishments*: The UCMJ, in format and substance, resembles a modern penal code. It includes both typically military crimes (such as AWOL, desertion, and disobedience of orders) and civilian crimes (such as murder and larceny). Although prior military codes claimed only limited jurisdiction over civilian crimes committed by servicemen, the UCMJ extended court-martial jurisdiction to all servicemen's crimes, military or civilian. It also established court-martial jurisdiction over certain civilians such as persons accompanying the Armed Force in the field in time of war or outside the United States. However, in a series of cases beginning in 1955, the Supreme Court struck down court-martial jurisdiction over discharged servicemen, civilian dependents overseas in peacetime, and civilian employees of the military overseas. Then, in June, 1969, in the landmark decision of *O'Callahan* v. *Parker*,[18] the Supreme Court held that courts-martial also lack jurisdiction over offenses committed by servicemen which are not "service-connected," finding no jurisdiction over a serviceman charged with attempted rape while off-post, off-

duty, and in civilian clothes. Thus the attempt of the UCMJ to create an all-inclusive court-martial jurisdiction has failed, and, in light of language in *O'Callahan* indicating that the Supreme Court feels courts-martial offer an inferior brand of justice, it is possible that further contractions of court-martial jurisdiction will take place.

Although most crimes in the UCMJ are defined with clarity and specificity, the UCMJ retained two types of traditional military offenses which, in a civilian context, would probably be held unconstitutionally vague and unduly restrictive of First Amendment rights. First, the UCMJ failed to remove certain traditional military crimes imposing particularly authoritarian limitations on servicemen, such as "contemptuous words against the President [and other government officials]" (Article 88), and "provoking or reproachful words or gestures towards any other person" (Article 117). Second, it left intact the two open-ended crimes: "conduct unbecoming an officer and a gentleman" (Article 133), and "all disorders and neglects to the prejudice of good order and discipline in the Armed Forces" and "conduct of a nature to bring discredit upon the Armed Forces" (Article 134). These offenses play an important role in the "disciplinary" function of the military justice system. The speech limitations of Articles 88 and 117 are rarely enforced and, because they set such rigid limitations, it is unlikely that uniform enforcement could be accomplished. However, they serve as a source of selective enforcement against certain non-favored individuals or groups, much like the old "no spitting on sidewalks" ordinances. Thus, the first prosecution under Article 88 since 1951 was the court-martial in 1965 of Lieutenant Henry Howe for carrying a sign reading "END JOHNSON'S FACIST AGRESSION IN VIETNAM" and "LET'S HAVE MORE THAN A CHOICE BETWEEN PETTY IGNORANT FACISTS IN 1968" [*sic*] in a peaceful off-post rally while off-duty and in civilian clothes.[14] The vague standards of Articles 133 and 134 also enable the commander to exact extensive conformity from his men by giving him a wide latitude as to what acts will be considered criminal. Since the commander also has the power to select the court from among his officers and to exercise a variety of administrative functions in connection with the trial, the court-martial serves as a deterrent which accomplishes far greater conformity to official standards and attitudes than does the civilian criminal law process.

The military establishment views these vaguely defined crimes not as setting a trap for the serviceman but as providing the commander with the tools which he needs for insuring good order and discipline. From the military point of view, efficiency in combat is the paramount consideration, and the idea that such efficiency can only be obtained by strict compliance of servicemen with military standards of conduct, guided by an unwritten code of honor, lies deep in military tradition. There is still a strong feeling among officers that the only alternative to strict discipline and absolute obedience to an undefined code of military conduct is chaos. Thus, the military sees the general articles as providing the commander the power to insure that his men live up to the "higher" standards required of servicemen and views the criminal sanctions of the court-martial as the ultimate means of enforcing these standards.

In a day when most servicemen will not see combat, when substantial numbers of servicemen live off-post and lead a nine-to-five military existence, and when even in combat such qualities as initiative, creativity, and intelligent reaction have replaced the old standard of blind obedience to orders, military emphasis on obedience to a rigid and unspecified code of conduct administered by commanders with criminal sanctions is subject to question. Thus, there is a basic policy conflict between military demands for broad tools, such as the general articles, to enforce the conformity it feels is necessary to maintain military efficiency and civilian demands for greater military concessions to individual diversity.

It appears unlikely today that there would be an adverse effect upon military efficiency if these vaguely worded crimes were either abolished or made applicable only in non-judicial punishment (under Article 15 a commander can assess a variety of punishments, including forfeitures of pay, demotion, and up to one month in custody, without using a court-martial). It is true that a commander would no longer be able to hold over his men's heads the threat of a court-martial for unspecified conduct which he considers prejudicial to good order and discipline. But he would still have substantial "disciplinary" powers, and these minor disciplinary powers, rather than the threat of court-martial, have always been the primary means of enforcing discipline in the military. Since the power to court-martial under vague standards tends to encourage an arbitrariness of command, it can itself have an adverse effect upon morale.

The structure of military punishments also reflects a disciplinarian philosophy. The *Manual for Courts-Martial* contains a table which sets the maximum punishments which can be given in a court-martial for various crimes. Some maximum punishments, especially for certain military crimes, are too high, and there are not enough subcategories so that findings of less culpable elements can result in a smaller maximum sentence. Also, since a military tradition still persists that courts-martial should give a high sentence in order that the commander will have the option of cutting it down on his review, unduly severe sentences are not uncommon in the military. This is especially true in courts-martial in which the command has displayed particular concern or in which the crime is particularly offensive to the military court members. Thus the first three men court-martialed for participating in a brief sit-down strike to protest stockade conditions and the shooting of a prisoner at Presidio, California, in October, 1968, were sentenced to fourteen, fifteen, and sixteen years respectively (later cut down to two years in an unprecedented intervention by the Judge Advocate General after intense public outcry).[15] Similarly, Vietnam war dissenters have received heavy sentences ranging from several years to ten years for such crimes as "conduct unbecoming an officer" and making "disloyal statements." The reflection of individual attitudes and biases in sentencing is, of course, also present in civilian courts. However, the fact that members of courts-martial are not chosen at random from the community, but are selected from the commander's officers, severely restricts the type of person chosen for court-martial duty and tends to encourage a disciplinarian approach to sentencing. Thus the procedure for sentencing in a court-martial—with high maximums, few sub-categories, unusual review powers in the commander encouraging court members to give too high sentences, and restriction of court members to the officer class—tends to encourage a "disciplinary" quality which is out of place in a modern criminal law system.

2. *Role of the Commander*: The most important difference between military and civilian justice after the passage of the UCMJ lies in the role of the commander in a court-martial. Under the civilian criminal law process, different functions are performed by independent individuals: the district attorney decides whether to prosecute; the grand jury determines whether to indict; the defense counsel has no connection with any of the other participants; the jury is picked at random from the community; the judge and

other court officials have no relation to the district attorney; and the appellate courts are independent tribunals. In a court-martial, the commander plays a role, in varying degrees, in all of these functions. He decides whether to prosecute; he has the power to handpick the jury from his command and, in some services, the trial counsel and defense counsel from his legal officers; he has certain supervisory powers over the administration of the trial; and he has the power to review the findings and sentence.

The Military Justice Act of 1968, by creating military judges independent of the commander convening authority, removed one court-martial function from the commander's control. And, it is true, commanders do not usually handpick court members or counsel, leaving this up to one of their staff officers, such as the staff judge advocate, and do not become involved personally in the administration of most courts-martial. However, the ultimate power still lies with the commander and, in cases in which he is particularly interested, he frequently takes a hand in the selection of court and counsel and in various administrative matters. The military cases have upheld the convening authority's power over a variety of supervisory and administrative matters connected with a court-martial. He has the power to enter into a pre-trial agreement with the accused whereby he promises to cut down the sentence in return for a guilty plea. This is an immensely important part of military justice prosecution; there are guilty pleas in two-thirds of all Army general courts-martial and almost three-quarters of these are negotiated pleas. The convening authority rules on defense motions to subpoena witnesses and obtain other evidence before trial. He can excuse court members both before and, in certain limited situations, after the trial has begun. The Court of Military Appeals has even held that the convening authority can, if he disagrees with the decision, reverse a court's dismissal of charges granted on such grounds as denial of a speedy trial, and order the court to try the man anyway.

The administrative functions in connection with the trial which are carried out by the commander's staff judge advocate are usually performed without direct supervision by the commander but are subject to his overall control. In a typical case, the staff judge advocate might confer with the commander about an individual concerning the commander's desire to court-martial. He might then advise the commander as to legal issues regarding the court-martial, select the counsel and court members with or without instructions from the commander, carry out a variety of impartial functions related to the preparation for and administration of the trial, including giving advice and instructions to counsel, and finally advise the commander concerning review of the conviction and sentence. The potential for conflict of interests is increased by the fact that the staff judge advocate is considered first and foremost to be the commander's lawyer, and the staff judge advocate's office to be the commander's law firm. As former Judge George W. Latimer of the Court of Military Appeals has stated: "If we look the facts in the face, we must realize that presently the staff judge advocate is the officer who is suspected of being a messenger of conviction. He is always pictured as the alter ego of the commander." [16]

The military defense of the command-dominated structure of the court-martial process rests on the concept of unified command authority. It is argued that if the commander could not demand the unqualified obedience and loyalty of all legal personnel, he would lose effective control of discipline within his unit. This is not to say that the military position assumes that the staff judge advocate or the defense counsel will compromise the interests of the accused under pressure from the commander. The military takes pains to emphasize that although the staff judge advocate and the defense counsel are directly responsible to the commander and are charged with insuring that the interests of the command are preserved, nevertheless they are also charged with insuring that the rights of the accused are protected. There is no problem in serving both the interests of the command and the accused, the military maintains, because they are the same.

The problem with this analysis is that, in fact, the commander and accused often have different views of what rights the accused has and what is a fair and impartial proceeding. Commanders, no matter how conscientious, can become personally involved in disciplinary matters and court-martial cases, and this involvement can color their view of how the case should be handled. Likewise, the juggling of interests by the staff judge advocate and his legal officers can become a difficult process, for they too experience the inevitable conflict which arises when they are expected to maintain loyalties to two individuals whose interests are not, in fact, the same. The military, which tends to minimize possible conflicts between the interests of the command and servicemen and puts great faith in the ability of officers to perform conscientiously in a variety of assignments, sees no conflict of interest here; civilians, who emphasize independence of administrators, do.

The UCMJ, although it preserved the commander's control over court-martial appointments and administration, attempted to prevent him from influencing the trial unfairly. Thus the commander-convening authority of any court-martial is forbidden from censoring court members, military judge, or counsel with respect to the outcome of a court-martial and from attempting to coerce or influence, by unlawful means, the action of a court-martial (Article 37).

The reformers had substantial doubts about the efficacy of this provision to prevent commanders from influencing courts-martial, as is indicated by the testimony of Arthur Farmer before a congressional committee in 1949:

> The provisions of Article 37 which prohibit the censure of the court and counsel and any attempt to coerce the court's actions will be valueless in a situation where the commanding general desires to circumvent them. It is naive to suppose that it will be necessary for the commanding general to use such direct means of influencing the court that they could form the basis for prosecution under Article 37.[17]

Farmer thus predicted that, first, commanders would find indirect ways of influencing a court-martial and second, that even when their actions went beyond the permissible boundaries, the prohibitions in the UCMJ probably wouldn't do much good. His predictions seem to have been accurate. There has never been a case, since the enactment of the UCMJ, in which a commanding officer was prosecuted for improper command influence, despite the fact that there is considerable evidence, from the testimony of ex-servicemen as well as affidavits filed in military cases, of direct and unlawful attempts by commanders to influence courts-martial. The Court of Military Appeals has become sufficiently concerned over the extent of unlawful command influence to establish a new procedure for dealing with complaints of command influence, observing that "in the nature of things, command control is scarcely ever apparent on the face of the record . . ."[18] The most serious case of command influence arose in 1967 when the commanding general of Fort Leonard Wood, Major General Thomas Lipscomb, was charged with improper command influence in ninety-three court-martial cases. There was evidence that General Lipscomb, who had decided on a "get tough" court-martial policy for the post, had indicated his displeasure to court

members and counsel when he felt court-martial verdicts or
sentences were too lenient, had widely disseminated his
views that court-martial sentences were too low, and had
taken personal control over a number of court-martial administrative functions to insure that courts-martial carried
out his disciplinary policies. A military investigation found
he had acted unwisely, although not illegally, but the Court
of Military Appeals reversed all ninety-three cases. No action
was ever taken against the General.

Although the weakness of the UCMJ prohibitions in pre-
venting improper command influence is a matter of concern, a far greater concern today is the extent of legal command influence. Commanders, exercising their legitimate
rights provided under the UCMJ, are in a position to have a
substantial effect upon the outcome of the court-martial
process. The degree to which commanders take an active
role in the operation of courts-martial varies a good deal
with the personality of the commander and the type of case
involved. New commanders sometimes tend to feel an obligation to "shape up" the unit by tightening discipline, and
therefore take a more personal interest in the court-martial
process. Most commanders view certain types of cases as
particular threats to discipline and order—such as cases involving alleged homosexual acts, barracks thefts, disobedience, and any kind of political organizing or dissent—and,
in a desire to have an example made for the rest of the men,
often become personally involved in the court-martial process.

The rise of anti-war dissent organizing in the military
during the Vietnam war period has been viewed by most
commanders, at both lower and higher echelons, as a serious challenge to the military. Thus, in most cases in which a
serviceman has been court-martialed for activities related
to anti-war dissent, the immediate commander, and often

higher commands right up to the Pentagon, have been directly involved in the court-martial process from initial investigation through final review. This command involvement has been so intense as to raise serious doubts about the impartiality of the courts-martial which have resulted. First, there has been tremendous command control over the process for investigating and bringing charges. Although the UCMJ requires investigation before charges can be referred to a general court-martial, the commander is not required to follow the recommendations of the investigating officer (unlike civilian law where, if the grand jury refuses to indict, the district attorney is not permitted to prosecute). Although the recommendations of the investigating officer are usually followed, commanders have disregarded them in a number of Vietnam war dissenter cases, notably in the well-publicized case of Lieutenant Dennis Morrisseau.[19] [See pp. 75–102—Ed.]

The 1969 Presidio courts-martial provide a similar example. A young legal officer, Captain Richard H. Millard, was appointed as investigating officer for six of the servicemen charged with mutiny for participating in the short sit-down strike. He was well aware that the commanding general, General Stanley R. Larsen, felt strongly that the men should be prosecuted for mutiny, and he was personally warned by his superior "not to investigate too deeply." [20] He enraged the command by finding, after conducting his investigation, that there was insufficient evidence, and recommending that the mutiny charges be dropped and that several of the men either be discharged or tried for lesser offenses in a special court-martial (where the maximum confinement would be six months). His recommendations were overruled, and the men were tried and convicted of mutiny in courts-martial which resulted in such severe sentences that there was an unprecedented intervention by the Department of the

Army, after intense public outcry, to reduce them. Similarly, in a recent Vietnam war dissenter case, certain court-martial charges against Seaman Roger Priest, arising out of his publication and distribution of an anti-war servicemen's newspaper, containing derogatory comments about government officials and encouraging anti-war activism, were dismissed as legally insufficient by a military judge, but reinstated on the order of the commander.

In addition to the commander's absolute power to court-martial a serviceman, command influence has been apparent in other phases of the courts-martial of Vietnam war dissenters. The choice of the officers to sit on the court-martial, which is at the sole discretion of the commander, has frequently indicated an attempt to select men whose attitudes, experiences, and prejudices will be in sympathy with the prosecution in dissenter cases. Thus, in the court-martial of Captain Howard Levy, in which Levy's civil rights activities in the South and anti-Vietnam war views were prominent issues, the commander chose a court of ten career Army officers, seven of them white Southerners and most of them recent Vietnam war veterans. Two Black Muslims, Corporal William Harvey and Private George Daniels, were sentenced to six and ten years respectively for making "disloyal statements" in a bull session to the effect that Vietnam was a white man's war and black men should not fight there. They were tried by courts made up, with one exception, of career Marine officers, one of whom stated that he disliked Black Muslims and would not want one in his unit, another that he did "not go along with demonstrations" because they "constitute a breach of the peace to the degree that they get notoriety," and another that he felt black Marines have no business concerning themselves with the problems of their race.[21] Similarly, the Presidio courts-martial were made up predominantly of career officers (the command had ordered that no second lieutenants or warrant officers be included), including an officer who bowled weekly with the chief prosecution witness, and others who stated that they felt even peaceful demonstrations lead to violence, disliked protests and the American Civil Liberties Union, and "deplored" demonstrations.

The role of the commander has been especially prominent in the conduct of the trial itself in many of the Vietnam dissenter courts-martial. Dissenter cases such as those of Levy, Morrisseau, "the Presidio 27," and "the Fort Jackson Eight" (involving eight members of G.I.'s United Against the War in Vietnam, who had been organizing among fellow soldiers at Fort Jackson in the spring of 1969) —all involved commanders who were intensely sympathetic to the prosecution and who personally directed or approved a number of the administrative activities connected with the court-martial. The commanders exercised such administrative powers as ruling on defense motions to subpoena witnesses and evidence (Captain Levy's lawyers claim they were denied the right to subpoena key witnesses and to see critical classified information, and military defense counsel in the Presidio cases were unable to obtain a number of military documents and letters claimed to be misplaced) and to obtain various due process procedural guarantees (military defense counsel in some of the Presidio cases were refused a verbatim transcript of the pre-trial investigation).

The fact that a commander is known to be personally interested in obtaining a conviction can itself create an atmosphere favorable to the prosecution. Military counsel and court members, especially career men dependent upon the command for duty assignments, ratings, and promotions, can be affected by the command position. In the Presidio case, one of the defense counsel, a young non-career captain, observed afterwards: "I know now that you should always get a civilian lawyer. We were under such tremendous pressure not to challenge the structure of the court, not to challenge the pre-trial advice, not to challenge the system." [22] Finally, the commander's influence has been especially felt in the sentencing and review in Vietnam dissenter cases. Most of the dissenter cases resulted in unusually high sentences (Lieutenant Howe received two years for carrying his sign, Captain Levy three years for anti-war statements and refusing to teach Green Berets, Corporal Harvey and Private Daniels six and ten years for disloyal statements, Privates Amick and Stolte four years each for distributing anti-war leaflets), and commanders have almost universally approved these severe sentences *in toto* despite the fact that court-martial sentences are usually reduced by commanders.

The Vietnam war dissenter cases, because they aroused intense antagonisms in military commanders, provide especially severe examples of the abuse of command control over courts-martial. The problem goes to the heart of the military justice system which has centralized too much power in the commander. As a consequence of his responsibility to insure order and discipline among his men, he is ill-suited to overseeing and carrying out supposedly impartial judicial functions. One might still be willing to overlook the capacity for abuse in command control if convinced that, as the military argued so forcefully when the UCMJ was being debated, it is essential to the proper functioning of the military. However, it appears more and more today that command control of courts-martial has little to do with efficiency in the military.

A reduction of commanders' powers over military justice is consistent with the trend which has been taking place in the military since World War II. There is a certain ana-

chronistic ring to arguments that any lessening of a commander's powers over the personnel and administration of
courts-martial would weaken his ability to maintain discipline among his troops. The truth is that the nature of the
military has changed dramatically since World War II, and
likewise the nature of discipline has had to change. Technology has transformed the military into a highly bureaucratic society. A whole new class of enlisted men, called
specialists, came into being after the Korean War, made up
of those who perform technical jobs outside a troop environment. Many servicemen work in jobs not much different
from that of a civil servant or a corporation employee, and
substantial numbers live off-post. Only about 10 percent of
today's servicemen have MOS's (job descriptions showing
their occupation speciality) which involve combat skills,
while 54 percent hold technical specialties (electronics,
mechanics, crafts, etc.) and the rest hold service specialties
(food, administration, clerical, etc.).[23] In short, today's military is a big business, with a substantial portion of its members being non-career civilian-soldiers who serve their
country in a service job or at a desk.

This change in the nature of the military inevitably calls
for a re-evaluation of traditional military attitudes towards
discipline and the role of the commander. Two of the traditional commandments of military discipline, absolute and
unquestioning obedience to commands of superiors and absolute conformity to official attitudes, have already been seriously undercut. After Nuremberg, men in the ranks cannot
escape individual responsibility for acts which they are ordered to do, and the Court of Military Appeals has further
undercut the concept of absoluteness of orders by creating a
number of areas in which a serviceman is not bound to follow the orders of a superior. The following language of a

board of review in *United States* v. *Kinder* (1953) indicates the change in attitude towards the relationship of a serviceman to his commander:

> The obedience of a soldier is not the obedience of an automaton. A soldier is a reasoning agent. He does not respond, and is not expected to respond, like a piece of machinery. It is a fallacy of wide-spread consumption that a soldier is required to do everything his superior officer orders him to do.[24]

A similar alteration of attitude has taken place concerning the obligation of servicemen to conform to official attitudes and demands. No young man who enters the service today has escaped the influence of the individualistic and democratic values of our society, and it is more and more difficult for the military to command the absolute conformity to official views it once could. The current movement for expanded servicemen's rights, particularly as regards exercise of First Amendment rights involving reading and expressing dissenting views, has already led to rewriting of regulations to permit certain of these activities. The substantial number of court cases still pending may further extend servicemen's individual rights.

These changes have significantly reduced the role and the power of the commander. Whereas once the commander possessed the authority to control virtually every aspect of the life of his men, today there are distinct areas where he lacks authority. In many ways, the military trust in the commander-soldier relationship as the keystone of an effective military is now subject to question. Many servicemen work in a bureaucratic or technical atmosphere, and the command structure, with its rigid notions of caste, rank, and absolute obedience, has little to do with their effectiveness on the job. The traditional view of the commander as an all-powerful *pater familias* is today something of an anachronism and, even among combat troops, the specialization of jobs has removed much of the need for the crude authoritarianism which has always characterized the command philosophy. Our civilian paramilitary, like police and firemen, demonstrate that men can function effectively in life-endangering activities under a normal civilian superior-subordinate relationship where the superior lacks absolute powers and criminal law sanctions. This is not to say that commanders are on the way out, but rather that the role of the commander, except with some modifications in a combat situation, must necessarily be closer to that of a civilian manager.

There is also something unrealistic about the notion that a commander must himself possess all effective powers over his subordinate personnel or his authority and effectiveness will be undermined. This, of course, is the premise behind the contention that a commander must control all functions of a court-martial. Today, with instant communications and easy mobility, there is no reason to believe that a commander's effectiveness would be destroyed if he had to rely upon other agencies to perform court-martial functions. Commanders may once have held their men in check by the fear which their disciplinary powers engendered, but discipline in the modern military is based upon more diverse and complex factors than crude displays of retributory powers. The fact that a commander's authority is not absolute, or that it must be shared with other officials, is not in itself a reason for rejecting that authority. In fact, the young servicemen of today are more sensitive to abuse of authority, brutality, and injustice than to the pettiness of bureaucracy. The fact that their commander, in order to court-martial them, must submit the charges to an independent court administered by impartial officials, is more likely to win their acceptance than the spectre of an all-powerful commander whose control makes a farce out of courts-martial.

Of course, it is difficult to judge what the reactions of millions of servicemen would be to removal of command control of courts-martial, and the foregoing analysis can hardly be considered a scientific prediction. However, it should indicate that there are complicated dimensions to this question, and that the obsession of the military with individual command powers as the only key to military effectiveness fails to take into account both changed conditions and a variety of other relevant factors. There is simply no concrete evidence on which to argue that removal of command control of court-martial appointments and machinery would adversely affect military discipline today.

3. *Membership and Selection of the Court:* The UCMJ provided for a limited right to enlisted men on courts-martial. Upon request, an accused enlisted man would be entitled to be tried by a court made up of one-third enlisted men(the rest would continue to be officers). However, the commander-convening authority continued to have discretion as to appointing court members, and since 1951, whenever there has been a request for one-third enlisted men, commanders have invariably chosen non-commissioned officers, who are usually considered even more disciplinarian and severe than officers. As a result, enlisted personnel are rarely requested (they were requested in only 2.6 percent of Army courts-martial in 1968), and so court-martial duty continues to be pretty much the exclusive province of the officer class.

The UCMJ also failed to provide for random selection of court members, and so a commander, or his subordinates, can still sit down with a list of officers and select those men he would like to have on the court. If court members were selected at random from the entire military community at the particular installation, as juries are chosen in civilian courts, it is likely that a heavy majority of the members would be young men in the lower ranks. The military views this as undesirable, arguing that class antagonisms might prevent lower-ranking servicemen from rendering an honest verdict and cause undue sympathy with the accused. The military has also raised the somewhat contradictory objection that low-ranking enlisted men might be overwhelmed by the presence of officers on the court and therefore not exert their own independence. Finally, the military has argued, low-ranking enlisted men are not qualified to serve on courts-martial because of their lack of experience in the military and their lack of understanding and appreciation of the purposes and objectives of military discipline.

These arguments actually go to the heart of the jury system itself. Permitting an accused to be tried by a jury of his peers chosen at random always involves the possibility that jurors will be sympathetic to the accused, swayed by other members of the jury, or will not appreciate the purposes and objectives of the prosecution and the criminal laws. These qualities, however, are only objectionable if they prevent a juror from judging a case with an open mind, and they have a valuable function in insuring trial by a jury whose members reflect the different experiences, attitudes, and biases found in the community. The all-officer court-martial is especially lacking in these qualities.

There seems to be little basis for arguing that lower-ranking servicemen are not qualified to sit as members of courts-martial. Today, when a high percentage of enlisted men have a high school education and a substantial minority are college-educated, they appear to possess as acceptable qualifications to determine the kind of fact questions which we seek from a jury as the average civilian juror. There may be, however, some risk that court-martial members from lower ranks will be more class-motivated and less objective than the average civilian juror. The young recruit, who has been forced to accept a highly disciplinarian way of life, may harbor deeper antagonisms against a military prosecution than does the average civilian juror towards the district attorney's case. The continued effects of anti-war and servicemen's union organizing in the military and of the movement for expanded G.I. rights have, no doubt, increased anti-establishment antagonisms among some servicemen. Of course, similar problems exist in civilian law, and it has not been suggested that the right to trial by jury of peers should be suspended because, for example, a high percentage of the jury in a prosecution for acts connected with a labor dispute might be sympathetic to the aims of the workers.

A number of military justice reformers have maintained that trial by peers is not adaptable to the military because of the potential bias inevitably created by the military caste system. This view has been expressed by Charles Morgan, Southern Director of the ACLU and counsel for Captain Levy,[25] and ex-JAG officer Luther West, and has been endorsed in a resolution by the National Conference on G.I. Rights which met in Washington, D. C., in November, 1969. They argue that military men can never shake off the disciplinarian attitudes which are basic to military life, and that since the military cannot provide the proper atmosphere for a fair and impartial criminal trial, all military crimes should be tried in civilian courts. The example of the West German army, which has no court-martial system, and of Great Britain, where civilian lawyers carry out the judge advocate functions, lends weight to the feasibility of this position. It seems clear that, at the very least, a broadening of the class from whom courts-martial are chosen and removal of the commander's power to handpick the court members is the one most important reform now needed in military justice.

4. *Post-Trial Proceedings and Appeals:* The UCMJ provides for three levels of review or appeal from a court-martial conviction. All general and special court-martial convictions are reviewed by the commander who convened the court. Only he has the power to remit or reduce the sentence, but, as the reformers have contended, this power tends to encourage courts to give higher sentences in order to give the commander the option of reducing it if he feels it appropriate with his disciplinary policies. The second level of appeal is to the Courts of Military Review (called boards of review before the Military Justice Act of 1968), which are composed of three lawyers, usually career officers, assigned to the Judge Advocate General's office. However, review by these courts is only available in cases involving generals or flag officers or sentences of death, dismissal, dishonorable or bad conduct discharge, or more than a year's confinement, and so many courts-martial do not qualify (there is an additional administrative review in such courts-martial by a legal officer, usually under the commander, and, in some special court-martial cases, by the commander exercising general court-martial convening authority). The final level of appeal is to the civilian Court of Military Appeals. There is no appeal of right to the Court of Military Appeals, which selects from those cases which have already been decided by a Court of Military Review only those which it chooses to review. As a result, it reviews only a tiny percentage of the total court-martial convictions.

The appellate structure of the military justice system needs a thorough overhauling. The administrative reviews by the commander-convening authority and legal officers all too often become a routine without real scrutiny of the record. The power of the commander to review sentences encourages the undesirable practice of courts giving the maximum sentence so that the commander will have the option to cut it down or not, and this power should be removed. The Courts of Military Review are not independent, their availability on appeal is too limited, and they should be extended full equitable powers so that they can provide a genuine forum for relief for servicemen in a variety of administrative matters. The Court of Military Appeals should be enlarged in membership, its writs and equitable powers extended, and its availability in a larger number of cases increased.

Conclusion

The reform of military justice has been a slow process, and the limited expansions of servicemen's due process rights have been painfully won. The court-martial is still an unsatisfactory mechanism for the trial of criminal offenses. The major defects, which have been examined here, go to the heart of the military justice system as it now exists, and substantial changes will be required to bring court-martial justice up to the level of civilian criminal law. It may be that instead of attempting to graft further civilian standards onto a fundamentally alien military law system, it would be better, as other countries have done, to abolish the court-martial system and refer crimes committed by servicemen to civilian courts. However, there are serious logistical problems involved in such a proposal, and the political realities, at least at the moment, do not appear to favor such a radical proposal.

The movement for reform which has been generated by the injustices and inadequacies of the court-martial system during the Vietnam war appears to be a viable force, and it is still to be hoped that genuine court-martial reforms may result from it. The Vietnam war movement has also brought to light basic defects in the overall system of order and discipline in the military and has raised troubling questions concerning the traditional military approach towards free speech rights of servicemen, methods used for training and discipline of troops, and requirements of conformity and obedience. It is to be hoped that the lessons to be learned from the Vietnam war—from the court-martial injustices in the dissenter cases to the horrors of Son My—will not pass unheeded and that, with hard work and determination, genuine reform of military law can still be accomplished.

Notes:

1. O'Callahan v. Parker, 395 U.S. 258, 265 (1969).
2. JOURNALS OF THE CONTINENTAL CONGRESS 1774–1789, at 90 (Lib. of Cong. ed., 1904–1937).
3. 346 U.S. 137, 140 (1953).
4. Quoted in *Hearings on H.R. 2498 Before a Spec. Subcomm. of the House Comm. on Armed Services,* 81st Cong., 1st Sess. 780 (1949).
5. Ansell, *Military Justice,* 5 CORNELL L.Q. 1 (1919).
6. Act of June 4, 1920, ch. 227, 41 Stat. 759, 787.
7. R. EVERETT, MILITARY JUSTICE IN THE ARMED FORCES OF THE UNITED STATES 9 (1956).
8. White, *The Background and the Problem,* 35 ST. JOHN'S L. REV. 197, 201 (1961).
9. Quoted in Letter from New York State Bar Association to Committee on Military Justice, Jan. 29, 1949, at 4, in VI Papers of Professor Edmund Morgan on the U.C.M.J., Treasure Room, Harvard Law School.
10. Statement of Arthur E. Farmer, *Hearings on H.R. 2498 Before Subcomm. No. 1 of the House Comm. on Armed Services,* 81st Cong., 1st Sess. (1949) in VII Morgan Papers.
11. 10 U.S.C. sec. 801–940 (1964) (originally enacted as Act of May 5, 1950, ch. 169, 64 Stat. 107).

12. Pub. L. No. 90–632 (Oct. 24, 1968).

13. 395 U.S. 258 (1969).

14. See United States v. Howe, 17 U.S.C.M.A. 165, 37 C.M.R. 429 (1967).

15. See F. GARDNER, THE UNLAWFUL CONCERT: AN ACCOUNT OF THE PRESIDIO MUTINY CASE (1970).

16. Latimer, *Improvements and Suggested Improvements in the Administration of Military Justice*, REPORT OF CONFERENCE PROCEEDINGS, ARMY JUDGE ADVOCATE CONFERENCE 54 (1954).

17. Statement of Arthur E. Farmer, *supra* note 10, at 2.

18. United States v. DuBay, 17 U.S.C.M.A. 147, 149, 37 C.M.R. 411, 413 (1967).

19. Sherman, *Buttons, Bumper Stickers and the Soldier,* 159 THE NEW REPUBLIC, Aug. 17, 1968.

20. GARDNER, THE UNLAWFUL CONCERT, *supra* note 15, at 99.

21. *Record of Trial of LCpl. William L. Harvey, Jr. by General Court-Martial,* Camp Pendleton, Cal., 72 (1967); *Record of Trial of PFC George Daniels by General Court-Martial,* Camp Pendleton, Cal., 124, 125 (1967).

22. GARDNER, THE UNLAWFUL CONCERT, *supra* note 15, at 143.

23. J. SHELBURNE & K. GROVES, EDUCATION IN THE ARMED FORCES 37 (1965).

24. United States v. Kinder, ACM 7321, 14 C.M.R. 742, 776 (1953) (quoting from the Nuremberg "Einsatzgruppen Case").

25. THE NEW YORKER, Oct. 25, 1969, at 63, 119.

The Army and
the First Amendment

Leonard B. Boudin

In November, 1965, Second Lieutenant Henry H.
Howe of the United States Army was found guilty of violating Article 88 of the Uniform Code of Military Justice
(UCMJ) by marching in a civilian peace demonstration
with a sign referring to "JOHNSON'S FACIST AGRESSION IN
VIETNAM" [sic].[1] Article 88, which he was judged to have
violated, provides that "[a]ny commissioned officer who
uses contemptuous words against the President, the Vice
President, Congress, the Secretary of Defense, the Secretary
of a military department, the Secretary of the Treasury, or
the Governor or legislature of any State, Territory, Com-
monwealth, or possession in which he is on duty or present
shall be punished as a court-martial may direct."

Both Lieutenant Howe's action and the punishment

The author wishes to acknowledge the assistance of Stacy Siegle, national secretary of the G.I. Civil Liberties Defense Committee, in preparing this article.

meted out to him have a long tradition, for problems related to self-expression in the Armed Forces are not new. To offer but one example that parallels that of Lieutenant Howe: In 1811, a British Army officer was found guilty of using "sundry expressions unbecoming an officer, highly disrespectful to His Royal Highness, the Prince Regent, and tending manifestly to the subversion of military discipline." [2]

The high value placed upon military discipline is reflected in the many code provisions which form part of a long Anglo-American history of rigid, even totalitarian control over soldiers. At a time when the Duke of Wellington could say that "It is quite impossible for me or any other man to command a British army under the existing system. We have in the service the scum of the earth as common soldiers . . ." [3]—at such a time the imposition of harsh control is understandable. But the world, and the armed forces, and the problems of military discipline have changed since then. And today the right of men in the Armed Forces of the United States to express their opinions on matters of public concern is of great and increasing importance.

In addition to Article 88 under which Lieutenant Howe was convicted, some of the provisions with possible impact upon free speech include "willfully disobeying a superior commissioned officer" (Article 90), failure to obey "any lawful general order or regulation" (Article 92), "mutiny or sedition" (Article 94), "riot or breach of peace" (Article 116), the use of "provoking or reproachful words or gestures towards any other person subject to this chapter" (Article 117), and the catch-all, "all disorders and neglects to the prejudice of good order and discipline in the armed forces, all conduct of a nature to bring discredit upon the armed forces, and crimes and offenses not capital, of which persons subject to this chapter may be guilty, shall be taken cognizance of by a general, special, or summary court-martial, according to the nature and degree of the offense, and shall be punished at the discretion of that court" (Article 134).

Regulations of this type have historically been directed against soldiers for isolated conduct, sometimes involving speech, deemed to violate military law. No period prior to the present one has presented the American military establishment with free-speech problems as widespread, organized and severe as those engendered by the current opposition to the Vietnam war. Soldiers and civilian populations have objected in the past to particular wars. The Revolutionary War had many instances in the military establishment itself; the so-called smaller wars of 1812, the Mexican War, and the Spanish-American War were opposed by large sectors of the civilian population, but—since service was on a volunteer basis—there was little objection in the Army itself.[4]

The conscription acts, beginning with that of 1917, for the first time gave us a truly conscript army of many millions. The constitutionality of the first draft law was upheld by the United States Supreme Court in 1918 after a limited attack upon it that made two points: first, that the States had a right to raise armies and, second, that the clause which allowed exemption on religious grounds was unconstitutional. The first argument is clearly weaker than the current assertion of the citizen's rights with respect to the federal government; the second has, in effect, been upheld by the Supreme Court in the Seeger and Welsh cases which have rewritten the draft statute to include all conscientious objectors to war. The Court had disposed of these two points in 1918 in a most inadequately reasoned decision, which held that a declaration of war entitled the Government to the services of its citizens and that the argument of religious discrimination was untenable.[5]

There was little disaffection in the ranks during the Second World War. But mass demonstrations of soldiers occurred thereafter when the Government assigned troops from Europe to the Pacific and failed to demobilize the Pacific troops, despite promises to do so following the end of hostilities.[6] In August, 1945, the White House acknowledged receipt of a telegram from 580 members of the 95th Division stationed at Camp Shelby, Mississippi, protesting the failure to demobilize them. At about the same time, the Army cancelled a troop transport scheduled to return men from Manila to the United States. This resulted in a Christmas-day march of 4,000 troops on the 21st Replacement Depot Headquarters in Manila carrying banners: "WE WANT SHIPS."

Demonstrations continued throughout the first week of January and, on the 7th, it was estimated that from 12,000 to 20,000 soldiers jammed the Philippine Hall of Congress to denounce United States military activities in North China and Indonesia and to demand that the Philippines be allowed to settle its own internal problems. A UPI dispatch described the capital on that day as "tense."

As news of the protests spread, G.I.'s in Europe began to demonstrate; 2,000 at Camp Boston, France, demanded a speed-up in European demobilization. On January 9th, 18,000 demonstrated in Guam. On the same day, 1,000 soldiers and WAC's at Andrews Field, Maryland, booed down their commanding officer when he tried to explain the delay in discharging them. A resolution issued by several thousand soldiers in Seoul, Korea, stated, "We cannot understand the War Department's insistence on keeping an oversized peacetime army overseas under present conditions."

The Truman Administration did not seek to discipline leaders of the massive upsurge because it feared even larger protests; it first directed that complaints be sent through

"normal" channels. Army newspapers were officially instructed not to report news of the G.I. protests. But by January 16th, General Dwight D. Eisenhower, Chief of Staff,
issued an order banning further demonstrations, and minor
reprisals such as transfers were taken against the leaders. At
the same time, the military began to demobilize troops. A
15-million-man war-time army had, by mid-summer 1946,
been reduced to 1.5 million troops.

Despite the fact that it was under United Nations
auspices, the Korean War posed politico-military problems
for our country. The problems, however, were largely
created by the Government itself, which dealt inconsistently
with people who had political views and associations it considered questionable. Some of these people were not inducted; others were. In some cases commissions were denied to physicians inducted under the Doctors Draft Act
because of their political activities, and they were forced to
serve in the ranks.[7] In other cases the Army gave administrative discharges of a less than honorable character to persons of whose pre-induction political associations it disap-
proved.[8]

While no American war has been the subject of such
widespread civilian and military protests as the present war
in Indochina, civilians, at least, are not generally prosecuted
by the Federal Government for expressing their dissent as
they were in World War I. There are some exceptions. Congress passed a statute making it a crime to destroy draft
cards, even one's own, and the Supreme Court in *United
States* v. *O'Brien* upheld the constitutionality of that statute;[9] in *United States* v. *Spock*,[10] while the Court of Appeals
for the First Circuit directed a judgment of acquittal for Dr.
Spock, it overruled the appellants' argument that the criminal conspiracy doctrine could not be applied to public statements on public issues. Only Circuit Judge Coffin agreed

with the defendants' free-speech argument. Non-criminal sanctions were applied by the Federal Government against protesting Selective Service registrants by revoking their deferments; this was ultimately held illegal by the courts.[11] On the other hand, state authorities have engaged in mass prosecutions of individuals for minor offenses arising from peaceful demonstrations.

The situation in the military establishment was quite different, at least in the early years of the Indochinese war. There were isolated examples of individual opposition to the war by servicemen and officers. They resulted in the prosecution of Dr. Howard Levy for refusing to teach Green Berets,[12] of Lieutenant Howe under Article 88, already discussed,[13] and of Captain Dale Noyd, who attempted to resign his Air Force commission on grounds of conscientious objections to the war in Vietnam, for refusing to train student pilots for active duty.[14]

Following President Johnson's election in 1964 and the massive increase in military operations in Indochina, the increase in the civilian opposition to the war was paralleled by a lesser, but still substantial, increase in opposition among the soldiers who, for the most part, had been inducted under the Selective Service System. Beginning with 1968, servicemen began to hold public meetings on posts, to engage in off-post demonstrations and to publish underground newspapers on and off the posts; at this writing, at least sixty such newspapers exist.[15] In addition, a series of G.I. coffee houses were put up near Army bases, the first—the UFO—in Columbia, South Carolina, in 1967, where soldiers on leave from active duty could discuss political issues.

The first well-publicized meeting of soldiers on post occurred at Fort Jackson, Columbia, South Carolina, in the spring of 1969. More than one hundred soldiers attended a spontaneous meeting held on the base to discuss civil rights and the Vietnam war; they had sought unsuccessfully to present petitions of grievances to their commanding officers. The Army retaliated by filing charges of disobedience for failing to disband the meetings, arrested the so-called Fort Jackson Eight, and detained them for more than two months prior to the anticipated trial. Then it accepted the recommendation of a hearing officer not to institute court-martial proceedings, and it got rid of the soldiers it regarded as troublemakers through administrative discharges.

The original leader of the group, Joseph Miles, was transferred to Fort Bragg, North Carolina. Here his organizing abilities led to meetings similar to those at Fort Jackson, to petitions and to the publication of an underground newspaper, *Bragg Briefs,* which the servicemen distributed off-base and sought permission, unsuccessfully, to distribute on the base.[16] The Army responded to these efforts by transferring him to Anchorage, Alaska, where he was ultimately followed by General Hollingsworth, his commanding officer at Fort Jackson.

The Army took note of this increase in G.I. opposition to the war. On May 27, 1969, the Adjutant General issued a document entitled, "Army Guidance on Dissent." In April, 1969, the Army promulgated Army Regulation 210–10 relating principally to "Protection of Loyalty, Discipline and Morale," and on September 12th, it issued Department of Defense Directive 1325.6 on the same subject. [See Appendix 3.] These three documents stated that soldiers as citizens were entitled to dissent under the First Amendment, that the Army encouraged a range of viewpoints, and that it would not interfere with publications because of their "poor taste" or "unfair criticism" of government policies. On the other hand, Army Regulation 210–10 stated that certain restraints might be necessary for "an effective and disciplined army," that some utterances might be punishable criminally, and that on-post distribution of publications could be limited by post commanders. Generally, distribution of publications is made through regular distribution outlets such as post exchanges by contracts with the Federal Government. This protects commercial publications. Other publications—those of soldiers particularly—can be distributed on-post only by special permission of the commanding officer. He is authorized to deny distribution where there is "a clear danger to discipline, morale and loyalty." Whatever these regulations might provide on their face, as a matter of practice very few G.I. newspapers have been permitted distribution on the bases themselves, although they are available to soldiers off-base in towns adjacent to their posts. Post commanders have promulgated regulations pursuant to A.R. 210–10, giving them power of censorship over G.I. newspapers.[17]

The legality of such regulations, as well as the restrictions upon public meetings and filing of petitions, is the subject of two lawsuits instituted in 1969 in Federal District Courts and still pending on appeal at this writing.[18] In both cases, lower federal courts declined to interfere with the censorship by post commanders.

The range of protests in and about the military establishment is not limited to these few examples. Anti-war activities by servicemen include the distribution of off-base literature, the participation in civilian off-base demonstrations, sometimes in uniform, attendance at G.I. coffee houses, and the making of statements regarded by the Army as inducing disloyalty among members of the Armed Forces. In addition, civilians have sought to enter Army posts to distribute literature.

The Army has responded with criminal and non-criminal sanctions. As I have noted, it has, inconsistently and erratically, refused to induct persons suspect because of their political associations. On the same grounds it has denied commissions to certain physicians. The courts are reluctant to review such disciplinary actions (as denial of commissions); they are even more reluctant to review such familiar methods as restrictions to posts or barracks, punitive transfers and extra work assignments, since these have traditionally been considered the internal affairs of the military. Analogous cases of discrimination in civilian life for the exercise of such First Amendment rights would probably be a basis for judicial review. The parallel that comes most readily to mind is the Supreme Court's decision reversing the exclusion of newly elected Julian Bond by the Georgia legislature because of his stated opposition to the war.[19]

Another sanction which it is most difficult to bring to judicial review is pre-trial detention after charges are filed but prior to formal court-martial proceedings. Three of the Fort Jackson Eight were detained without trial for two months.[20] Article 13 of the UCMJ provides that "no person while being held for trial or the result of trial may be subject to punishment or penalty through arrest or confinement upon the charges pending against him nor shall the arrest or confinement imposed upon him be any more rigorous than the circumstances require to insure his presence, but he may be subjected to minor punishment during that period for infractions of discipline." A Federal District Court declined to consider the legality of the pre-trial detention[21] until an application was made to the United States Court of Military Appeals; that court summarily denied the application.[22] An appellate court remanded the case to the District Court, rejecting the argument of the servicemen that the only criterion for detention is insurance of the servicemen's presence at trial. Instead, the court relied upon the *Courts-Martial Manual* which noted another criterion for pre-trial detention: the seriousness of the offense. This is a dangerous example of the kind of pre-trial detention sought by the Government from Congress for use outside the military. Its potential for the dangerous suppression of political dissent is obvious.

The more critical problem, of course, arises from criminal prosecutions for violations of the UCMJ. On April 27, 1970, Roger Priest was given a bad conduct discharge by a court-martial following conviction for "promoting disloyalty and disaffection." [See pp. 191–214—Ed.] The conviction stemmed solely from statements in an anti-war newspaper, *OM*, which Priest had published.

Perhaps one of the most dramatic cases is that of the Presidio 27. On October 14, 1968, twenty-seven prisoners in the stockade of the Presidio of San Francisco staged a sit-down to protest the conditions of the stockade and the killing, three days earlier, of an AWOL G.I., Richard Bunch, by one of the guards. They were charged with mutiny, subjected to the longest court-martial in U.S. military history and prison sentences of up to seven years.[23]

Court-martial proceedings were instituted against four servicemen at Fort Gordon for "attempting to promote disloyalty" as well as for the unauthorized distribution of literature; they had published a leaflet calling for the formation of a G.I. war crimes commission, hoping to "open new avenues of investigation and to arouse public opinion to the real nature of the war in Vietnam." Two were acquitted, one was convicted of unlawful distribution, and the fourth of both charges.

Lieutenant Susan Schnall, a Navy nurse, and Airman First-Class Michael Locks were convicted of violating Army Regulations 600–20 and 600–21, which prohibit members of the Armed Forces from participating in off-post demonstrations in uniform.[24] They had, while in uniform, taken part in a huge anti-war rally in San Francisco the weekend of October 12, 1968. Both were convicted. Locks received one year at hard labor, forfeiture of all pay and allowances, reduction to Airman Basic and a bad conduct discharge. Schnall served her six months' sentence as a nurse in a pediatric ward, after which she was dismissed from the Service.

The technique of undesirable discharges for speech and acts of political dissent is not a new phenomenon. Following World War II, several soldiers were given less than honorable discharges which the Supreme Court, in *Abramowitz* v. *Brucker*[25] and *Harmon* v. *Brucker,*[26] held to be improper since, under Army regulations, one's military records and not one's political record or attitude determines the type of discharge one receives. More recent undesirable discharges for similar reasons involved Howard Petrick, whose political attitudes antedated his induction, and Andrew Stapp, the founder of the American Serviceman's Union, who was charged with post-induction political associations. A federal district judge applied to the *Stapp* case the *Abramowitz* principle—that political attitudes are not a proper criterion for undesirable discharge—and thereby skirted, as had the Supreme Court, the basic First Amendment issue.[27]

In support of its restrictions upon freedom of speech in the military service, the Army argues that it is a military establishment whose purpose, the waging of war, is impaired by the free expression of viewpoints conflicting with those of the Army and the Government. This was most dramatically reflected by the Government's brief in the Fort Bragg case, *Yahr* v. *Resor*, where it said:

> In such a community, at least while on the post, there can be no vigorous championing of minority views. Matters which are otherwise still open to public debate, such as the United States' role in Vietnam, are not open to public challenge by the soldier, at least on post, once they have become part of the national military policy. The role of the United States in Vietnam is such an issue.

While the ordinary citizen can condemn it, and refuse to support it, the soldier has no such option. It is well known that the President, as Commander-in-Chief, has directed military participation in Vietnam. Thus, any comment concerning Vietnam which would cause soldiers to reduce their effort, or challenge their orders, is clearly a danger to good order and discipline and cannot be permitted. Nothing which will detract from the authority of the commander can be tolerated, and this must include words as well as actions. Anything less would adversely affect discipline and, ultimately, the national security. Accordingly, just as with civilians in specialized situations, the general rules pertaining to the exercise of First Amendment rights cannot always under all circumstances obtain on military reservations.

In the view of the Government, the decision of the post commander as to the effect of particular statements on discipline, morale and loyalty must be conclusive because he is the person most qualified to know that effect and because courts should not interfere, except in extreme cases, with the running of the Army. The Army further argues that if soldiers were permitted to express their views on national policy they might themselves espouse military policies contrary to those of the President of the United States; indeed, it argues this is the kind of activity which can lead to a putsch against the government.[28] The clash between President Truman and General Douglas MacArthur illustrates the potential danger of independent judgment.

The truth is, of course, that the danger of a putsch comes not from the dissenting servicemen but from the General Staff and bureaucracy of the Army. It is ludicrous to treat the Pentagon as a compliant servant of the civilian Commander-in-Chief; its power and influence and its gigantic and expensive propaganda machine is an independent force affecting our domestic and foreign affairs. This is thoroughly documented by Professor Melman's recent book, *The Power of the Pentagon*. But what greater proof is needed than the invasion of Cambodia?

The legal or moral right of the military establishment to ban meetings, statements and periodicals because they challenge governmental policies is inconsistent with an increasing line of Supreme Court decisions that emphasize the preferred position in our constitutional system of such fundamental rights as freedom of speech, association and press.[29] The abridgement of these rights "impairs those opportunities for public education that are essential to effectuate exercise of the power of correcting error through the process of popular government." [30] "Speech concerning public affairs," said the Supreme Court in *Garrison* v. *Louisiana*,[31] "is more than self-expression; it is the essence of self-government," and such speech was most recently described by the Court as "a powerful antidote to any abuses of power by governmental officials." [32] Indeed, the Supreme Court has said that the government has the affirmative duty "to implement this profound national commitment to the principle that debate on public issues should be uninhibited, lawful and wide open." [33]

The Army does not deny that its censorship cannot be reconciled with these basic principles. Instead, as we have seen, it insists that the military machine is exempt from First Amendment demands. This claim cannot be limited to the control of public meetings and the public distribution of periodicals on the post; logically, it must be extended to private discussions of political issues among soldiers and to statements made and publications distributed off the post by and to servicemen. This is a power not claimed by any other agency of government. Even the Louisiana state judges were unable by reason of the First Amendment to punish District Attorney James Garrison for contempt when he charged them publicly with criminality.

The military establishment avails itself of the argument of the critical importance of national defense, an argument courts will not readily disregard. But the same national defense argument, based on the need of the nation to have war-waging capability, has been held insufficient for discriminatory disregard of First Amendment rights in cases involving passports,[34] employment in defense plants and employment in the Merchant Marine.[35] In *Youngstown* v. *Sawyer,* the Supreme Court rejected a similar war emergency claim when it declared President Truman's seizure of the steel mills during the Korean War to be illegal;[36] it is true that property rights were involved in that case, but the personal liberties of the citizen-soldier are surely entitled to equal weight.

The Army reminds us often that the Constitution expressly authorizes the President to make rules for the governing of the land and naval forces. That constitutional provision does not authorize governmental disregard of the First Amendment. Thus, for example, even more explicit congressional powers—to tax, regulate interstate commerce, and make postal laws—are subject to the mandate of the Bill of Rights. The Supreme Court has told us that the power to regulate the Army must be exercised "in harmony with the Bill of Rights." [37] Even the Court of Military Appeals has recognized, with some limitations, the right of soldiers to freedom of speech and expression.[38] Less authoritative, but perhaps more telling, is the Army's recent sensitivity to such rights and its attempt to spell them out in the promulgation of the documents and regulations previously noted.

The serviceman is a citizen with the duties and rights of citizens, including the right to speak, the right to vote, the right to try to persuade others how to vote, and the right to affect the course of national policy. He has the same need for constitutional protection as have other citizens; in fact, his may be greater, because his movement is restricted and he is subject to military discipline and, of course, to its hazards. The soldier has a greater need to talk and to hear, to write and to read, since the Army's system of indoctrination and regimentation and controls has a pervasive effect upon the young men who are truly a captive audience. Freedom of speech is a wholesome antidote mandated by our constitutional system.

There is another reason why freedom of speech and thought in an army is necessary. The Rules of Land Warfare of the United States Army expressly adopt the Nuremberg Judgment's principle that superior orders are not a defense to violations of the laws of warfare. The Uniform Code of Military Justice speaks of disobedience to "lawful" orders. This harmonizes with the demands of international law by recognizing the individual judgment of every serviceman and his duty to exercise it under proper circumstances. This will sometimes entail the open expression of skepticism or disbelief about the legality and morality of particular orders.

The Army, sometimes retreating from its advanced position limiting the right to censor a soldier wherever he is, also argues that a military reservation is "not a place habitually dedicated to such expressions." [39] That type of insulation from freedom of speech has been rejected in cases involving company towns, defense plant towns and educational institutions.[40] It has even been questioned in a case involving the right of civilians to distribute anti-war leaflets on a military post.[41] Governmental property dedicated to a particular purpose is a proper place for the exercise of First Amendment rights.

It has often been stated that in the area of public affairs there is no single truth; there is certainly no established political doctrine binding upon soldiers or civilians. The Government's views, even when expressed by the military establishment, are entitled to no greater weight than those of its citizens, including those in the military service.

We should be turning a blind eye to reality, however, if we did not recognize that governments, in the area of foreign affairs and military policy, among others, often engage in half-truths, untruths and concealment. One is horror-stricken to realize that some of the current prosecutions for war crimes came about only after letters were written to congressmen by servicemen subsequent to their discharge (when Army officers on high levels in the Army put reports of massacres in file cabinets) and only after newspapermen made their own investigations. A single Seymour Hersh, who exposed the horror of My Lai, has turned out to be more successful in unearthing such crimes than the Inspector General or the Criminal Investigation Division of the Army.

I challenge the Army's premise that an army deprived of the right to express opinions is a better army. On the contrary. When human beings are treated as robots or animals, they behave as such. When men lose faith in the government they serve, perhaps the government is at fault. A democratic army, rather than a prussianized one—like a democratic civilian society—is the best kind of army for a democratic country.

Notes:

1. a) United States v. Howe, 17 U.S.C.M.A. 165, 37 C.M.R. 429.
   b) Kester, *Soldiers Who Insult the President,* 81 HARV. L. REV. (June, 1968).
2. W. HOUGH, PRECEDENTS IN MILITARY LAW (1855), 120–22.
3. From DISPATCHES, vol. vi, p. 575, as quoted in HALÉVY, HISTORY OF THE ENGLISH PEOPLE: England in 1815 (1961).

4. S. E. MORISON, F. MERK, F. FREIDEL, DISSENT IN THREE AMER-ICAN WARS (1970).

5. Selective Draft Law Case, 245 U.S. 366.

6. M. A. WATERS, GIS AND THE FIGHT AGAINST THE WAR (1967).

7. Orloff v. Willoughby, 345 U.S. 83 (1953).

8. Abramowitz v. Brucker, 355 U.S. 579.

9. United States v. O'Brien, 391 U.S. 367.

10. United States v. Spock, 416 F.2d 165 (2d Cir. 1969).

11. See (a) Wolff v. Selective Service Local Board 16, 372 F.2d 817 (2d Cir. ———), (b) Gutknecht v. U.S., 396 U.S. 295 (1970).

12. Levy v. Corcoran, 389 F.2d 929 (D.C. Cir. 1967).

13. See *supra* note 1(a).

14. Noyd v. Bond, 395 U.S. 683.

15. GI Press Service, c/o Student Mobilization Committee, 15 E. 17th St., N.Y., N.Y.

16. Yahr v. Resor ——— F.2d ——— (#14423, 4th Cir., Aug. 1970), *aff'd., remanded.*

17. See, e.g., Fort Dix Regulation 210–27 (May 8, 1968).

18. Dash *et al.* v. Commanding General ——— F.2d ——— (#34390, Aug. 1970), *aff'd.;* and see *supra* note 16, Yahr.

19. Bond v. Floyd, 385 U.S. 116.

20. HALSTEAD, GIS SPEAK OUT AGAINST THE WAR (1970).

21. U.S.A. *ex rel* Chaparro *et al.* v. Resor, Civil Action 69, 350 (DSC 1969).

22. Cole *et al.* v. Resor *et al.* misc., Docket 69–16 (U.S.C.M.A. 1969).

23. For a full discussion of this case see F. GARDNER, THE UN-LAWFUL CONCERT (1970).

24. Locks v. Laird, 300 F. Supp. 915 (N.D. Cal. 1969).

25. See note 8 *supra.*

26. Harmon v. Brucker, 355 U.S. 579.

27. Stapp v. Resor, 69 Civ. 5345 (SDNY) 1970.

28. See note 18 *supra,* Dash.

29. See EMERSON, THE FIRST AMENDMENT (1970).

30. Thornhill v. Alabama, 310 U.S. 88, 95.

31. Garrison v. Louisiana, 379 U.S. 64.

32. Mills v. Alabama, 384 U.S. 214.

33. New York Times v. Sullivan, 376 U.S. 254, 270.

34. Kent v. Dulles, 248 F.2d 600.

35. (a) United States v. Robel, 389 U.S. 258.
    (b) Schneider v. Smith, 390 U.S. 17.

36. Youngstown v. Sawyer, 343 U.S. 539.

37. O'Callahan v. Parker, 395 U.S. 258.

38. United States v. Wysong, 9 U.S.C.M.A. 249 26 C.M.R. 30–31.

39. See government brief in Yahr, *supra* at note 16.

40. (a) Marsh v. Alabama, 326 U.S. 501.
    (b) Tinker v. Community School District, 393 U.S. 503.
    (c) Tucker v. Texas, 326 U.S. 517.

41. Kiiskila v. Nichols, —— F.2d —— (7th Cir. 1970).

Command Influence

Luther C. West

The American people can hardly postpone any longer a close examination of military criminal "jurisprudence." When Green Beret assassinations are planned by almost the highest levels of government—and the perpetrators go untried—or when a massacre of several hundred unarmed women and children is buried for well over a year, we should suspect the system that allows it.

Under this system of "justice" military defendants for almost two hundred years have been subjected to despotic military judicial actions. To name only a few of the more common travesties that are or have been visited on victims of the system: denial of legal counsel, increase of adjudged sentences, rigged verdicts and sentences, reversal of acquittals, and outrageous intimidation of both assigned military defense counsel and members of the court.

Neither the concept nor practice of military justice could have developed as they have within the Armed Forces of the United States were it not that the Supreme Court and the American people have been tragically indifferent to the plight of the military defendant. Neither our people nor our courts acknowledge that military commanders and military staff judge advocates are not fair-minded men in the judicial sense of the word; that they are, basically, incapable of operating a system of justice along democratic principles. The ethical motivation of military officers is command oriented, their integrity all too often indistinguishable from the principle of undeviating obedience to superior orders.

Military justice decisions as well as court-martial verdicts and sentences may, thus, revolve around such non-legal issues as what is considered best for the military establishment, the desire to please superiors, or to maintain a tightly disciplined command, ambition for promotion, fear of failure, whim, and a host of related factors. The builders of future military law must recognize these factors as well as the historical errors and historical horrors of the past. They must recognize the inherent weaknesses of military morality as well as the refusal of young Americans to accept military solutions to ethical problems. The individual-destroying element of present-day military "training" must be recognized, and the dehumanizing, spirit-breaking games that our military leaders have traditionally imposed upon drafted American youth in the name of military discipline and military necessity must be terminated.

But of first importance is the removal of the *entire* military judicial-law enforcement system from the operational control of the military commander. The military commander simply cannot be trusted to operate a judicial system in which military officers serve as judge and jury as well as defense counsel; and where the commander determines what charges are to be investigated, what defendants shall stand trial, who will prosecute and defend each case, and who shall serve on the juries involved. Under this system it is not surprising that commanders tip the scales of justice so frequently. Thus the entire system should be stripped from the military and placed in the hands of civilian administrators, preferably under the control of the Attorney General of the United States. Civilian trial lawyers and civilian judges should perform the functions now performed by military judges, defense counsel and legal officers in every branch of military justice. And of equal importance, convening authorities who insist upon tampering with military courts should be indicted and prosecuted in U.S. District Courts.

Only when the system is removed entirely from military control will abuses such as those in the following cases be removed or substantially lessened.

DON'T PICKET THE WHITE HOUSE

The case of the *United States* v. *Second Lieutenant Dennis J. Morrisseau* began in the spring of 1968 when Lieutenant Morrisseau, while stationed at Fort Devens, Massachusetts, attended a McCarthy-for-President rally, in uniform.[1] Subsequently, the Lieutenant put an anti-Vietnam war sticker on the bumper of his automobile at Fort Devens, and then capped his performance by conducting a one-man picket of the White House, resplendent once again in full Army uniform and carrying a sign reading "120,000 AMERICAN CASUALTIES. WHY?"[2] Lieutenant Morrisseau's picketing of the White House occurred on Saturday, March 9, 1968. He was arrested on the spot by military policemen, and was returned immediately to Fort Devens. By the following Monday he found himself on orders to Vietnam, via Panama for jungle war training.[3] Furthermore, he was to board a commercial flight in Boston on March 13 to take him on the first leg of his journey to Panama.[4] His military superiors, however, apparently had a nervous conviction that

Lieutenant Morrisseau was not going to board the commercial flight as scheduled and provided another aircraft.

The personal aircraft assigned to Major General K. B. Lemmon, Jr., Commanding General, Fort Devens, was allegedly made available to fly another lieutenant to Fort Bragg.[5] Since the aircraft "was going in the same general direction," Morrisseau's unit commander, a lieutenant colonel on the staff at Fort Devens,[6] decided that it would be a good idea to have Morrisseau fly the first leg of his journey to Panama aboard this aircraft. Hence, on the morning of March 13, without permitting him to make a telephone call or to pick up his clothes that were off-post at the time, Morrisseau was whisked away to the general's waiting aircraft at the Fort Devens Airport, and ordered to board the aircraft forthwith.[7] He refused to board the plane, and was immediately charged with the offense of refusing to obey a military order to board the aircraft, an offense punishable by five years imprisonment.[8]

The order had allegedly come from one Lieutenant Colonel John J. Cauley, Morrisseau's commanding officer. It was this same Lieutenant Colonel Cauley who signed charges against Lieutenant Morrisseau for his refusal to board the military aircraft as ordered.[9] Two days later, after Morrisseau had been placed in arrest of quarters pending disposition of court-martial charges, his legal advisor, Lieutenant Nicholas Bizony, a qualified lawyer from the California Bar (but not a member of the Judge Advocate General's Corps), was himself offered non-judicial punishment under the provisions of Article 15 of the Uniform Code of Military Justice for failing to go to his appointed place of duty on the Saturday morning when Lieutenant Morrisseau picketed the White House.[10] Lieutenant Bizony had on that morning accompanied Lieutenant Morrisseau to Washington, but did not participate in the picketing. On March

22, Lieutenant Bizony accepted non-judicial punishment for the offense of being absent from Saturday work call, a punishment which was imposed upon Lieutenant Bizony by Major General Lemmon personally. This punishment provided as follows:

> Restriction to the limits of the main post, Fort Devens, Massachusetts, for sixty days, further provided that you do not enter the Fort Devens Officers' Open Mess after 1900 hours daily during the period of this restriction; and forfeiture of $50.00 pay per month for one month.[11]

At the time Lieutenant Bizony received this punishment, he was officially designated as defense counsel for Lieutenant Morrisseau, whose charges were still pending. In addition to the imposition of Article 15 punishment, Lieutenant Bizony was recommended for non-promotion to captain.[12] On March 25, Lieutenant Bizony appealed his punishment under appropriate provisions of military law to the Commanding General, First United States Army, Fort Meade, Maryland.[13]

At the time of the receipt of the appeal, I was serving as Chief of Military Justice, First Army Headquarters, and accordingly, the appeal came to my desk for initial action and review. I was aware of the existence of the *Morrisseau* case at Fort Devens, but this was the first indication I had that a second officer was involved, or that the second officer was also acting as defense counsel for Lieutenant Morrisseau. I also noted that Lieutenant Bizony's appeal was based in large part upon the common-sense ground that the punishment imposed would severely hinder his ability to prepare a defense for Lieutenant Morrisseau. While I personally knew none of the parties involved in Lieutenant Morrisseau's case, and knew very little more of the facts involved than I had read in the local Washington, D.C., newspaper, I was more than willing to render whatever assistance I could in any situation that smacked of command influence, and my immediate reaction was that this case reeked of it.

I first asked an associate to telephone the staff judge advocate at Fort Devens to obtain a written account of the facts involved in the imposition of non-judicial punishment upon Lieutenant Bizony. I explained to this officer that he should request an "in-depth" statement, a statement that would include a detailed account of the type of Saturday morning work that Lieutenant Bizony usually performed, whether he had in the past always been present for Saturday morning work, and, if he had in the past from time to time missed Saturday morning work, whether he had been expressly excused in advance of such absences, or whether such absences were in the past generally tolerated without formal excuse.

Two days after the call to Fort Devens, the requested written statement had not yet arrived. Therefore I myself called the staff judge advocate at Fort Devens, Major D. A. Fontanella, acting staff judge advocate following the retirement of his predecessor (who had taken most of the action in the *Morrisseau* case). I explained that my request for a written statement was official, and that the statement was necessary in order to rule upon Lieutenant Bizony's appeal to First Army Headquarters. I also explained, pointedly, that I did not like the looks of the action that was taken against Lieutenant Bizony, and that I felt it very unwise to punish him at all inasmuch as he was acting as defense counsel for Lieutenant Morrisseau. I also suggested to Major Fontanella that he keep detailed memoranda for the record concerning his future actions in the case, since it might be required in the future development of the case that he explain exactly what action he took in the case and when he took such action.

Several days later, on April 3, Major Fontanella answered my request for details in a formal letter to the Commanding General, First Army Headquarters, attention staff judge advocate.[14] The letter was two pages long, and explained in considerable detail that Saturday morning work at Fort Devens was a very real and substantive matter, and that Lieutenant Bizony's commander was quite concerned and upset with his unexcused absence from work on the Saturday morning involved. The letter then specified that the command decision to punish Lieutenant Bizony was motivated solely by his absence from work, and had absolutely nothing to do with the fact that Lieutenant Bizony was acting in conjunction with Lieutenant Morrisseau on the morning involved, or the fact that Lieutenant Bizony was currently acting as defense counsel for Lieutenant Morrisseau. In his final paragraph, Major Fontanella stated:

> In my opinion, based upon informal inquiry into the facts of the case, the non-judicial punishment would have been administered regardless of any later developing events. I am sure my predecessor, who provided counsel to the Commanding General in this matter, was fully cognizant of its ramifications and the implications by LTC West, and personnel of his office, that the action was taken with other motives, is indeed unfortunate.[15]

The full extent of the "unfortunate" implications made by LTC West were to be spelled out in the succeeding weeks.

Immediately after receiving Fontanella's letter, I recommended to my superior, the First Army Staff Judge Advocate, that the Bizony appeal be granted; that, under the circumstances, the punishment of Lieutenant Bizony was of the utmost illegality and would result in the reversal of any subsequent conviction that might be obtained in the *Morrisseau* case. My superior, however, agreed with me only in part. He recommended that the restriction to the post for sixty days and the prohibition of the use of the

Officers' Club at Fort Devens be lifted, and the Commanding General, First Army, acted on the appeal accordingly. Lieutenant Bizony's appeal of his punishment under Article 15 was thus in large part granted.[16] The case against Lieutenant Morrisseau, however, was far from over.

At the Article 32 investigation of the charges against Morrisseau, which was being conducted during the period of Lieutenant Bizony's Article 15 appeal, several fairly well-known provisions of military law figured prominently. According to the Uniform Code of Military Justice, it is "unlawful for an accuser to convene a general court-martial for the trial of the person so accused." [17] Both the *Manual for Courts-Martial* and the UCMJ defined an "accuser" as a person who "signs and swears to charges," or "who directs that charges nominally be signed and sworn by another," or simply as "any other person who has an interest other than an official interest in the prosecution of the accused." [18] The *Manual* also provided, however, that a commander whose only interest in the case is official will not be barred from further acting in the case, nor will he become an accuser simply by directing a subordinate to "investigate an alleged offense with a view to formulating and preferring appropriate charges if the facts disclosed by such investigation should warrant preferring charges." [19] But both the *Manual* and the Uniform Code expressly provided that when a commander is an accuser, he shall refer the charges to a *superior* competent convening authority for disposition.[20]

The defense counsel—made up, in addition to Lieutenant Bizony, of Captain Thomas P. Dugan of the Fort Devens' Judge Advocate office and Mr. Edward F. Sherman of the Harvard Law School faculty—hoped to demonstrate that not only had the commander overstepped the bounds of official interest which would bar his acting as convening authority but had, indeed, set the stage for the commission of the contemplated offense and then, through his maneuvering and direct orders, placed the prospective offender in position to commit the desired offense. Specifically, if the defense counsel could establish that the Commanding General at Fort Devens had a personal interest in the case—by having ordered Lieutenant Morrisseau's shipment date advanced, by ordering that he be shipped by military air rather than commercial aircraft, by arranging to have him delivered to the Fort Devens Airport at the desired moment, by making the General's own aircraft available for the flight, and by seeing to it that every aspect of the case was kept from the defendant and his counsel until the last moment—it might then be argued that the Commanding General, either expressly or by necessary implication, had also made it clear that Morrisseau was to be charged with refusing to obey a military order in the event he refused to board the aircraft in question. As such, the Fort Devens Commander would have been deemed an "accuser," and accordingly would have been ineligible to refer Morrisseau's charges to trial at Fort Devens.

Had defense counsel been successful in proving these factors at the Article 32 investigation, it would have been necessary for the Commanding General at Fort Devens to have forwarded the case to a superior general court-martial convening authority for disposition. Had this in fact been accomplished, and had the case been transferred to a higher command, little would have been gained for the defense. The charges would have been routinely referred to trial by general court-martial, the accused would have been convicted and would have been sentenced to from three to five years in military prison.

But matters of great command concern, such as are involved in the *Morrisseau* case, are seldom dealt with by military commanders in an open and direct fashion. To have played it by the book, and to have admitted his own participation in the case, and to have transferred jurisdiction in the case, would have been an admission by the Commander at Fort Devens that he could not handle his own "dirty wash," a singularly unpopular admission by military commanders. And such an admission and transfer of jurisdiction would also have lessened the chances of personal vengeance by the Fort Devens command element against the defendant, an important consideration in the game of playing local God, as military commanders are sometimes prone to do. At any rate, the military command at Fort Devens, for reasons known only to themselves, resolved to cover up the activity of their Commanding General in the case, and to play it as though this most unusual of cases was just another insignificant case in which the command had only a passing, *official* interest.

This decision was a costly error for the Fort Devens command. That the error was a blunder in legal judgment, as well as in common sense, is a matter almost beyond dispute. First, the facts themselves cried out in advance that the *Morrisseau* case had to have considerable command involvement, as well as high-level command decision, for it was a case that generated national and international news coverage. Lieutenants in American Army uniform seldom take part in anti-war demonstrations at the White House. Anyone faintly aware of things military would have little doubt that such a matter would be referred immediately to the Department of the Army for instant cognizance. Nor could anyone of adult mentality fail to grasp the fact that generals in the Pentagon might make the decision as to what course of action to take in the case involved. This, then, was the first danger signal that the Fort Devens command failed to observe when it resolved to cover up the fact that their Commanding General was personally involved in the *Morrisseau* case. In a case of this importance, the local commander cannot afford to be out of the picture. He must be centrally involved, for when the top brass at the Pentagon want instant answers, they are not going to call the Fort Devens public information officer. They call the Fort Devens Commanding General, and he personally accounts for the case.

The second danger sign that the Fort Devens command failed to observe when they resolved to hide the role played by their Commanding General in the *Morrisseau* case, was the series of obvious facts of the case. Ordinarily, officers from Fort Devens were flown by commercial aircraft from Boston on the first leg of their trip to Panama, and thence to Vietnam. With the advance knowledge that Lieutenant Morrisseau would probably refuse to board the aircraft and that it might prove embarrassing if he had arranged press coverage at plane side to publicize the event, a decision was made to transport Morrisseau by military aircraft, from a military airport, and to do so with no advance notification to Lieutenant Morrisseau. As such, there would be less embarrassment to the Army if he refused to board the aircraft. There would be no civilian witnesses to the disagreeable incident, no civilian lawyers present to make speeches, and no newsmen to take pictures. Thus, the second danger sign the military failed to observe was the simple fact that defense counsel for Lieutenant Morrisseau might analyze the facts themselves. Additionally, since the aircraft involved was the personal aircraft assigned to the Fort Devens Commander, no one subordinate to that commander at Fort Devens would have dared formulate a plan of action in this most critical case, utilizing the General's own aircraft, without the personal approval of the Commanding General himself.

But these signs went unread by the military command at Fort Devens when it came time to formulate a course of action at the Article 32 investigation. The planners therefore resolved to make it appear at the pre-trial investigation that the decision to fly Lieutenant Morrisseau to Fort Jackson by military aircraft, as opposed to a commercial flight, was the sole decision of his group commander, Lieutenant Colonel John J. Cauley, Jr., who was ordinarily responsible for issuing orders to Lieutenant Morrisseau. Furthermore, to make the story more plausible, it was to appear that Lieutenant Colonel Cauley made this important decision in this case without any prompting, direction, or coaching of any sort from the Commanding General at Fort Devens, his Chief of Staff, or other command representatives, or from higher military authorities.

Had the plotters been successful here, it would have permitted the Commanding General at Fort Devens to convene the general court-martial that was to try Lieutenant Morrisseau. It would also have given the impression that General Lemmon knew what he was doing, and could handle a touchy situation without calling on outside command assistance. That the decision would involve dishonesty and perjury, and might also backfire, apparently failed to register with those responsible for making it. Hence, the danger signals in the *Morrisseau* case were ignored, and "Operation Fraud" was given full speed ahead by the military command at Fort Devens.

With this background of the case, let us now look at the Article 32 investigation that was conducted in the *Morrisseau* case. An Article 32 investigation is roughly comparable to the grand jury indictment procedure in civilian practice, except that the military investigation is far more thorough than that made by the usual grand jury. The military defendant is entitled to be present, with counsel, throughout the Article 32 investigation. And of utmost importance, all government witnesses will generally be called if the defendant should so desire, and he and his counsel will be given the opportunity to cross-examine all witnesses for the government, as well as the opportunity to present defense witnesses. The usual rules of evidence do not apply at this hearing, and counsel may ask any question he desires. In fact, he may and sometimes does, cross-examine a witness for hours on any point he deems relevant.

Lieutenant Colonel John J. Cauley, Acting Commander of the 46th Direct Group, Fort Devens, Massachusetts, was called as a witness at the Article 32 investigation. Portions of his testimony follow:

Questions by Investigating Officer.

Q. Did you issue your verbal orders from higher authority, or did you issue this order to Lieutenant Morrisseau at the plane-side, Fort Devens Airfield, on your own volition?

A. The specific order that I gave [to board the plane]?

Q. Yes, sir.

A. I issued it on my own volition.

Q. You had no instructions from any higher headquarters towards the issuing of this order?

A. Well, I'd have to clarify that insofar as the plane and the resources being made available, but the decision was left to me. Yes, the plane was made available and I was informed where it would be going, but the decision was left to me to be made as to whether or not these instructions would, or would not, be issued.

Q. So, you did have an option as to the other means of travel for Lieutenant Morrisseau?

A. I did, yes.

Q. You could have exercised that option yourself?

A. Yes, there were no restrictions at any time that had been placed on me.[21]

Captain Dugan, military defense counsel, next questioned Lieutenant Colonel Cauley as to why Lieutenant

Morrisseau was ordered to board a military aircraft some several hours prior to the scheduled departure of his commercial flight.

Questions by Captain Dugan.

Q. Could I ask you, sir, why the change and why it appeared to be a matter of sudden urgency?

A. In what regard?

Q. In connection with Lieutenant Morrisseau's departure from the area.

A. No particular sudden urgency that I know of. I am not sure that I understand you.

Q. Well, let me take it one part at a time. Why was the decision made to change his mode of travel from here to Fort Jackson from commercial conveyance to military aircraft?

A. Well, one of the reasons was the fact that he had been held up almost to the point of delay as far as reaching his destination. There was only one aircraft left, or two, I believe it was. I forget how many he could catch out of Boston to South Carolina.
I was advised that the aircraft was available and to move Lieutenant Morrisseau by military air to Fort Jackson, South Carolina.

Q. Excuse me, sir, did you say you were advised to do so?

A. No, I didn't. I said I was advised that the aircraft was available.

* * *

Q. Was it your idea, sir, that is, did the idea originate with you that it might be possible to move Lieutenant Morrisseau by military airplane?

A. No, it didn't.

Q. Where did the idea originate?

A. As far as I know by the Chief of Staff.

Q. How was it communicated to you by the Chief of Staff? Was it in the form of a suggestion or could you relate exactly what it was that he said in relation to that?

A. That the plane was available and would I entertain a motion to have Lieutenant Morrisseau use it, and I did.

Q. Did you understand at that point, sir, that it was strictly your decision?

A. Oh, yes.

Q. In other words, you felt free to say no at that point had you wanted to do so?

A. Absolutely, absolutely.[22]

Mr. Sherman, civilian defense counsel for Lieutenant Morrisseau, conducted the major portion of the cross-examination of the Chief of Staff, Fort Devens, one Colonel Hugh F. Queenin. Colonel Queenin had a slightly different recollection of events, particularly as to whether or not he had given Lieutenant Colonel Cauley notice of the fact that the military aircraft was available in the event he wanted to order Lieutenant Morrisseau aboard it. He testified, in essence, that the decision to move Lieutenant Morrisseau by military aircraft was made by Lieutenant Colonel Cauley, and that neither he, nor the Commanding General, Fort Devens, had anything to do with the formulation of the decision. Excerpts from his testimony in this regard follow:

Questions by Mr. Sherman.

Q. Is it usual for the Chief of Staff and his officers to plan transportation for a lieutenant when he is clearing Post?

A. I didn't say that the Chief of Staff planned it.

Q. You did say that you discussed it?

A. I stated this, that transportation was available, and it was the decision of the Commanding Officer of the 46th Group [Lieutenant Colonel Cauley] who made the decision of the transportation, not my decision, nor was I the one to suggest it.

* * *

Q. Is it usual for the installation to send a lieutenant to his next assignment on a special plane?

A. It was not the Installation Commander's decision. It was the Commanding Officer's decision of the 46th Group.

* * *

Q. Did you make the decision to make the plane available to the Commander of the 46th Group?

A. I did not make the plane available to him. I wish, once and for all, for the record to state, unequivocally, that the plane was not made available to the Commanding Officer of the 46th Group.

A seat was vacant on that aircraft, which was going in the direction Lieutenant Morrisseau was traveling, was made available. A seat, whether he be a lieutenant or a general, a seat was available.

If there was an enlisted man traveling, he would have had the same seat made available to him, and that is normal as far as military transportation is concerned.

Q. Now, did Colonel Cauley know that there was a seat available on the plane?

A. I could not state that. I could not. Certainly, I did not make him knowledgeable of this.

Q. Did he come of his own free will to you and ask you if a seat was available?

A. Let me put it this way. He would not come to me and ask if a seat was available. He might have gotten the information from the airfield.

* * *

Q. The thing I am not clear about, Colonel. After your explanation as to the nature of the flight and the fact that it had been set up, the day before, but what I am not clear about is exactly how the decision to put Lieutenant Morrisseau on the plane came about.

A. I couldn't tell you that either. The decision was the CO's of the 46th Group.

* * *

Q. In other words, there was no initial action from you or anyone above the Commander of the 46th? He came to you?

A. That is true.

Q. He came to you, and did he state how he had found out about this seat on the plane?

A. No, I do not recall that he did, but I didn't make it my point to find out.

Q. Somehow or other, he had found out about this seat, and he asked if Lieutenant Morrisseau could go on it and you said?

A. I said, there's no reason why not.

* * *

A. I think one misapprehension that people may have is this, that the Chief of Staff is going around running the Commander's business. I turned Lieutenant Morrisseau's case over to [the former Commanding Officer] of the 46th Group. From that point on, it was his business.[23]

Questions by Captain Dugan for the defense.

Q. And you weren't aware that Lieutenant Morrisseau was going to be given a direct order, and be given one hour in which to prepare himself?

A. The circumstances of the order were not discussed with me.

Q. Was there any discussion between you and Colonel Cauley about getting Lieutenant Morrisseau on that plane?

A. There was no discussion about getting Lieutenant Morrisseau on that plane. I have stated quite frankly, I believe, that the only thing that was brought to my attention was to approve the request for space aboard the aircraft, which I did.

Q. For all you knew, Lieutenant Morrisseau wanted to go at that time. You were told that he wasn't going against his wishes?

A. That is of no concern to me. The Commanding Officer of the 46th Group came to me and asked me for the space aboard the aircraft, which I provided because the space was available.

* * *

A. I am returning to what I previously said. Lieutenant Morrisseau's case was referred to the Commanding Officer of the 46th Group, who, as his commander, would take whatever action would be deemed appropriate and would consult, I am sure, whatever legal counsel is necessary.

In so doing I stepped out of the picture because it was the Commanding Officer's apparent matter of concern to him, not to me.[24]

Captain Dugan then asked Colonel Queenin if Lieutenant Colonel Cauley received instructions from a higher headquarters on what actions to take in Lieutenant Morrisseau's case. Colonel Queenin answered in the negative.

A. Well, as a Commanding Officer, I think he would be remiss if he waited for some word from higher headquarters as to what he would do. This is his responsibility and prerogative as a CO.

Q. Then, to your knowledge, nothing had transpired to indicate that the matter was under consideration at a higher headquarters?

A. I don't know that the matter was . . . under consideration at higher headquarters. I know that his actions were of concern at higher headquarters, all the way to the Department of the Army, but to my knowledge, there was no requirement by any higher echelon to take any action against Lieutenant Morrisseau whatsoever.[25]

* * *

Question by Mr. Sherman.

Q. No decisions were made?

A. Because any decision pertaining to Lieutenant Morrisseau would be made by the CO of the 46th Group.[26]

* * *

Questions by Captain Dugan.

Q. Sir, one final question. Was it ever expressed or made known to the Commanding Officer . . . of the 46th Group, or, in fact, to anyone in general, that there was any desire on the part of the Chief of Staff or any of the Staff Sections, or perhaps the Commanding General himself, to expedite Lieutenant Morrisseau's departure from Fort Devens in any way?

A. I do not know of any statement made by the Commanding

General, nor did I make any such statements, as far as expediting him.[27]

* * *

Q. Do you know of any desire along those lines that might have been discussed by any other Staff Section?

A. I know of no official comment on this.

Q. Any unofficial comment?

A. I would not comment on that. I have no knowledge of any official or unofficial statement made by anybody in their position as a Staff Officer in charge of this installation.[28]

Leaving the official record of the Article 32 investigation at this point, the scene shifts to the action of the Fort Devens' Staff Judge Advocate, Major Fontanella, who, following the submission of the report of investigation on May 1, 1968, prepared his formal pre-trial advice on the *Morrisseau* case. Major Fontanella made a brief review of the facts involved in the case, noting that the investigating officer had recommended that the charge be dropped because he was of the opinion that Lieutenant Colonel Cauley's order to board the aircraft, under the circumstances, was an illegal order. Major Fontanella, however, disagreed with the investigating officer, and recommended that the charges be referred to trial by general court-martial.[29] The Commanding General, Fort Devens, personally reviewed the file and recommendations in the case, and ultimately agreed with his staff judge advocate; on May 2, 1968, the charges were referred to trial by general court-martial by command of Major General Lemmon.[30] The trial was scheduled to be held on May 14 at Fort Devens, with a court-martial, all of whose members were subject to the command of Major General Lemmon.[31]

On May 3, 1968, Captain Dugan served notice on the military that defense counsel were going to strike at no less a figure than Major General Lemmon himself. On that date,

Captain Dugan formally requested that Major General Lemmon and his former Staff Judge Advocate, Colonel Willis E. Schug (Retired), who had been on duty at the time Lieutenant Morrisseau refused the order to board the military aircraft, be made available for defense examination at the formal trial of the case.[32] The General himself was thus to be called into court, told to raise his hand and swear to tell the whole truth just as any ordinary mortal. It is conceivable that this intention on the part of defense counsel put somewhat of a damper on the joy of bringing Lieutenant Morrisseau to his heels at Fort Devens.

Ten days after this request was submitted to the Fort Devens command, the trial counsel (i.e., the prosecutor) in the *Morrisseau* case advised the Commanding General at Fort Devens to withdraw the charges from trial at Fort Devens. This advice, in pertinent part, read as follows:

. . . Evidence discovered in the course of preparation for trial indicates that a substantial question will be raised at the trial concerning your involvement in Lieutenant Morrisseau's case and your capacity to act as convening authority.

. . . Accordingly, I recommend that the charge be withdrawn from trial and that the case not be referred to trial before any court convened by you.[33]

Two days later, on May 16, General Lemmon threw in the sponge, his appetite for Lieutenant Morrisseau's blood having gone somewhat stale. He withdrew the charges from trial at Fort Devens, and forwarded them to First Army Headquarters for ultimate disposition. The Commanding General's reasons of record for referring the matter to First Army are quoted in pertinent part below:

2. Pursuant to the advice of the trial counsel, I have withdrawn the charges from the court to which it was referred since I have been advised that my involvement in Lieutenant Morrisseau's case might be construed to indicate a personal interest on

my part in the prosecution of the case, which would disqualify me from acting as convening authority.

3. Although I personally feel that my interest in this case has not gone beyond my official interest as commander of the installation to which Lieutenant Morrisseau is assigned, I wish to avoid even the suggestion that the government has not provided an impartial forum for the disposition of the charge against Lieutenant Morrisseau.

4. Accordingly, the charge sheets and allied papers are forwarded for such disposition as you deem appropriate.

5. I recommend trial by general court-martial.

K. B. Lemmon, Jr.
*Major General, USA
Commanding*[34]

While the General's letter did not admit "even the suggestion that the government has not provided an impartial forum" for the trial of Lieutenant Morrisseau at Fort Devens, a second piece of correspondence from Fort Devens, dated the same day and signed by Major Fontanella, presents a different picture. This second letter, in fact, indicates that some of the key command actors at Fort Devens had an exceedingly light regard for sworn truth at the Article 32 investigation.

This correspondence reads, in its entirety:

16 May 1968

MEMORANDUM FOR RECORD

On 15 May 1968 I spoke with the Commanding General concerning his involvement in the case of United States v. 2LT Dennis J. Morrisseau.

At that time he indicated to me that he had accepted a suggestion that Lieutenant Morrisseau be transported to Fort Jackson, South Carolina, by military aircraft. After checking on aircraft availability, the Commanding General authorized a flight set up to take the G-3 officer to attend a meeting at Fort Bragg, North Carolina, with a scheduled drop-off of Lieutenant Morrisseau at Fort Jackson, South Carolina, en route to Fort Bragg. His agreement with, and authorization of, this arrangement was in his opinion the best course of action under the existing circumstances as known by him at the time. Although implementation was left up to the Chief of Staff, the Commanding General indicated that after authorizing military air travel for Lieutenant Morrisseau, he expected that this action would be accomplished unless the matter were again referred to him.

When questioned as to his reasons for authorizing this course of action, the Commanding General indicated that he was in receipt of information that indicated that Lieutenant Morrisseau was lagging in his installation clearance procedures and departure arrangements to the point that there was a question as to his ability to effect timely compliance with his Department of Army orders if left to his own devices. He stated that his decision was influenced by the following considerations:

1. Interested in taking all possible measures to insure compliance by Lieutenant Morrisseau with his Department of Army orders.

2. To minimize public exposure of Lieutenant Morrisseau in connection therewith to preclude occasions for repetition of Lieutenant Morrisseau's conduct in New Hampshire [the McCarthy rally] and Washington, D. C. [picketing the White House].

The Commanding General indicated that he considered this to be the most reasonable and appropriate course of action in view of Lieutenant Morrisseau's recent activities.

D. A. Fontanella
Major, JAGC
Staff Judge Advocate

Only the bracketed material has been added. Otherwise the memorandum is a verbatim copy, material which, if true, reveals not only a questionable regard for truth by the supporting staff at Fort Devens, but also a doubt as to General Lemmon's own regard for truth.

It will be recalled that a general court-martial convening authority and his staff judge advocate are required by law to review an Article 32 investigation prior to referring charges to trial by general court-martial.[35] Thus, if General Lemmon read the report of investigation, as would appear reasonable under the circumstances of this very unusual case, he would

surely have known at that time that his own participation in
the decision to move Lieutenant Morrisseau to Fort Jackson
by military aircraft was seriously misrepresented by his subordinates at the Article 32 investigation—assuming, that is,
that the memorandum of May 16, 1968, signed by his Staff
Judge Advocate, is truthful as it relates to the General's actions in the *Morrisseau* case. Additionally, if the memorandum is accurate, had the General been briefed orally by his
Staff Judge Advocate on the issues involved in the Article
32 investigation—another standard course of action in a
case as important as the *Morrisseau* case—he would have
received news of his own purported absence of participation
in the case, a notification that would have instantly alerted
him to the dangers of further proceedings in the case. Yet,
following his own review of the Article 32 investigation of
the charges against Lieutenant Morrisseau, and following
the receipt of the staff judge advocate's written pre-trial advice in the case,[36] and, of course, well knowing the extent of
his own participation (if we are to believe the memorandum
of his staff judge advocate), General Lemmon nonetheless
proceeded to refer the case to trial by general court-martial.
If Major Fontanella correctly recounted his May 15 conversation with General Lemmon, a most serious question arises
—why a general officer in the United States Army would
associate himself with such a reckless, cruel and senseless
venture that was obviously designed to hide the fact that the
jurisdictional basis of the *Morrisseau* case (insofar as its being referred to trial at Fort Devens was concerned) was
supported entirely by fraud and perjury. Those who would
advance military necessity as a justification for this type of
conduct would indeed carry a most heavy burden.

The charges against Lieutenant Morrisseau, together
with the report of the Article 32 investigating officer, and
the staff judge advocate memorandum of May 16, were ulti-

mately referred to me as Chief of Military Justice at First
Army Headquarters, for initial review. I reviewed the entire
file, including the memorandum signed by Major Fontanella, and concluded that the request of the Fort Devens'
Commander—that jurisdiction in the case be assumed by
First Army—was indeed proper, albeit a bit tardy. Rather
than act on the matter at First Army Headquarters, however, the Army Commander determined that the case
should be referred to a third court-martial jurisdiction for
final disposition. Thus, the entire file was forwarded to the
Commanding General, Fort Belvoir, Virginia, for appropriate action. That same day, I telephoned the Belvoir staff
judge advocate and advised him of the nature of the case. I
also gave my opinion of the importance of the memorandum signed by Major Fontanella, and suggested that this
memorandum be studied in detail before referring the
charges against Lieutenant Morrisseau to trial by general
court-martial. It was not too long after this conversation
that the charges against Lieutenant Morrisseau were
dropped by order of the Commanding General at Fort Belvoir. A short time thereafter, Lieutenant Morrisseau accepted a mild reprimand and forfeiture of pay, under the
provisions of Article 15 of the Uniform Code of Military
Justice,[37] as his punishment for his refusal to board General
Lemmon's airplane as ordered, thus ending this most unusual case. At the time Morrisseau accepted Article 15
punishment, he had less than one year to serve in the Army,
and was, reportedly, reassigned to military duty within the
United States for the completion of his obligated military
service.

Rather than litigate the honesty, truthfulness, and integrity of its top brass at Fort Devens, the Army, in typical
military justice fashion, simply dropped the charges against
Lieutenant Morrisseau. To my knowledge, Lieutenant Mor-

risseau was the first and only individual in the Army who openly and publicly denounced the Vietnam war and who openly and publicly avoided military service in that ignoble war as a matter of conscience, all without suffering court-martial conviction and prison sentence for his efforts. Morrisseau's head was bloodied in the process, and he came close to martyrdom. But he came through with his honor and principles untarnished. It is probable that, at some date not too distant in our country's future, men such as Morrisseau, and his less fortunate compatriots who were sentenced to prison for their decision to stand on their moral convictions on this same question, will be recognized as the true patriots that they are; and that the flag-waving, war-seeking military chieftains who bite so viciously and, at times, so dishonorably, at their heels, will be relegated to the proper level of public disdain reserved for the common enemies of mankind.

Notes:

1. See Sherman, *Buttons, Bumper Stickers and the Soldier,* THE NEW REPUBLIC, August 17, 1968, at 16.

2. *Id.*

3. See the testimony of Lieutenant Colonel John J. Cauley, Commanding Officer, 46th Direct Support Group, Fort Devens, Massachusetts, in the Report of the Investigating Officer of the case of the United States v. Second Lieutenant Dennis J. Morrisseau, United States Army, dated May 1, 1968, at pages 26–35.

4. See testimony of Lieutenant Morrisseau, at page 377, Report of the Investigating Officer, note 3, *supra,* wherein Morrisseau testified that he "fully intended to take an Eastern Airlines flight . . . which had been arranged for me . . . at 7:09 PM, the 13th of March . . . to eventually reach Fort William Davis, Canal Zone, for two weeks of jungle training."

5. See testimony of Colonel Hugh F. Queenin, Chief of Staff, Fort Devens, at pages 283–7, Report of the Investigating Officer, note 3, *supra.*

6. *Id.* at 288. Also see testimony of Lieutenant Colonel Cauley, pages 39–40. Report of the Investigating Officer, note 3, *supra.*

7. See the written deposition of Major Jerry M. Hendrick, pages 12–28, attached as an Exhibit to the Report of the Investigating Officer, note 14, *supra,* wherein Major Hendrick testified that the possibility that the accused might not make his civilian flight was "ever present in anyone's mind," and that "I had a personal feeling that Lieutenant Morrisseau would not comply with his Department of the Army orders." Also see the testimony of Lieutenant Colonel Cauley, the individual who allegedly made the decision to move Lieutenant Morrisseau by military aircraft as opposed to commercial. Cauley stated: "Lieutenant Morrisseau had indicated to me in one way or another that he wasn't moving in the manner that he should be, and that he wasn't preparing himself to make the move that the order had directed . . ." Page 35, Report of the Investigating Officer, note 3, *supra.*

8. See page 1 of the pre-trial advice in regard to charges against Lieutenant Morrisseau, dated May 1, 1968. Charge sheets were prepared the very day that Morrisseau refused to board the aircraft, were signed and sworn by Lieutenant Colonel Cauley, and Morrisseau was formally advised of the charges on the same day. See page 3 of the Charge Sheet wherein these matters are recorded as a matter of record.

9. See note 8, *supra.*

10. Lieutenant Bizony's record of non-judicial punishment is contained on Department of Army Form Number 2627–1. The offer to impose punishment for a failure to go to his appointed place of duty on March 9, 1968, is dated March 15, 1968, and is signed by Thomas J. King, an Assistant Adjutant General at Fort Devens, for the Fort Devens Commander.

11. See page 2 of Department of Army Form Number 2627–1, note 10, *supra.*

12. This information was furnished at my request by the Acting Staff Judge Advocate at Fort Devens. See Letter, dated April 3, 1968, entitled: *Nonjudicial Punishment in the Case of 1Lt Nicholas Bizony,* from Major D.A. Fontanella, Fort Devens,

Massachusetts, to the Commanding General, First United States Army, Attention: Staff Judge Advocate, Fort Meade, Maryland. Major Fontanella reported in this letter:

> Based upon his performance and the Article 15, Lt. Bizony was not recommended for promotion to Captain. LTC Calahan reiterated that his recommendation for disciplinary action in this case was based solely upon the offense without any consideration of Lt. Bizony's relationship to Lt. Morrisseau.

13. Lieutenant Bizony's appeal is found at page 3, Department of Army Form Number 2627–1, note 10, *supra.* In his appeal he noted that his absence "would not have been noticed were it not for a set of circumstances involving me with one 2LT Dennis J. Morrisseau, who is now awaiting a General Court-Martial." He further noted in his appeal that the punishment imposed would "seriously hamper my effectiveness as Defense Counsel for the above mentioned 2LT Morrisseau."

14. This letter is the same letter that is referred to in note 12, *supra.*

15. See the concluding paragraph of Major Fontanella's letter, dated April 3, 1968, noote 12, *supra.*

16. See page 1, Department of Army Form 2627–2, dated April 4, 1968, in which the Commanding General, First Army Headquarters, granted Lieutenant Bizony's appeal insofar "as it pertains to the 60-day restriction, including your right to enter the Fort Devens Officers Open Mess." To my knowledge, however, nothing was done in regard to the recommendation not to promote Lieutenant Bizony. Hence it is quite likely that Bizony was never promoted to Captain.

17. Articles 22*b* and 23*b*, Uniform Code of Military Justice.

18. Article 1 (11), Uniform Code of Military Justice; paragraph 5*a* (4), MANUAL FOR COURTS-MARTIAL, United States, 1951.

19. Paragraph 5*a* (4), MANUAL FOR COURTS-MARTIAL, United States, 1951.

20. Articles 22*b* and 23*b*, Uniform Code of Military Justice; paragraph 5*a* (3), MANUAL FOR COURTS-MARTIAL, United States, 1951.

21. Pages 26–7, Report of the Investigating Officer, note 3, *supra.*

22. *Id.* at pages 31–4.

23. *Id.* at pages 283–90.

24. *Id.* at pages 290–3.

25. *Id.* at page 296.

26. *Id.* at page 304.

27. *Id.* at page 308.

28. *Id.*

29. See the pre-trial advice of the staff judge advocate, dated May 1, 1968, Fort Devens, Massachusetts, in regard to court-martial charges against Lieutenant Morrisseau.

30. See page 3 of the Charge Sheet, United States v. Second Lieutenant Morrisseau, Fort Devens, Massachusetts, dated March 13, 1968.

31. See Court-Martial Appointing Order Number 10, Headquarters, Fort Devens, Massachusetts, dated May 2, 1968.

32. See Letter, entitled *Subpoena of Witnesses,* dated May 3, 1968, from Captain Thomas R. Dugan, addressed to the Commanding General, Fort Devens, attention: Staff Judge Advocate.

33. See Letter, entitled *Withdrawal of Charges against 2LT Dennis J. Morrisseau,* dated May 13, 1968, from Captain Charles P. Malone, Trial Counsel, addressed to the Commanding General, Fort Devens, Massachusetts.

34. See Letter, entitled *Disposition of Charges against 2LT Dennis J. Morrisseau,* dated May 16, 1968, from Major General K. B. Lemmon, Jr., Commanding General, Fort Devens, Massachusetts, addressed to the Commanding General, First United States Army, Fort Meade, Maryland.

35. Article 34, Uniform Code of Military Justice, reads in pertinent part:

> Before directing the trial of any charge by general court-martial, the convening authority shall refer it to his staff judge advocate or legal officer for consideration and advice.

See also Weaver, *Pretrial Advice of the Staff Judge Advocate Under Article 34, Uniform Code of Military Justice,* 19 MILITARY L. REV. 37, at 37 (1963), who explains the philosophy behind the pre-trial advice:

> The proper selection of cases to be tried by general court-martial is an important step in the administration of military justice. This selection can be made only after the staff judge

advocate or legal officer has made a careful, impartial, independent and professional review of the report of investigation made under Article 32(b) of the Uniform Code of Military Justice, and the accompanying papers. Careful analysis and mature, independent recommendations woven into a persuasive pretrial advice will assist the convening authority in the discharge of his judicial function of determining whether charges should be referred for trial by general court-martial.

36. The staff judge advocate's pre-trial advice in Lieutenant Morrisseau's case, contained no reference to Morrisseau's picketing the White House. There was no background explanation at all, just a bare summation of the fact that he received an order to board an airplane and refused to do so. This, and nothing more, rated a recommendation by the staff judge advocate that he be tried by general court-martial. The pre-trial advice also made no reference whatever to the matter of General Lemmon's personal involvement in the case. Nor did the pre-trial advice mention the painful fact that a month *before* the completion of the formal pre-trial investigation of charges against Lieutenant Morrisseau, the Fort Devens command element was laying the groundwork for his general court-martial, to wit: On March 29, some five weeks before the Commanding General at Fort Devens referred Morrisseau's case to trial, the Fort Devens Chief of Staff saw fit to issue a directive, in the name of the Commanding General, directing the Provost Marshal to prepare a plan to exclude "curious visitors and trouble makers" at the trial of Lieutenant Morrisseau. And on April 1, the command specified that the currently convened general court at Fort Devens would not try Lieutenant Morrisseau, but that a specially appointed court-martial would be convened for this purpose, which would include at least two lieutenants as members, both of whom were to have had "combat experience."

37. Under the provisions of Article 15, a commanding officer may impose certain punishments upon officers, warrant officers and enlisted personnel of his command without the intervention of a court-martial. In the Army no individual may be punished under Article 15 if the individual concerned demands trial by court-martial in lieu of punishment under Article 15. Under Article 15, officers may be punished by imposition of restriction to specified limits, suspension from duty, and forfeiture of pay. The MANUAL FOR COURTS-MARTIAL, 1951, which was in

effect at the time Morrisseau was punished, provided that Article 15 punishments were reserved for "minor offenses," unless it appeared "that punishment under that article would not meet the ends of justice and discipline." Paragraph 129, MANUAL FOR COURTS-MARTIAL, 1951.

COMMAND INFLUENCE—THE WORKING LEVEL

The case of *United States* v. *Wells*[1] originated almost a year after my transfer from Third Army Headquarters at Fort McPherson, Georgia. The facts of the case were relatively simple.[2] Several black soldiers stationed at Fort Bragg, North Carolina, got into an altercation with several white soldiers over the use of a phone booth at Fort Bragg, on January 8, 1964. A fight took place between one of the white soldiers and one of the black soldiers, and during the fight the white soldier was threatened with a knife. The two groups then split, but both met again at the barracks of the white soldiers where another fight ensued in which one of the white soldiers was stabbed to death, another cut over the right eye. Charges of premeditated murder, aggravated assault and conspiracy to commit murder were charged against the defendant Wells and three of his black companions. The charges were eventually referred to trial by general court-martial at Fort Bragg, and second-degree murder convictions were returned against all four defendants on May 16, 1964. Sentences ranging from three to ten years were imposed against the four defendants.

First Lieutenant Wayne Loudermilch, who defended Wells at the trial of the case, conducted a vigorous defense. He initially asked for, and was granted, a continuance for further preparation of the defense case by the law officer. There is little doubt that this continuance, coming as it did on the first day of the scheduled trial, upset the ordinary timetable of the prosecution, and required the entire case to be delayed for several days. During the subsequent trial, Lieutenant Loudermilch—loaned to Fort Bragg by the Third Army Staff Judge Advocate at Fort McPherson, Georgia, as counsel for Wells only—raised the matter of command influence in the preparation of the pre-trial advice of the case. He, and counsel for the remaining defendants, alleged that the executive officer in the Staff Judge Advocate Section at Fort Bragg had directed the criminal investigation of every stage of the case; that he had prepared the charges in the case and had directed the accuser to sign them; and that he had thereafter written a supposedly impartial and judicial pre-trial advice in which he recommended that the convening authority refer the same charges to trial by general court-martial—in short, that the pre-trial advice was illegal and in contradiction to Article 6c of the Uniform Code of Military Justice.[3] Among other tactics, defense counsel for all defendants made frequent objections to evidence, and in particular objected to the rulings of the law officer when, under the provisions of the Jencks' Act,[4] they demanded the production of statements in the hands of the government.

Following the trial, and after Lieutenant Loudermilch's return to Atlanta, he found his superiors unenthused about his defense tactics. In fact, the reception was so hostile, that Lieutenant Loudermilch filed a detailed brief with the Secretary of the Army, setting forth in detail what he felt to be illegal command reprisal actions taken against him by the Third Army Staff Judge Advocate, a Colonel Harold Luren.[5] Loudermilch alleged that upon the day following his return to Fort McPherson he was personally interviewed and threatened by Colonel Luren. He stated that he was informed by Luren that "a lot of unethical tactics" were employed in the *Wells* trial, and that Colonel Luren was not going to tolerate cases "being defended like that at Army headquarters." What is more, Loudermilch's brief continued, Colonel Luren "demanded" to know why he asked for a continuance on the first day of the trial, and that, without giving him time to reply, remarked that "it was damned stupid." [6]

Loudermilch recorded that on the next day, Colonel Luren summoned all officers of his staff into the office library to hear a "critique" on the conduct of the *Wells* trial. At this critique, Loudermilch stated, Luren asked the law officer who presided at the *Wells* trial, and a reservist on active duty for two weeks, a lieutenant colonel from north Alabama, to conduct the critique. The latter, according to Loudermilch, conducted the major portion of the critique, praising the prosecutor in "laudatory terms, such as 'highly commendable' and 'outstanding' " but finding very little of a complimentary nature to say about the defense counsel. Then, according to Loudermilch's brief, this reserve officer stated that the defense counsel engaged in "a lot of borderline tactics," and that Loudermilch "made repeated requests for instructions with slight change of phraseology," and that it appeared that he "was either trying to trick the Law Officer or make it appear that he didn't know what he was doing." [7] In addition, again according to Loudermilch's brief, counsel for the defense were "collectively criticized for what was alleged to be a major effort to subvert the Law Officer," with multiple motions and objections. One defense counsel was accused of deliberately misstating law to the Law Officer in regard to the Jencks' Act, while others made pointless objections. Quoting from Loudermilch's brief:

> Throughout this critique, Colonel Luren was positioned at one end of the table in full view of the rest of his staff. His initial remarks were confined to a few questions concerning some of the

"borderline tactics." Each time a defense counsel's name was used, Colonel Luren would start writing, giving the appearance of taking copious notes on the mentioned counsel. Toward the conclusion of the meeting, he inquired as to the "possibility of contempt action or even disbarment proceedings against some of the counsel" and asked whether the Law Officer could suggest any corrective command measures or disciplinary actions that were in order. The Law Officer stated that he was certainly not aware that that was the purpose for which Colonel Luren had called the meeting, and that it was his opinion that no action should be taken against any of the officers, but that if that was the purpose of the meeting then he would like to withdraw from further discussion and he would refuse to participate further in meetings of that nature . . .[8]

Loudermilch noted that after one and a half hours the critique was called to a close, and alleged that, shortly thereafter, Colonel Luren communicated with the Staff Judge Advocate Office at Fort Bragg about bringing possible disbarment proceedings against one of the defense counsel involved, Captain Smaltz.[9] Six days after the critique, he stated, he received a telephone call from the personnel branch of the Office of the Judge Advocate General in the Pentagon, and was told that he was being transferred to Fort Sheridan, Illinois. Two days later, while still assigned at Fort McPherson, Loudermilch was relieved of duties as Chief of Legal Assistance, and was moved into the Military Justice Section of Colonel Luren's office, where he was given non-trial duties and would not be in position to interview clients of any description.[10] A week later he was required to read and initial the Canons of Professional Ethics.[11]

Loudermilch closed his initial brief with a request that the post-trial review of the *Wells* case be written by the Staff Judge Advocate at the United States Continental Army Command, the next superior Headquarters to Third Army.[12] This request was immediately ordered by the Secretary of the Army who, at the same time, ordered an Inspector General's investigation of Lieutenant Loudermilch's allegations against Colonel Luren, to be conducted, of course, by very senior Judge Advocate personnel from the Department of the Army.[13]

A second brief from Lieutenant Loudermilch was soon to follow.[14] In this second brief, he reported his actual transfer to Fort Sheridan, Illinois, on July 8, 1964.[15] He further noted that only fourteen days after the trial of Private Wells, Colonel Luren personally rendered an unusually low efficiency report upon him.[16] The first three efficiency reports he received at Fort McPherson, he recalled, were "near perfect," with scores of 230, 229.7 and 231.5 (out of a total maximum of 240). His fourth report, however, the one which he received from Colonel Luren fourteen days after the trial of Private Wells, reflected a total score of 172.6, representing a drop of some 58.9 points from his last rating of 231.5.[17]

In his second brief, Lieutenant Loudermilch also asked that he be given a copy of the Inspector General's investigation of his allegations against Colonel Luren.[18] As officially stated, he was requesting a copy of the report to perfect the appellate brief that he was writing in behalf of Private Wells' eventual appeal to the board of review, and ultimately to the Court of Military Appeals. Loudermilch knew, of course, that an Inspector General's report of investigation in the Army is a secret process, from beginning to end, and that as such, the report relating to his allegations against Colonel Luren would be read only by trusted members of the Army establishment. Loudermilch also knew, or at least correctly predicted, that under no circumstances would the Army release a copy of the report to him, because of what its contents would reveal as to the nature of military justice at Third Army Headquarters. Hence, it was largely with tongue in cheek that this request was made. But in another context, it was a serious request, for once the Army turned it down, the Army would be legally precluded from going further either with the appellate review of Private Wells' conviction, or his re-trial in the event the present conviction were reversed upon appeal. In other words, both the short and long-range prospects for a successful prosecution in the *Wells* case were in serious jeopardy; the Army either had to produce the Inspector General's report (a report which took several weeks to complete), or throw in the sponge and completely dismiss charges against Private Wells. Both Lieutenant Loudermilch and I, who were in quite close correspondence at the time, were of the opinion that the Army would elect to dismiss the charges (second-degree murder) against Private Wells rather than release the report of investigation.

Loudermilch resolved, therefore, to bring the entire matter formally before the Court of Military Appeals, hoping for some censure of the Army by that Court before the Army mooted the case via the expedient of dismissing the charges against Private Wells. Loudermilch, accordingly, filed two writs with the Court of Military Appeals, asking for extraordinary relief. He formally requested the Court of Military Appeals, through its inherent powers as a federal court, and pursuant to its authority under the All Writs Act,[19] to dismiss charges against his client on the basis of the unconstitutional reprisal action taken against him as counsel following the trial of the case. As an alternative, he attacked the jurisdiction of the convening authority involved to convene general courts-martial, and asked that his client be released on a writ of habeas corpus.[20] In a second writ, a writ of mandamus,[21] he asked the Court of Military Appeals to order the Secretary of the Army to furnish him a verbatim copy of the Inspector General's investigation of his charges against Colonel Luren, for the purpose of perfecting an appeal of his client's conviction. In each of his petitions to the Court of Military Appeals, Lieutenant Loudermilch set forth in detail the reprisal action taken against him that preceded his transfer to Fort Sheridan. He also included copies of his briefs to the Secretary of the Army as exhibits to his petitions for extraordinary relief. The Court of Military Appeals denied, or dismissed, his petitions summarily, without comment on their merits,[22] and on January 12, 1965, some eight months after his client was convicted, the Staff Judge Advocate, Continental Army Command Headquarters, recommended that the Continental Army Commander disapprove the convictions in each case, and this was done. Re-trials were ordered in two of the cases, but the charges against Private Wells and a second defendant were *dismissed* on the basis of a "failure of proof" at the original trial.[23]

The most that came of the punitive action that was taken against Lieutenant Loudermilch in this case was a critical comment relating to it, read into a Senate subcommittee hearing by Judge Homer Ferguson in 1966.[24] The Court of Military Appeals, as we have seen, did less than nothing in regard to this case. The Army, of course, did not release the controversial report, nor did it reassign Lieutenant Loudermilch to Fort McPherson, Georgia, and he thus remained at Fort Sheridan in a non-trial assignment until he was relieved from active duty. While still assigned at Fort Sheridan, on March 30, 1965, Loudermilch received a letter from the Judge Advocate General of the Army, who made reference to the two briefs and affidavits he had filed with the Secretary of the Army alleging command influence and illegal command reprisal action against him in the *Wells* case. The Judge Advocate General advised Loudermilch in this regard:

Those matters referred to in your briefs and affidavits not directly related to proceedings in the *Wells* case have been exhaustively and impartially investigated pursuant to direction by the Secretary of the Army. Based upon this investigation and the investigating officer's findings and recommendations, the Secretary of the Army has determined that no disciplinary or unfavorable administrative action will be taken with respect to any personnel involved in the investigation.[25]

The sad commentary upon this statement was the fact that very much unfavorable administrative action had *already been taken* against Lieutenant Loudermilch. He had first been castigated by Colonel Luren, then threatened, then publicly embarrassed and slandered at the "critique," then relieved of his job at Fort McPherson's Legal Assistance Office, then given an extremely low efficiency report by Colonel Luren, and then transferred to Fort Sheridan, Illinois. The Judge Advocate General's assurance that "no disciplinary or unfavorable administrative action" would be taken against anyone involved in the case was therefore not only a bit wide of the mark, but outright ludicrous. The immediate loser was Lieutenant Loudermilch, if physical inconvenience and military "one-up-manship" are considered as yardsticks of victory. If, however, the case is judged from the viewpoint of moral integrity, Lieutenant Loudermilch was a decided winner; his fight was a well-directed effort by a dedicated young lawyer against overwhelming odds; and, as usual in such cases, he stood almost alone against the eye of the hurricane.

Notes:

1. Private Thomas L. Wells, U.S. Army, and others were tried at Fort Bragg, North Carolina, by general court-martial, pursuant to Headquarters, Fort Bragg, Court-Martial Appointing Order Number 3, dated April 28, 1964. The defendants were identically

charged with premeditated murder, assault with intent to inflict grievous bodily harm, conspiracy to commit murder, and conspiracy to commit grievous bodily harm. The trial commenced on April 29, and concluded on May 16, 1964.

2. The facts of the case are taken from a Post Trial Review of the conviction by the Staff Judge Advocate, Headquarters, United States Army Continental Command, Fort Monroe, Virginia, dated January 12, 1965.

3. See Defense Brief and Affidavit submitted pursuant to Article 138(c), Uniform Code of Military Justice, in behalf of Private Thomas L. Wells, dated July 27, 1964, at 1–2.

4. 18 U.S.C. sec. 3500 (1958). Also see Jencks v. United States, 353 U.S. 657 (1957).

5. Colonel Luren's true identity has been withheld.

6. See Defense Brief, *supra,* note 3, at 3–4. Lieutenant Loudermilch stated in his brief that he reminded Colonel Luren that all the defense counsel involved did the best they could do for all their clients, all of whom were charged with capital offenses. The brief continues:

   . . . it was beyond my comprehension how he could characterize my conduct and that of the other defense counsel as unethical. Moreover, were the cases being tried tomorrow, I would handle the defense of my client in the same manner. As for the continuance, I enumerated the grounds that I had raised at the trial and remarked that I couldn't say anything further on that except that the law officer considered that I had given more than enough reasons to satisfy him that I was entitled to a continuance. Colonel Luren then concluded the conference with the statement that: "I hope what I have said on these matters is clear." Defense Brief, *supra,* note 3, at 4.

7. Defense Brief, *supra,* note 3, at 4–5.

8. *Id.* at 6.

9. *Id.* at 7.

10. *Id.* The trial was completed on May 16, 1964 (see note 1, *supra*), and, according to Loudermilch's brief, he received the telephone call from the Pentagon informing him he was being transferred to Fort Sheridan, Illinois, on May 25, 1964. On May 27, he was told by Colonel Luren that he was to be moved

out of his job as Chief of Legal Assistance at Fort McPherson. Defense Brief, *supra,* note 3, at 7.

11. Defense Brief, *supra,* note 3, at 7.

12. *Id.* at 12–3.

13. See unclassified electrical message, Department of Army 980332, dated July 31, 1964.

14. See Defense Brief and Affidavit submitted pursuant to Article 138(c), Uniform Code of Military Justice, in behalf of Private Thomas L. Wells, dated October 23, 1964. As the former brief, the second brief was addressed to the Secretary of the Army.

15. Defense Brief, *supra,* note 14, at 1.

16. Defense Brief, *supra,* note 14, at 1–2. The efficiency report in question was rendered on May 31, 1964.

17. *Id.* at 2.

18. *Id.* Loudermilch stated in his brief, in this regard:

> Following the submission of my initial brief in this case, the Department of the Army ordered an investigation of the command influence allegations contained in my brief. Two senior Judge Advocate officers conducted the investigation. A certified court reporter accompanied these officers, and took verbatim statements from witnesses, including a statement from me. I herewith request that the reviewing authority, prior to writing the post-trial review in this case, and prior to taking post-trial action in the case, obtain a verbatim copy of this report of investigation for post-trial review purposes. I further request that the reviewing authority furnish me a complete verbatim copy of the entire investigation for my use in perfecting the appeal in this case. [In a subsequent letter to me dated December 22, 1964, Loudermilch estimated that the report of investigation contained the testimony of 44 witnesses, and had been reported to him as being in excess of 1200 pages in length.]

19. 28 U.S.C. sec. 1651 (1964). The statute provides in pertinent part as follows:

> (a) The Supreme Court and all courts established by Act of Congress may issue all writs necessary or appropriate in aid of their respective jurisdictions and agreeable to the usages and principles of law.

20. See Writ of Habeas Corpus in the matter of Private Thomas L. Wells, to the United States Court of Military Appeals, dated November 23, 1964.

21. See Writ of Mandamus in the matter of Private Thomas L. Wells, to the United States Court of Military Appeals, dated December 7, 1964.

22. The Writ of Habeas Corpus was denied, and the Writ of Mandamus was dismissed. See Order of the Court of Military Appeals, in the matter of Private Thomas L. Wells, dated December 17, 1964. In Gale v. United States, 17 U.S.C.M.A. 40, 37 C.M.R. 304, at 307 (1967), the Court of Military Appeals rendered its first opinion in regard to an extraordinary writ submitted to that Court to stay further judicial proceedings in a pending case. In this landmark case the Court held that it "clearly possesses the power to grant relief" in extraordinary situations, pursuant to its authority under the All Writs Act.

23. See Post Trial Review, *supra,* note 2, at Inclosure Number 7.

24. See *Joint Hearing before the Senate Subcommittee on Constitutional Rights of the Committee on the Judiciary and a Special Subcommittee on Armed Services on S. 745–62 and 2906–7,* 89th Cong., 2d Sess., January 18, 19, 25, and 26; March 1, 2, and 3, 1966, at 302 wherein Judge Ferguson, in a written statement to the Subcommittee, in regard to the Wells case, noted:

> Recently, we had another case . . . in which a senior staff judge advocate similarly gave extremely bad efficiency reports to two young defense counsel and had both of them transferred, one actually being relieved from active duty. Upon this becoming known, the Secretary of the Army ordered these cases reviewed in another jurisdiction. They were set aside on the basis of other errors, but a lengthy investigation of the matter again came to naught, with no action, to my knowledge, being taken. On the retrial [of two of the accused] the new defense counsel was intimidated by the same staff judge advocate and ended up with an equally bad efficiency report for defending his client with vigor. Yet, despite this repetitive violation, we are aware of nothing that has been done.

> Also see Lieutenant Loudermilch's written statement which was submitted to the same Subcommittee, *Joint Hearings on S. 745–62, and 2906–7, supra,* at 658–60.

25. The letter was signed by Major General Robert H. McCaw, the Judge Advocate General of the Army, under date of March 30, 1965.

SEX AND WHISKEY IN PARIS, GEORGIA

My only occasion to practice law before a branch of military service other than the Army revealed that the Services were consistent in their desire to avoid embarrassing litigation. This case originated in Paris, Georgia, in the spring of 1960. Sergeant James Foster of the United States Marine Corps Reserve Detachment at Paris—a small unit of about sixty enlisted men and three officers who were assigned to service Marine Reserve personnel in the area, and to look after the Marine drill hall—had allegedly committed bigamy.[1] Sergeant Foster was a twenty-five-year-old Marine with almost seven years' service in the Corps. His first wife, some six years his senior, had long ago separated from him and only kept her legal relationship to draw the family living allowance which the Marine Corps sent to her so long as she was the Sergeant's lawful wife. As a result of the long separation from his wife, and because Sergeant Foster had filed suit for divorce and expected his decree to come through at any minute, the Sergeant permitted himself to fall in love. The young lady, Miss Wanda Lane, apparently fell for the man too and, believing him to be lawfully divorced from his first wife, was soon discussing matrimony. Despite Sergeant Foster's attempts to delay the pressing question, he soon found himself engaged to be married, with the wedding day rapidly approaching. Rather than risk losing Miss Lane, the Sergeant felt compelled to proceed with the ceremony, and he and Miss Lane were in fact married by a local minister. Several months after their marriage, the young lady's mother made an official inquiry of Sergeant

Foster's commanding officer, in an attempt to learn why her daughter was not receiving a family living allowance from the Marine Corps as were the wives of other enlisted men. Back came the reply that Sergeant Foster's first wife was receiving the allowance. The fat was in the fire.

After a thorough informal investigation by his unit commander, the Sergeant found himself on the receiving end of several related charges, of which the principal offenses were bigamy and adultery. Since the Marine Corps prided itself on being short of lawyers, and the Army had several to spare, I found myself assigned to represent the Sergeant at the formal Article 32 investigation of his court-martial charges. For several years I had contemplated defending a bigamy charge along what I considered to be untried lines of defense. The gist of my contemplated defense lay in the fact that bigamy is charged under the general Article of the Uniform Code of Military Justice, namely, Article 134; thus, in addition to the expected elements of the offense of bigamy, the government was required to prove that the conduct of the accused, under the circumstances, brought "discredit upon the Armed Forces." [2]

Thus when Sergeant Foster reported to my office in Atlanta prior to the official investigation, I made sure to ask him how many houses of prostitution, if any, were located in Paris, Georgia. He answered that there were two full-time houses of prostitution operating within the city limits, one with about five girls and the second with as many as ten. I asked him if Paris was wet or dry insofar as alcoholic drink was concerned. He assured me it was dry, but added that anyone could get a bottle within five minutes by dialing a certain telephone number. Thereupon, the Sergeant and I departed for Paris to verify his statements, and after questioning ten to fifteen Marines stationed in Paris, and a scattering of other citizens, I was convinced that the Sergeant's statements were true and provable. I was also convinced that the existence of vice in Paris, Georgia, was a matter of common knowledge to the man in the street.

Several days later, when the investigating officer, Major Roy J. Leite, Jr., of the United States Marine Corps Headquarters in Atlanta, was ready to proceed with the formal pre-trial investigation of the charges against the defendant, I advised him of my theory of defense, and added that, under the circumstances, I could not understand how the defendant's act of bigamy would rate much attention in Paris, much less tend to bring serious discredit upon the reputation of the Marine Corps in that city. I also advised Major Leite that, in the event the matter went to trial, I was surely going to litigate in the nation's press the Christian virtue of Paris, Georgia. I had suspected that the Major might immediately excuse himself and report the subject of our conversation to his Headquarters, and in that event I would have expected serious command interference—all of which I would have attempted to utilize against the Marine Corps in the trial of the case. But to my great surprise, Major Leite was fascinated with the theory and indicated his wholehearted support. Not only would he proceed forthwith, but he advised me that he would cooperate with me to the maximum in exposing as much of the story as possible to support my defense. Thus, upon our arrival in Paris, Major Leite got right down to business at hand.

The first witness at the investigation was the defendant's immediate commanding officer, Major Richard P. Wells, United States Marine Corps, who had preferred the charges against the defendant. Major Leite swore in this witness, and had him give a brief account of the evidence which led him to prefer charges against Sergeant Foster. At this point only a verbatim report of this witness' testimony can begin to do it full justice. The testimony, in pertinent part, follows:

Questions by Major Leite; answers by witness Wells.

Q. I would like to ask you your opinion, based upon your position in the community of Paris, why the actions you have just described could or would likely cause discredit to the Armed Forces?

A. It would most certainly bring discredit upon the Armed Forces, particularly the Marine Corps, as we have a very good reputation in this town, and anything of this nature would certainly bring discredit upon the Marine Corps.

Q. Are you referring there to the alleged bigamy only or the matter of adultery as well?

A. To both, the bigamy and adultery.

Q. It is generally looked down upon by the community here, the practice of engaging in illicit sexual intercourse with another person when he is not married?

A. Yes, it is looked down upon.

Questions by Captain West.

Q. Major Wells, how long have you been in the Marine Corps, sir?

A. Better than twenty years, almost twenty-one years.

Q. And you have served as an enlisted man in the Marine Corps? How many years?

A. Eight and a half years.

Q. What rank did you hold as an enlisted man?

A. Private through Staff Sergeant.

Q. Are you a Regular Marine Officer or a Reserve?

A. I'm a Regular.

Q. So . . . off and on or continuously from what date again have you been in Marine Corps?

A. Since 8 January 1940.

Q. Since 8 January 1940 you have associated on a close personal relationship with both enlisted men and officers?

A. Yes, I have.

Q. Would you say as a general rule illicit sex or intercourse is frowned upon by enlisted men in the Marine Corps?

A. I would say yes.

Q. How about officers?

A. Why certainly.

Q. Is it completely unknown?

A. Absolutely not.

Q. In other words, members of the Marine Corps do occasionally from time to time engage in illicit sexual intercourse.

A. It would be a presumption on my part if I said yes.

Q. You assume that this illicit sex, from your knowledge in the Marine Corps both with enlisted and officer status, has taken place both in the United States as well as overseas theaters, has it not?

A. As I say, I would only be making an assumption if I answered in the affirmative. I have no proof of it.

Q. But you tend to answer in the affirmative, do you not?

A. That's true.

Q. Now in this town of Paris, Georgia, do you say that you have illicit sex among the civilians here perhaps, or not?

A. I would say if you had it in any city, you'd have it here.

Q. In other words, illicit sexual intercourse is not the worst thing in the books by any means, is it, Major?

A. Well, naturally not.

Q. It's not so much service discrediting then as it would appear?

A. Well, this is my first occasion to ever be connected with such, so I really can't express an opinion there as to whether or not this act of illicit sexual intercourse is service discrediting in Paris, Georgia.

Q. In other words, you have no opinion . . .

A. That I do have. As far as the one concerned here, it would be very discrediting to the Marine Corps if the general public knew about it.

Q. Does the general public know about it?

A. They do not.

Q. This act of sexual intercourse involved in this case, involving the accused and Miss Lane, certainly it wouldn't stir up any more antipathy on the part of the general public than any other illicit sexual acts that took place in Paris, Georgia, would it?

A. As far as the Marine Corps is concerned, yes, because we enjoy a very high reputation here. So consequently, the Marine Corps would be looked down upon if a member of this unit was connected with such.

Q. Is it a fact that the Marine Corps would look down upon the member, or would the community look down upon the Marine Corps?

A. The community would look down upon the Marine Corps and the member concerned.

Q. You're sure of that fact?

A. I'm positive of it.

Q. Why do you say you're positive of it, sir?

A. Well, this community here has more churches per capita than any other small city in North Georgia. They are real church-going people and they will not condone such wrong doings. That's what I base my opinion on.

Q. You have no direct knowledge of that, it's strictly your opinion?

A. That's right.

* * *

Q. This Paris, Georgia, has more churches than almost any other city of this particular size?

A. That's right.

Q. And for that reason you conclude that this is a very Christian community?

A. That's true.

Q. And being a Christian community [it] would be endowed and imbued with all the attributes of Christians?

A. That's right.

Q. Including holding illicit sexual intercourse with this woman . . .

A. That's true.

Q. Alright, Major Wells, let's tackle another topic . . .

Major Leite, the investigating officer, subsequently returned to the subject of illicit sexual intercourse in Paris, Georgia, with Major Wells, and after drawing an answer from the witness that he knew of no public or private condoning of illicit sexual intercourse or the illicit sale of alcoholic beverages in Paris, Georgia, Major Leite pointedly asked him if he knew there were houses of prostitution operating in Paris. The witness replied:

Yes, I believe it is publicly known that there are several houses of prostitution here.

Question by Major Leite; answer by Major Wells.

Q. Here is the question that I am personally concerned about. In view of the two-faced attitude toward offenses of this nature, that is one the public avowment and the other the quietly condoning, the condoning attitude, would the sum total of this offense concerning bigamy and adultery really amount to a serious blow to the status of the Armed Forces, the Marine Corps in this town?

A. If the alleged crime were general knowledge, it is my belief that the Marine Corps Reserve Unit here would suffer substantially.

* * *

Questions by Captain West.

Q. It's general knowledge that there are, to be exact, two houses of prostitution, is that correct?

A. That I cannot prove. I have no proof. It's just general knowledge.

Q. And they operate in the city limits?

A. That I could not say. I have no idea whether they are in the city limits or not.

Q. And also there is the sale of illicit alcoholic beverages taking place in Paris, is that correct?

A. Well, I believe you can find that anywhere in the State of Georgia.

Q. So this fine community, even though it has the most churches of any other city its size in the United States, does condone certain types of criminal activity, would you say?

A. Well, certain people condone it.

Q. Certain people condone it, so therefore, the city does nothing about it?

A. I have no idea whether they are trying to do anything about it or not. I believe there was an article in the paper a couple of days ago where the sheriff came out and said he was going to back the temperance league here of which their drive is to stop illegal sale of whiskey and illicit houses of prostitution.

Captain West: I have no further questions.

Major Leite: I have no further questions.

Captain West: Thank you very much.

Following the completion of the Article 32 investigation, in order to convince the Marine Corps that I really intended to litigate the matter of illicit whiskey and women in Paris, Georgia, as well as to question other Christian attributes and church-going qualities of its citizens, I forwarded a letter to the local Marine Commandant in Atlanta and spelled out my intentions in considerable detail. I did point out, however, that if the Marine Corps would refer the charges —which included bigamy, adultery, and forgery of a marriage document—to trial by special court-martial, with the further agreement that no sentence in excess of a one-grade reduction in rank would be approved, my client would plead guilty to all charges; I would then and there withdraw from the defense of the case, and the integrity of Paris,

Georgia, and its Christian ways would not be litigated at all.

Despite much initial growling and some local command interference, the Marine Corps saw the wisdom of trial by special court-martial, and accepted the proffered deal. In the ensuing trial, Sergeant Foster was defended by none other than Major Leite and was sentenced to a bad conduct discharge and six months' confinement. Upon review, however, the convening authority was as good as his word, and approved only so much of the sentence as reduced the defendant to the grade of Corporal—and thus ended the court-martial of Sergeant James Foster, USMC.

Notes:

1. The facts of this case as related in the accompanying text are taken from the Report of the Investigating Officer in the case. Some names and the name of the town concerned have been changed to protect the identity of persons involved.

2. Offenses under the General Article (Article 134) were originally covered in very simple instructions to the court-martial. The elements were taken from paragraph 213 of the MANUAL FOR COURTS-MARTIAL, and were considered to be (a) That the accused did or failed to do the acts as alleged; and (b) the circumstances were those specified. The Court of Military Appeals, however, held these elements of proof far too general and inadequate to cover disorders and neglects and discreditable conduct under the General Article. Hence, the specific act complained of must be identified, and its essential ingredients explained to the court-martial. Additionally, the court must be instructed that under the circumstances the conduct of the accused must be proven beyond a reasonable doubt to be prejudicial to good order and discipline within the Armed Forces, or was of such a nature to bring discredit upon the Armed Forces. See, e.g., United States v. Sadinsky, 14 U.S.C.M.A. 563, 34 C.M.R. 343 (1964); United States v. McIntosh, 12 U.S.C.M.A. 474, 31 C.M.R. 60 (1961); United States v. Grosso, 7 U.S.C. M.A. 566, 23 C.M.R. 30 (1957); United States v. White, 2

U.S.C.M.A. 439, 9 C.M.R. 69 (1953); United States v. Marker, 1 U.S.C.M.A. 393, 3 C.M.R. 127 (1952).

MILITARY JUSTICE—FORT LEONARD WOOD STYLE

The recent Fort Leonard Wood command influence cases, some ninety-three in number, and the various legal battles engaged in by the major participants in those cases, almost defy description within the limited boundaries of this paper. I will attempt only a brief discussion of the cases, with the suggestion that for more complete information the reader refer to the "good offices" of the Judge Advocate General of the Army for copies of the briefs involved, or to the participants themselves. My *own* efforts to obtain facts from the Office of the Judge Advocate General of the Army were largely unavailing, I should say. Requests simply went unanswered. Equally unavailing were my efforts to obtain information from the participants themselves. Participants in command influence cases, particularly those connected with the defense, do not discuss the facts of the case with strange lieutenant colonels who express a "professional" interest. Thus I had to ask a captain in my office if he would request copies of defense briefs from his personal friends assigned at the Office of Appellate Defense in Washington, D. C. This maneuver produced two very detailed briefs, excellent in scope, but directed more to the facts in the particular cases than to the broad general picture that prevailed at Fort Leonard Wood during the litigation of the cases under consideration.[1] I was most fortunate then in the arrival of Captain Juan Keller, JAGC, at our office at Fort Meade, an officer stationed at Fort Leonard Wood during the time in which these cases were litigated. Captain Keller had reviewed a large portion of the proceedings involved and was kind enough to fill me in on many gaps in the overall story.[2]

The story opens on August 5, 1965, at Fort Leonard Wood. A Sergeant, driving home from a company party at night along a poorly lit road, drove his automobile into the rear of a marching body of troops, killing two and injuring many more. Just before the accident, the Sergeant had had to drive his car over a small rise in the road; just prior to the accident, too, another car had passed him from the opposite direction, possibly with its high-beam headlights on. The troops involved were trainees, and they were being marched by a trainee. All were wearing dark fatigue uniforms without protective markings. Post regulations provided that on the marching of "company size" units after dark, protective, reflective devices were to be worn. But there were no regulations concerning the marching of units of less than company size. The number of men in the unit involved here was thirty-two, far less than company size.

Immediately after the accident, the defendant was whisked away to the Fort Leonard Wood Hospital by the military police, for the purpose of taking a blood alcohol test. A blood sample was taken, and sometime later a second sample was taken. The two samples were, however, inadvertently mixed by laboratory personnel and were thus not reliable as evidence. It was also discovered that on the day previous to the accident, the Sergeant had had two wisdom teeth extracted and that he had been issued medication by the dentist to kill the pain. The Sergeant was still taking the pain-killing drug when he attended a party on the evening of the accident given by his unit commanding officer to celebrate the successful completion of the unit's training cycle. At this party the Sergeant appeared to be in pain, but he drank two beers.

Within three days of the accident, the Commanding General of Fort Leonard Wood convened a board of officers to determine the cause of the accident and to make recommendations as to its disposition. The findings of the board were not made public, although the Sergeant involved was represented at the board hearing by qualified military defense counsel. It was at this point that a new Commanding General, Major General Thomas Lipscomb, arrived at Fort Leonard Wood and assumed duties as installation commander.

Charges of negligent homicide were in time preferred against the Sergeant and formally investigated at an Article 32 hearing. The Article 32 officer, after completing the investigation, recommended that the charges against the defendant be dismissed for lack of evidence. The Staff Judge Advocate of Fort Leonard Wood, Colonel James C. Starr, also formally recommended, in his pre-trial advice to General Lipscomb, that the charges be dismissed. Colonel Starr pointed out that the results of the blood tests were legally inadmissible as evidence and, as such, there was absolutely no evidence of negligence of any sort against the defendant. General Lipscomb, however, for reasons of his own, referred the charges to trial by general court-martial. At the trial of the case the law officer held the results of the blood tests were inadmissible, and the court-martial returned a verdict of not guilty.

Following the acquittal, General Lipscomb asked the trial counsel and the staff judge advocate to furnish him a written explanation as to why the case had been lost. As a result of his efforts, he received a reiteration of what he had been told before he referred the case to trial—namely, that the results of the blood tests were inadmissible, and that without this evidence there was no evidence of record to sustain a conviction of negligent homicide. The General refused to accept this explanation, and demanded others, but there were no other reasons to give. In response, the General began his valiant effort to move a mountain, and thus began the strange saga of the unorthodox general court-martial appointing order at Fort Leonard Wood.

The "Final Brief" for the Appellant, Private First Class Edward V. Moore, CM 414897, picks up the story at this point.[3] Prior to the publication of this rather strange court-martial appointing order at Fort Leonard Wood which, for the first time in the history of the Army, placed the court members' names ahead of that of the law officer's name, General Lipscomb had expressed dissatisfaction with the status of the law officer in military practice, and with the "decrease in status of the presidents." [4] Line officers who served as presidents of general courts-martial were almost always senior in military rank to legally trained law officers, yet these same line officers were constantly required to defer decisions during the trial of military cases to the law officer. This, General Lipscomb found difficult to appreciate and, apparently, to understand. Colonel Starr, the staff judge advocate, attempted to explain the relative roles of the officers involved, but related "it was obvious that he [General Lipscomb] was not satisfied." A day or two later, Lipscomb directed the staff judge advocate to prepare a list of duties that presidents of general courts-martial were authorized to perform during the trial of military cases. The General specified that he was going to distribute this list to the three senior ranking officers on every general court-martial convened at Fort Leonard Wood.[5]

It was shortly after this conversation that the Acting Chief of Staff, G-1 (Personnel), at Fort Leonard Wood issued a new format for general court-martial appointing orders. As related previously, this format listed the names of the court members first, in order of seniority of rank, and then listed the name of the law officer. This highly unusual change in format was ordered without the knowledge or consent of the staff judge advocate at Fort Leonard Wood.[6] A few days later, Lipscomb ordered that, henceforth, the staff judge advocate would not participate in the nomination of officers for court-martial duty at Fort Leonard Wood, nor would he be responsible for the publication of court-martial appointing orders in the future. This duty was given to General Lipscomb's G-1 section.[7] Colonel Starr subsequently stated that he did not try to persuade the General to change his mind on these matters because the General had informed him on a number of occasions "that the violation of Army regulations did not concern him." [8]

It was during this period, Colonel Starr reported, that he and a number of his officers first noticed that the general court-martial sentences at Fort Leonard Wood were on the upswing in severity. Colonel Starr stated that he was of the opinion that the court members "got the word" from the General.[9] His opinion in this regard was further buttressed by his report of a subsequent conference attended by himself, a representative from the Judge Advocate General's office in the Pentagon, and General Lipscomb. At one point in this conference, Colonel Starr recalled, General Lipscomb observed that his general courts were "now" making the dissident soldier "pay for his refusal to serve" in Vietnam, referring to the ever-increasing number of young American soldiers who absent themselves from military duty without authority.[10] General Lipscomb reportedly observed that these soldiers were just as guilty of avoiding the draft as the common draft dodger, and should receive the maximum sentence.

In a memorandum for record, subsequently submitted by Colonel Starr to the Office of Appellate Defense of the Judge Advocate General's Corps, in Washington, D.C., Colonel Starr quoted the General as stating that he would order law officers to admit blood alcohol tests in future trials, or have the Chief of Staff of the Army do so.[11] In another conversation—when the General was advised by Colonel Starr that the Judge Advocate General of the Army opposed pre-trial lectures, such as those contemplated by General Lipscomb, to prospective court members—General Lipscomb, according to Colonel Starr, advised him in clear language that he, Lipscomb, and not the Judge Advocate General of the Army, was in command at Fort Leonard Wood, and that he would himself determine what was necessary to maintain the discipline of his command.[12]

In further support of Colonel Starr's observation that General Lipscomb "got the word" to his court members, appellate defense counsel cited a statement in an affidavit submitted by one of the general court-martial presidents involved, which read in pertinent part as follows:

> Before the first case, I discussed certain principles with the members of the court in the deliberation room out of earshot of anyone. The principles generally were as follows:
>
> a. *I* was appointed the president of the court and would make decisions at any time we were in this room.
>
> b. Although I was senior, I would not try to influence the members of the court and all closed proceedings would be handled in accordance with the *Manual for Courts-Martial* and the law officer.
>
> c. That at any time any member of the court thought I was wielding undue influence, he was bound to leave by the rear door and discuss my actions with the convening authority, or the appointed law officer.[13]

As further noted by appellate defense counsel, the president of a general court-martial has no lawful authority to "make decisions" while in the deliberation room, nor to excuse jurors during the deliberation of a case, nor to direct jurors to discuss the case with outsiders during the deliberation— much less, to do so via "the rear door."

Appellate defense counsel cited another instance in which the president of a general court-martial at Fort Leonard Wood, during the critical time frame involved, instructed his fellow court members "off the record." This same president was described as also prone to admonish both trial and defense counsel involved for their trial tactics. On another occasion he admonished the accused for the poor appearance of his uniform.[14]

The battle between General Lipscomb and his military lawyers thus brewed on, and ultimately reached a climax when General Lipscomb published a letter intended to discourage the use of speedy trial motions by defense counsel. The General's letter specified that thereafter, if such defenses were raised, it would be the burden of the defense to prove why the delay was unreasonable. Otherwise, the General directed, the motion would be denied.[15] Colonel Starr refused to implement the directive and was relieved of duty as staff judge advocate of Fort Leonard Wood by General Lipscomb.[16] Within a short time after this occurrence, a military defense counsel stationed at Fort Leonard Wood directed an affidavit to Appellate Defense in Washington, D.C., and the Fort Leonard Wood command influence cases were soon making headlines in the Judge Advocate General's Corps.

Army Board of Review Number Two first heard several of these cases, and directed that an investigation be conducted by the Judge Advocate General of the Army to determine the true facts involved.[17] The Judge Advocate General, of much more conservative timber, felt that the cases were not sufficiently severe to justify an independent investigation, and did nothing to implement the board's directive.[18] Board of Review Number Two also requested a copy of the disposition form utilized at Fort Leonard Wood to direct the use of the unauthorized court-martial appointing order, but was advised by Colonel Starr's successor in office that the disposition form was not available and would not be furnished. Board of Review Number Two then evened the score by reversing the findings of guilt in all Fort Leonard Wood cases pending before the board,[19] citing, among other factors, the refusal of the staff judge advocate at Fort Leonard Wood to furnish it with a copy of the requested command disposition form, and the refusal of the Judge Advocate General of the Army to conduct a further investigation into the facts of the allegations against General Lipscomb.[20]

The Judge Advocate General countered this action by certifying the reversals involved, as he is entitled to do, for further review by the Court of Military Appeals.[21] More significantly, the Judge Advocate General did not refer any subsequent Fort Leonard Wood convictions to Board of Review Number Two for review. Fort Leonard Wood convictions that were received, subsequent to this, in the Judge Advocate General's office for initial review were referred to Board of Review Number Three, where that board proceeded to hold that the issue of command influence was not raised, and that Colonel Starr's affidavit in the matter was "chiefly distinguished by its length." [22] Board of Review Number Three further chastised Colonel Starr's affidavit as being in poor taste, and as a violation of his attorney-client relationship with General Lipscomb, and further, as against "legal precedent." Board of Review Number Three summed up the entire Fort Leonard Wood situation as follows: "In military justice matters the General was dynamic and the Colonel cautious." [23] The board further held that nothing was presented which would require further investigation in the cases. As expected, however, when these cases from both Board of Review Number Two and Number Three began to find their way to the Court of Military Appeals, not all was to go well for the government.

In the first series of these cases to reach the Court of Military Appeals, the Court in a *per curiam* opinion held that a very serious question of command influence was indeed raised in the records, and returned all cases concerned to Fifth Army Headquarters (a superior convening authority), with directions to refer the cases to a general court-martial whose law officer was to conduct an out-of-court hearing on the question of command influence.[24] If, in the determination of the law officer, after receiving evidence on the issue, command influence was present, he was to set aside the findings and sentences in the cases involved and proceed with rehearings on the merits. In the event the law officer then determined that no command influence was present, he would return the records, together with his opinion to the convening authority, who would then review the cases in regular fashion, and if affirmed at this level, forward them for regular appellate review by the boards of review and the Court of Military Appeals.[25]

At the hearing on the issue of command influence, which was conducted under the general court-martial jurisdiction of the Commanding General of the United States Fifth Army, the cases were consolidated and only one hearing was conducted on the matter of command influence.[26] The law officer at this hearing, despite having to caution Major General Lipscomb against further conversing with military defense counsel in the hallway of the court building, found that no command influence was present in the cases, and thus returned the cases to the convening authority where they were approved and forwarded to Washington for review by a board of review.[27] Upon review of these cases, the board found, contrary to the findings of the law officer, that the government had not in fact overcome the presumption of unlawful command influence that arises where there is the appearance of such influence. The board of review reversed the cases, or, in the situation of guilty pleas, reduced the sentences proportionately to the prejudice found.[28] All in all, some ninety-three general court-martial cases were involved.

General Lipscomb was ultimately transferred from command at Fort Leonard Wood, and subsequently retired from the Army. Thus ended his strange fight to turn back the clock on military justice, a fight that reflects as poorly upon the good faith administration of military justice as any in the history of our country.

Notes:

1. The two briefs were both defense briefs and both were addressed to the United States Court of Military Appeals. The first brief was a "Reply Brief Under Rule 41" in the case of the United States v. Private Robert L. DuBay, et al., CM 415047, Docket Number 20,149. The second brief was a "Final Brief Under Rule 41" in the case of the United States v. Private First Class Edward V. Moore, CM 414897, Docket Number 20,179.

2. Captain Keller furnished me a detailed three-page statement relating to the background of the Fort Leonard Wood cases prior to and after the arrival of Major General T. H. Lipscomb on the scene, as well as a recount of Lipscomb's subsequent difficulties with his staff judge advocate. Most of the details in the text, subsequent to this note, are taken from Captain Keller's statement, unless indication is made to the contrary.

3. See note 1, *supra*.

4. Page 4, Final Brief for Private Moore, note 1, *supra*.

5. *Id*. at page 5.

6. *Id*.

7. *Id*.

8. *Id*. at page 6.

9. Quoting from the Moore Brief, note 1, *supra*, at page 6:

During this period of time Major General T. H. Lipscomb revised the entire procedure involving the selection and appointment of general courts-martial, including the notification of those selected for duty by the G-1. Colonel Starr's affidavit relates that he and a number of other judge advocate officers noticed that the general court-martial sentences increased in severity after these changes took place, and they were generally of the opinion that the court members "got the word." See affidavit of Colonel Starr, pages 4–5.

10. Quoting from Colonel Starr's affidavit, which was repealed in part in the Moore Brief, note 1, *supra,* at pages 6–7:

> . . . I do not recall what trend the conversation had taken nor what prompted the remark, but I do remember a remark laughingly made by the General substantially as follows: "Well, with the general courts-martial I have now, the man will really pay for his refusal to serve."

Colonel Starr further noted in his affidavit that he recalled this remark so "vividly only because it made me wonder whether the General had ever communicated with any of the court members concerning the sentence problem . . ."

11. Colonel Starr reported that he once advised General Lipscomb that a law officer in a pending court-martial would probably not admit the results of certain blood tests in evidence. Colonel Starr stated that the General replied that he would "order the Law Officer to do so." Colonel Starr continued:

> . . . and when I informed him that the Law Officer was not a member of his command, he stated that he would get the Judge Advocate General to do so. When I advised him in my opinion that the Judge Advocate General would not do so, he inquired of me as to who was the Judge Advocate General's "boss." When I advised him that I supposed the Chief of Staff, United States Army, was the superior in line of command to the Judge Advocate General, he stated that he would get the Chief of Staff to issue the order . . . He did ask me if it were not true that the worst that could happen would be to have the Court of Military Appeals reverse the decision and give him "hell." I replied that this was true. Footnote 8, pages 7–8, Moore Brief, note 1, *supra.*

12. See footnote 10, page 8, Moore Brief, note 1, *supra.*

13. Page 14, Moore Brief, note 1, *supra*.

14. Page 3, statement of Captain Keller, note 2, *supra*.

15. Paragraph 8, page 3, statement of Captain Keller, note 2, *supra*. The paragraph in question reads:

> On the 17th day of October, 1966, the CG published a command letter intending that it should discourage the use of the Speedy Trial Motion, indicating that if it was raised, it would thereafter be the burden of the defense to show why the delay was unreasonable, and if it could not be so shown, then the motion was to be denied. The SJA refused to enforce this, and was relieved from command. Within a short time of this, one of the Defense Counsel submitted an affidavit to Appellate Defense in Washington, and the present problem came to light. [Author's note: my efforts to corroborate Captain Keller's statement from other parties involved, proved futile. While I requested statements from most of the parties concerned, statements were never forthcoming. My inquiries to Government Appellate, both formal and informal, were ignored. I specifically asked for government briefs, and while I was promised that such briefs would be forwarded to me, I have yet to receive them.]

16. See note 15, *supra*.

17. Board of Review Number Two apparently was in the process of reviewing thirteen cases from Fort Leonard Wood, all of which were tried during the period September to November, 1966. While General Lipscomb's feud with his legal section began almost as soon as he assumed command in September, 1965, it did not get into high gear until August, 1966, when the General directed the use of the unauthorized court-martial format for appointing general courts at Fort Leonard Wood, and culminated in late October, 1966, when Colonel Starr was relieved as Staff Judge Advocate. Of the thirteen cases before Board of Review Number Two, referred to initially in this note, seven involved maximum sentences, and five near-maximum sentences. The names of the soldiers involved in these thirteen cases are listed on pages 1–2 of the Reply Brief of Private DuBay, note 1, *supra*, as DuBay, Lieurance, Liverar, Fitzgerald, Jones, Phenix, Tell, Buchanan, Richmier, Scott, Baxter, Farmer, and Johnson.

18. The Judge Advocate General waited almost six weeks before he denied the order of the board of review for an investigation of the allegations against General Lipscomb. He notified the board through the Clerk of Court of his denial on March 10, 1967. See page 4, Reply Brief of Private DuBay, note 1, *supra.*

19. The board of review reversed the cases on March 17, 1967. The board's opinion is set forth in part, as follows:

   In view of the radical and sudden change in format of the court-martial appointing orders promulgated at Fort Leonard Wood, from one complying with Appendix 4*a* (1), Manual, *supra,* to one not so complying, it cannot be said that the change was inadvertent. The change was deliberate and with intent. What that intent was we will endeavor to ascertain from an analysis of Court-Martial Appointing Order Number 37 and the record of trial now before us in view of the futile effort of this Board to secure legally admissible evidence which might have shed some light on that intent. CM 415047, DuBay, dated March 17, 1967, pages 7–8.

   * * *

   . . . [W]e are constrained to find, under the total circumstances with which we are faced and on the record before us, that improper command influence so permeates this record of trial as to require the setting aside of the findings of guilty and the sentences.

   Accordingly, the findings of guilty and the sentence as to each appellant are hereby set aside. A rehearing may be ordered by a different convening authority. CM 415047, DuBay, dated March 17, 1967, page 13.

20. *Id.*

21. Article 67(*b*)(2), Uniform Code of Military Justice.

22. See page 2, Final Brief for Private Moore, note 1, *supra.*

23. *Id.* at pages 2–3. In a footnote on page 3, appellate defense counsel note that the board of review apparently felt that a "staff judge advocate is bound to condone the exercise of command influence through silence, at the risk of public castigation by military tribunals, out of loyalty to his commander."

24. United States v. DuBay, 17 U.S.C.M.A. 147, 37 C.M.R. 411 (1967).

25. 37 C.M.R. at 413.

26. United States v. Jacobson was one of ninety-three cases forwarded to the Commanding General, Fifth Army, under the mandate of the Court of Military Appeals in United States v. DuBay, note 24, *supra*. The right of the new convening authority to consolidate the cases into one hearing, without affording all accused counsel at the consolidated hearing (on the question of command influence) was affirmed by a board of review. See CM 416093, Jacobson, dated May 28, 1968. That this procedure would meet the right to counsel qualifications set forth in Escobedo v. Illinois, 378 U.S. 478 (1964), and Miranda v. Arizona, 384 U.S. 436 (1966), is extremely doubtful.

27. CM 416093, Jacobson, dated May 28, 1968; CM 414955, Berry, dated June 7, 1968.

28. CM 414955, Berry, dated June 7, 1968.

The Military
and the Individual

Peter G. Bourne, M.D.

D oes military service make an individual more
mature, more responsible, and more psychologically stable,
or does it destroy individual identity, warp idealism, and
mutilate the minds of innocent young men? Does the draft
result in better citizens with a fuller appreciation of a democratic society, or does it produce only subjugated, submissive
conformists, brainwashed with the self-righteous ideologies
of the military-industrial complex? While each viewpoint
has its own strong body of adherents in our society, the truth
probably contains elements of all of these positions. The
effects of military service are by no means the same for
every inductee. Personality characteristics, attitudes in the
home, age at induction, political sophistication, educational
level, and the prevailing political attitudes in the larger society are but a few of the factors that modify the experience
for each individual. Yet there are certain sociological and
psychological events that are common to the experience of

all draftees, and provide a more valid understanding as to what are the short and long-term effects of the military on the individual and the implications which they have for his subsequent participation in a democratic society.

Of all military institutions, basic training has become the most symbolic of the spirit, attitudes, and philosophy of the armed services. At the interface between the civilian and military cultures, it is the point at which the inductee is made most aware of the profound difference between life in the military and in the larger society and the enormity of the change which he is compelled to undergo in shifting from one environment to the other. Basic training is also designed to provide a symbolic concentrated distillation of everything that is the military so that the transformation of the new recruit will be maximal.

During my own military service, I was assigned to study basic training at Fort Dix, New Jersey, and the observations here are drawn largely from that experience.

According to *Army Training Program Manual,* N21–114, "Male Military Personnel Without Prior Service," April, 1964, the mission of basic training is ". . . to develop a disciplined, highly motivated soldier who is qualified in his basic weapon, physically conditioned, and drilled in the fundamentals of soldiery." Not stated is the fact that it also involves an intense forced acculturation to an alien social system and a careful denuding of the recruits' previous identity, values, and allegiances. Basic training stands outside the normal flow of time and is essentially ahistorical. It has no proud tradition from the past, and its existence is predicated on a future with which it has little continuity. It lacks any great opportunity for excelling, and is characterized by punitive retributions for failure. The nine weeks at the training center comprise, in effect, a temporal cocoon in which a phenomenal social, psychological, and political metamorphosis takes place.

All recruits entering basic training encounter a series of psycho-social events that they are unlikely to have encountered previously, certainly to this degree. The processes which these men undergo can be conveniently conceptualized by dividing them into four separate stages. Although each stage is consistently present and occurs at a chronologically predictable time in basic training, its impact on each recruit may vary significantly. In addition, there may be considerable overlap and blurring of one stage with another. I have termed these four stages (1) the period of environmental shock; (2) the period of engagement; (3) the period of attainment; (4) the period of termination.

The Period of Environmental Shock

When the recruit first arrives in the Army he is immediately plunged into an environment completely alien to his previous life experience. Not only is he in a strange and unfamiliar place, but he is also surrounded by people he does not know, who treat him in a disdainful and often hostile manner. From the start, demands are made on him that he is not sure how to meet, and at the same time he is deprived of many of the comforts and sources of psychological support he had taken for granted as a civilian. Perhaps worst of all, he is enveloped in the situation twenty-four hours a day without relief and without any opportunity to modify the environment significantly in any way. The net effect is that he is stunned, dazed, and frightened. For many recruits this is a period of anxiety which far exceeds anything in their previous experience.

The severity of this shock on each recruit in terms of

acute psychological stress had probably not been fully appreciated in the past. Recent studies have been made of basic trainees to determine chemical changes in the body which are a reflection of psychological stress. These investigations showed biochemical changes occurring in basic training which exceeded those found in almost any other circumstance, including combat. The point of maximum stress for most recruits seems to occur on their first day in the Army, when the shock of the environmental change is at its greatest. Although the men may remain extremely anxious for several days, there is a slight diminution after the first twenty-four hours. The recruits at this stage exhibit a picture of dazed apathy. There is a tendency to withdraw from direct involvement with the new environment, and conversation, which is often cursory, dwells almost exclusively on the more threatening aspects of the environment, both present and future.

Despite the fact that most recruits are between seventeen and twenty-three when they enter the Army, many have lived at home throughout their lives: often they have never changed residences, and have never previously had to form entirely new sets of friends and acquaintances. Entering the Army is frequently the most acutely shocking event of their lives. It also represents the most destructive threat to their adaptive capacity that they have ever had to endure. The stunned, frightened behavior of the young men in this situation bears a striking resemblance to that seen in physical disaster situations such as bombing raids, fires, or earthquakes. Sociologist Irving Janis has pointed out the similarity in psychological effect of natural disaster and disasters of the social environment:

> . . . psychological phenomena of this type can also be studied in a variety of extreme situations other than large-scale disasters —in financial depressions where people face extreme economic

insecurity; in personal disasters such as those involving health, status, prestige, or the breaking of affectionate ties; in emotionally traumatic accidents where a person undergoes a narrow escape from death; and in concentration camps where men are subjected to severe deprivations or are constantly threatened with punishment and torture.[1]

On the basis of the behavior observed among inductees when they first arrive in basic training, the experience does seem to represent in many ways a personal disaster, particularly in terms of loss of prestige and fear of physical and mental injury, with the first twenty-four hours being equivalent to the period of catastrophe in a civilian physical disaster situation.

For the recruit, the shock of the strange and unfamiliar is accentuated by a number of other factors. First, almost every recruit enters the Army with a highly colored and fanciful conception of what basic training will be like. This stems from the wealth of information he has obtained from the popular press, fictional accounts of Army life, and the composite picture of basic training held by the civilian population as a whole. As one recruit admitted to me, "I really believed they would be waiting for us with whips when we got off the buses." Many such expectations and fears which the inductee brings with him into the Army prove to be unfounded, but it takes some time for him to appreciate this. During the first few days after he arrives at the basic training center he receives very little, and generally erroneous, information about what to expect in the forthcoming weeks, which tends to maintain his state of anxiety.

A second factor is that much of the time after the recruit first arrives in the reception center is devoted to administrative processing. During this period he spends a considerable amount of time sitting around awaiting specific directions. The Army has in the past expressed sympathetic concern for the anxiety and apprehension experienced by the new recruit, and occasionally one hears the belief stated that it is good to allow the new inductees several days "to get on their feet" before placing any rigorous demands on them. However, judging by the study at Fort Dix, the level of anxiety apparently begins to decrease markedly as soon as the more strenuous regimentation and direction begins. The period during which the recruits are expected to "get on their feet" actually serves to prolong the severe anxiety produced by the initial sudden environmental change. It is probably true, in general terms, that whereas this initial phase of Army life when anxiety is extremely high is inevitable, it can be made extremely short by engaging the troops in active training as soon as possible after arrival.

Two features of the recruits' behavior during this initial period further reflect the similarity between this circumstance and the civilian disaster situation, with respect to the psychic adaptation used in dealing with it. First, a marked lack of independence is apparent, with a strong tendency to cling to persons in authority. The extent to which this is true seems to be in direct relation to how soon after the recruits arrive they are given access to an authority figure who professes a desire to help them. This person is usually the platoon sergeant, who will remain with them throughout basic training, and it seems that the earlier he meets the recruits, the more clinging, dependent, and trusting a relationship they will form with him. The effects of the initial strength of this relationship seem to last throughout the nine weeks of contact.

A second rather striking phenomenon, which frequently continues through much of basic training, is the tendency of the recruit to seize upon some relatively minor event and turn it into the most important aspect of his life. Such things as the possibility of being assigned to K.P. assume catastrophic proportions in the mind of the recruit, and it is common to hear an inductee say that for much of the previous day he had been unable to think of very much else except whether or not he would receive the detail. It is clear that the fear of the event has been enlarged out of all proportion to how great a threat it should actually be. A similar phenomenon has been described both in concentration camp populations[2] and in populations that have just experienced a nuclear attack.[3] The simplest explanation seems to be that in a person who is already under a great deal of stress there is tremendous fear that any further burden, however small, may prove to be "the straw which breaks the camel's back."

The extent to which an inductee experiences stress after his initial entrance into the Army is probably much more a reflection of how greatly the new environment differs from anything he has experienced in civilian life than it is of his psychological adjustment. The recruit who has been away from home at college, on an athletic team, or even in jail, will experience less stress from induction than his less-experienced colleague. This appears quite unrelated to the degree of psychological disturbance the recruit has demonstrated in his past life. However, although this seems to hold true for the first few days in the Army, it certainly cannot be said to be true for basic training as a whole.

Past experience with any remotely comparable event seems therefore to be the major factor in ameliorating the high level of stress during the period of environmental shock occasioned by entering basic training.

Period of Engagement

After spending several days in the reception center, the recruit is moved to the basic training company, where he will spend the next eight weeks. Again, as much as three or four days may go by during which he is involved only in the issuance of his equipment, becoming familiar with the geographical layout of the company area, and in acquainting himself with the personnel who will be responsible for his training. At the end of this period the actual training begins, with a conscious effort by the cadre to increase disciplinary demands, to provide continuous scheduling of activities up to twenty hours a day, and to impart to the recruit a feeling of engagement with the job at hand. At this point there is a noticeable drop in the anxiety level among the recruits. Many of them had not anticipated the period in the reception center or the days of administrative processing and therefore feel a degree of gratification in starting on the job they feel they are there to do.

Coincident with the start of involvement in the job of learning to become a soldier, and the very real drop in anxiety which it produces, a second process which has been occurring since their arrival begins to make itself felt by the men. This process is very much akin to what Goffman described in institutionalized mental patients as a mortification process.[4] Basic training is in every sense a total institution, with the recruits more isolated from society as a whole than any other group which is not undergoing some type of punitive action. They are forced into a role of total submission, the helpless victims of the whims of those who control the institution.

The trainee brings with him to basic training what has been termed by Goffman a "presenting culture." He has taken for granted a whole framework of supporting cultural factors, a concept of himself and his achievements which reflects the status he has been accorded in his past social environment, and a set of defensive maneuvers which has been consistently reinforced as he has dealt with conflicts, failures, and other personal adversity. Particularly he has come to expect his social environment to accord him the status he feels his own achievements or qualities warrant.

During this stage of basic training the recruit is no longer allowed the element of sympathy he received when he first arrived, and instead is subjected to a series of stripping processes whereby the mortification of the self occurs. This process is by no means unique to basic training, but is characteristic of any total institution. Personally identifying items are removed and institutional equivalents are substituted. Particularly meaningful to the late adolescent are the loss of personal clothing and the shaving of his head; the latter factor reaffirming in his mind the Army's right to do with him what it wishes, even in terms of such intimate areas as one's physical appearance. He is humiliated still further by being forced to pay out of his own pocket for the haircut. As Goffman summarizes the process:

> In addition ego-invested separateness from fellow inmates is significantly diminished in many areas of activity, and tasks are prescribed that are *infra dignitatem*. Family, occupational and educational careers are chopped off, and a stigmatized status is substituted . . . Areas of autonomous decision are eliminated through the process of collective scheduling of daily activity. Many channels of communication with the outside world are restricted or closed off completely. Verbal discreditings occur in many forms as a matter of course. Expressive signs of respect for the staff are coercively and continuously demanded. And the effect of each of these conditions is multiplied by having to watch the mortification of one's fellow inmates.

The authority structure of basic training is of the echelon type, which is characteristic of all total institutions and especially the Army; any member of the staff class has the right to discipline any member of the recruit class. Furthermore, in this type of situation, infraction of the rules in one area of one's life can be held against one in any other area. For example, failure to clean one's shoes adequately may result in a decrease in allowed sleep time or assignment of unpleasant work details.

The recruit is denied awareness of events going on in the outside world, and even the right to think, not because it is forbidden but because he is kept too busy or too exhausted for it. Even his accustomed language pattern must be renounced, and college graduates are reduced under the taunts of sarcastic drill sergeants to a vocabulary of monosyllables interspersed with obscenities adopted from their mentors. More recently, drill sergeants with Vietnam experience have been noted for boasting to recruits about the way they have tortured prisoners and committed other atrocities. It is primarily a way of mocking the humanitarian beliefs that the recruit brings with him from civilian life, but it is also effective in persuading many individuals that to be accepted and to survive in the military system they must adopt the same values as these clearly very powerful sergeants.

This type of institution operates primarily by means of the system of privilege and punishment and this is a major factor controlling all of the recruit's behavior. In civilian life he has largely associated punishment with animals and children, and its presence serves to deepen his feelings of belittlement and degradation.

Although the recruit may philosophically submit to this state of affairs, he finds very quickly that he is receiving very little in return for the sacrifices. This stage of basic training is in many ways devoid of pleasurable rewards, and contact with the outside world via letter and telephone becomes the sole focus of gratification. As many recruits complain, they are even deprived of sufficient privacy for masturbation. Also, despite the Army's demand that they accept its way of life, the Army does not reciprocate, and they remain in the stigmatized status of outsiders. Before the end of the fourth week of training they have achieved nothing tangible and have learned nothing for which the Army will give them credit. At the same time they are constantly reminded that any skills or other attributes brought with them from civilian life mean absolutely nothing in the Army.

The net result is that although the anxiety drops markedly during the first few days when the men begin to engage in the task, the status stripping process produces a slowly swelling tide of anger. This anger, which assumes tremendous proportions, continues to mount until around the fourth week of basic training, or about halfway through the cycle. The anger tends to be poorly directed, and although the recruit knows he is angry with "the Army," it is hard for him to find anyone on whom to vent his feelings.

The effect of the mortification process—unlike the initial stage of basic training—is probably felt most severely by those who have achieved highest status in civilian life. The process above all else is one of equalization, attempting particularly to strip the individual of those acquired characteristics which may previously have made him unique. For those who, prior to their entry into the Army, have acquired most in terms of individualizing achievement, the process will seem most demanding. On the other hand, for some persons—for instance, high school dropouts—some features of this period may represent an elevation in status. Bettelheim has described a comparable situation among concentration camp inmates.[5]

Although the denuding of identity and status can affect almost all areas of endeavor in the recruit's past life, certain areas remain immune, and some characteristics cannot be "scraped" away. This is primarily true of individuals who exhibit markedly superior physical stature and prowess, and has been particularly noticeable with recruits who have been professional athletes in civilian life. It also held true for a popular recording star while he was in basic training.

The Period of Attainment

During the third and fourth week of basic training the recruits spend the majority of their time on the firing range learning to handle a weapon. At the end of this time there is a two-day period during which they are tested on their proficiency with the rifle, and they fire for scores that will go on their permanent record. At the beginning of the second week on the range the anger reaches its peak, and then begins to steadily diminish. The rifle scoring seems to mark the turning point for the trainee: It is the first time that the Army gives him credit for an acquired skill, particularly one on which such a high premium is placed in the military. The very fact that he is being tested on his ability to fire a rifle implies to the man that the Army feels he must have acquired some degree of proficiency with it. Frequently there is great leniency in the scoring so that the majority of recruits score higher than they had anticipated, and their performance on "record fire" is the first major reinforcement they have received from the Army. For the first time since the recruit arrived in basic training, the Army has implied that the man has been accepted in his new role as "a soldier."

From this point on in basic training, the recruit constantly achieves new skills and attains a modicum of status in what has become for the present his total world, the Army. In quick succession after "record fire," he attains proficiency in hand-to-hand combat, the use of the bayonet, and tactical skills, and he experiences and survives the gas chamber. In a short period of time, beginning at about the fourth week of basic training, his bruised self-esteem is bolstered, and his injured identity is repaired by constant reinforcement in his new role. The result is that the fomenting anger, which usually reaches a peak in the fourth week, is rapidly dissipated. At this time, also, there is a perceptible shift in the group identity. Early in basic training the recruits identify only with the other members of their platoon, as a group of individuals caught in the same unfortunate situation. Their allegiance is to this group as a group of fellow sufferers, and not with the group as a military unit or as part of the Army as a whole. However, around the fifth week they begin to think of themselves as part of a platoon in a company which in turn is part of the total organization.

The striking change in effect seen at this stage is further enhanced by a number of secondary factors. First, since their own arrival on post, new inductees have arrived, so that although they remain in a stigmatized position, they are no longer on the very lowest rung of the ladder. Second, not only is the end of basic training now in the reasonably foreseeable future, but there is also a possibility of a weekend pass during the remaining period of time. Third, many of the recruits develop upper respiratory illness during the earlier part of the training, and this diminishes rapidly after the fourth week. Since hospitalization and absence from training can result in the recruit's having to repeat one or more weeks and being "recycled" into another company, illness in the platoon is a constant threat. The disappearance of illness around the fourth week can be very reassuring to the trainee in terms of the likelihood of his completing basic training. It is of interest that the period of highest incidence of illness should coincide with the period of basic training when the recruits seem to be under greatest stress. A more comprehensive review of this phase of the study is currently being prepared for publication.

This period then is characterized by the attainment of proficiency in many skills, for which the recruit receives acceptance and some degree of status, a rising anticipation of the end of basic training, and a very marked diminution in the high level of anger experienced in the preceding weeks.

The Period of Termination

Basic training is very much a finite event, and from its beginning the recruits do little to conceal the eagerness with which they await the day of departure. However, the point at which that day becomes a meaningful reality, having a major effect on behavior, is not always clear-cut. Generally, about one week before the end of basic training there is a shift toward a feeling of euphoria and a preoccupation with discussion of what the recruits will do during their forthcoming leave. However, very frequently they receive a weekend pass two weeks before the date of termination, and they may return at that time in a state of elation which is maintained for the rest of the training period.

This phase is marked by great euphoria, a feeling of immense confidence, and open expression of a sense of invincibility. With the end of basic training well in sight, there is a general consensus that they are capable of tolerating anything the Army wants to throw at them. Much of this type of behavior seems to stem from a feeling of relief at having successfully survived a period about which they all initially had considerable apprehension, and which they feel is generally regarded as the toughest part of one's Army career. Although fear of failure is always present early in basic training, the course is actually geared to ensure a tremendously high level of success, and the dropout rate is around 1 percent. A somewhat higher number, around 10 percent, are "recycled"—having to repeat part or all of the course. However, even among this group the direct cause is usually absence because of illness rather than failure in the training itself. This means that, though fear of failure may play an important part in the mind of the recruit, it has little basis in reality.

Despite the overwhelming feeling of achievement which is readily perceptible among recruits at this stage, one also hears frequent complaints that basic training was not tough enough; many recruits feel that they were capable of enduring much more rigorous training, and express anger towards the Army for not giving it to them. This somewhat paradoxical attitude seems to be related to the manner in which many recruits conceptualize the process and aims of basic training. For a large number of men entering basic training, the process is viewed as a form of masculine initiation rite, with the implied message from the Army, "Allow yourself to be subjected to this process with its indignities and discomforts and at the end, if you can take it, you will have achieved manly status." Many recruits find at the end of basic training that they do not feel very different from the way they felt at the start, and they feel that in some way the Army has broken faith with them. To many it seems that the only explanation for their failure to achieve the promised transformation is that somehow the Army has failed to make the appropriate demands on them to give the desired result. This is particularly true of physical training. During the nine weeks of basic training there are constant complaints about the discomforts of P. T., but at the end the recruits complain that they did not receive enough, as evidenced by the fact that they are not the superb physical specimens that they feel the Army had promised them they would be.

Unlike other groups, particularly much smaller groups, there is little evidence of apprehension or mourning about the disruption of the platoon at the end of the nine weeks. It might be anticipated that among a group of people who have lived in very intimate surroundings for this length of time, and who have been subjected to severe stresses, there would be attempts to deny that the group would disintegrate, and one might expect to hear plans to maintain it in some form, particularly in continuing individual relationships. However, although one might occasionally hear the comment, "We must get together again after we get home," it is clear that no one believes this, and in individual discussion with the recruits it is apparent that almost none of them expect to see their fellows again, or particularly wish to. Very few of these relationships are in fact maintained subsequently.

Of the many possible explanations of this attitude, the one which seems most plausible is related to the quality of the relationship itself. When the men enter basic training not only are they floundering, but they are also forced into a highly infantile role in which they are both extremely dependent and deprived of their right to determine any of their day-to-day activities. They are also subjected to punishment, and their choice of friends is considerably restricted.

Perhaps as a result of being placed in this type of position, their interpersonal relaltionships tend to be of a highly infantile and selfish form. There is a tendency, often expressed overtly, to use other members of the platoon for emotional support in a very demanding but often nonreciprocating manner. The individual tends to relate at a very superficial level and is able to terminate very rapidly what ostensibly is a much deeper relationship, with very little effect on himself. The recruit in basic training certainly seems to be able to make and break relationships with other recruits with this type of facility. The somewhat ephemeral nature of the relationship between the recruits may also reflect needs and pressures to form broader levels of group integration. This might well be expected as there is constant verbal exhortation from the training cadre for the recruit to view himself in turn as a member of the company, the regiment, and the Army. Perhaps there is a wish not to be reminded of the many dependent needs which are often exposed in situations of extreme stress.

Although we hear frequently of the cost of maintaining our extensive military forces, it is frequently forgotten that these costs must be calculated not merely in money or inconvenience, but in terms of the effects which military training and military life have upon the individual draftee and upon the general health and quality of our society.

Miltary training and military organization embody the concrete realization of attitudes and activities that are diametrically opposed to the practice and spirit of democracy. Obedience, the keystone of military order, is incompatible with the candid expression of opinion and the right to question and critically examine courses of action, prerogatives that are inherent in the role of the mature citizen in a democracy. Obedience further leads to dependence, with a reliance upon and acceptance of the will of others. Responsibility even for one's own welfare must be relinquished because it habitually remains in the hands of superiors. At the same time there is no reward for foresight or interest in the long-range consequences of actions or policy, only for servility, acquiescence, and the silent acceptance of the decisions of those in authority. By contrast, the central thesis of a democratic society is to develop and encourage in its citizens active participation in the decision-making and policy-making process. What the military reveres in the individual, democracy rejects; what democracy demands, the military expressly and vigorously forbids.

What, then, is the effect on young citizens of two or more years of indoctrination and total immersion in a subculture that espouses a value system which is the antithesis of that to which the larger society is committed? It can be persuasively argued that the military establishment so indoctrinates the young men it inducts that when they are seeded back into civilian life they carry with them implanted values and attitudes which not only guarantee the perpetuation of the military system, but enhance its slow and steadily increasing control over the entire society.

Forming the interface between the antithetical worlds of the military and a democratic society, basic training must be a crucial point of transformation during which these new values and beliefs are instilled. Three important processes can be identified as effecting these changes in the recruits. First, they must reject their pre-existing identity and envelop themselves instead in the institutional identity of the military organization. Second, they must accept their impotence in the face of military discipline and recognize the crushing recrimination it can inflict if they should seek to challenge it. Third, they must be convinced of the legitimacy of the system. These objectives and the psychological techniques by which they are accomplished show an interesting similarity to the methods of thought reform or "brainwashing" that are so vigorously criticized when employed by other nations. Both processes rely upon techniques of harassment and degradation to facilitate the stripping of the old identity, followed by a "rebirth" with constant recognition for accepting a new self-image prescribed by their captors in an otherwise rewardless environment. The techniques of basic training—sleep deprivation, isolation from the rest of society, and the critical role of the platoon sergeant as castigator, mentor, and omnipotent redeemer—differ, however, from those of "brainwashing" in that they were not deliberately contrived, but have instead evolved over time by virtue of their efficacy. It is this lack of conscious decision that has perhaps allowed the methods of basic training to remain largely free from criticism in our society, which normally frowns upon explicit attempts to control the minds of its citizens against their wishes.

In addition, basic training has evolved in the guise of a masculine initiation rite, a role that gains for it added acceptance at a time when the traditional ways of proving manhood are fast disappearing. Not only is the ethos of basic training one of conferring manhood, but the wearing of a uniform, the awarding of medals, and heroism in combat are all closely identified with the concept of masculinity. This provides particular appeal to the late adolescent struggling to establish a masculine identity for himself in society. Yet while the right to officially confer recognition of manliness is an indispensible part of the military reward system, and particularly of basic training, it is largely a deception, for military life offers not the attributes of mature manhood, but more nearly a permanent attenuation of adolescence.

The individual variation in the manner of handling and tolerating the military experience is considerable. By and large the older the individual, the less he is likely to become permanently inculcated with the military value system and the more likely he is to have the internal strength to resist the demand to relinquish his personal identity. However, it is not age alone which is the issue. It is related more closely to the extent to which the individual has developed a concept of his own identity, his worth, his accomplishments and his place in society. In its decision to draft nineteen year olds, the government seeks to secure those who are most vulnerable to the military objectives. Right out of high schools, these young men are more malleable and more easily intimidated than those even three or four years older.

College graduates and others with accomplishments that enhance their self-image have usually developed an emotional lifeline to their civilian identity and are not as easily drowned in the military sea.

Related closely to the question of pre-existing identity in resisting military engulfment is the ability to maintain nonmilitary associations while on active duty. The individual soldier is able to resist the militarization process much more effectively if he has ongoing reinforcement for his civilian identity from those outside the military structure. Whether it is emotional support from friends, access to reading material, or merely the opportunity to get out of uniform and off the post, the draftee is better able to resist total emotional surrender to the system.

In observing many hundreds of draftees as they passed through the militarization process, I noted one style that appeared particularly effective in minimizing the effect of the Army on the individual. Certain rather mature people were able to emotionally dissociate themselves from the experience and view it with extraordinarily objective detachment. It was as though they allowed their minds and bodies to be put through the experience while keeping their real selves apart and uninvolved. Maintaining a constant sense of humor, they never allowed themselves to become emotionally aroused by what they were enduring, but viewed it with aloof cynicism, secure in the knowledge that if they could tolerate it for long enough they would eventually be safely back in civilian life. This type of approach, while highly effective, demands a very mature individual with considerable inner strength and self-confidence.

Perhaps the danger of military service lies not so much in its potential to damage irrevocably the mind of the young inductee, but more in its ability to proselytize for its own ends during the two years that the draftee is within its grasp.

While he may reject the military value system with its authoritarian basis as inappropriate to civilian life, the draftee is frequently convinced, as a result of his own experience, of the unassailable authority and power of the military in its own domain and of the wisdom of unquestioning acceptance of military objectives. He also often retains an element of identification with the military in his new status as a veteran, and any limitation of military power is perceived as an incursion on his own influence. One result is that society has adopted a posture of special concession towards the military, making its power and expenditures largely immune from the criticism that legitimately controls other government operations.

In recent years, the military has enjoyed increasing influence and control over many spheres of civilian life through the mushrooming power of the military-industrial complex. While the military exists in theory to protect society, it has frequently become a law unto itself, acting with scorn for the values and cherished ideals of the system it was developed to serve. In recent years there has been increasing awareness that the organization we created to preserve our way of life may insidiously destroy it. The vulnerability of the adolescent in the grips of the draft might well stand re-examination in this light.

Notes:

1. Irving L. Janis, "Problems of Theory in the Analysis of Stress Behavior," *Journal of Social Issues*, 10 (1954): pp. 12–25.

2. Viktor E. Frankl, *From Death Camp to Existentialism* (Boston: Beacon Press, 1959).

3. Robert Vineberg, "Human Factors in Tactical Nuclear Combat," Technical Report 65–2 HUMRRO (April, 1965).

4. Erving Goffman, "Characteristics of Total Institutions," in *Symposium on Preventive and Social Psychiatry,* (Bethesda, Md., Walter Reed Army Institute of Research, April, 1957).

5. Bruno Bettelheim, "Individual and Mass Behavior in Extreme Situations," *Journal of Abnormal and Social Psychology* 38 (1943): 417–452.

Personal Testimony

Howard Levy, M.D.

Howard B. Levy, M.D., has been called "the most admired figure in the G.I. movement." In a movement that has spawned many local and temporary heroes he remains one of the most celebrated and most durable. As Captain Levy, stationed at Fort Jackson, South Carolina, he had, in 1967, refused to train Special Forces medical airmen, on grounds of medical ethics and conscience. Levy's civilian defense counsel at the trial, which in retrospect seemed like an inevitable step in his progress, was Charles Morgan, Jr., the Southern director of the American Civil Liberties Union. In his summation Morgan said, "This trial has to do with free men and responsibility. I truly do not want a martyr. I want a free man." The court responded by sentencing Captain Levy, M.D., to three years at hard labor.

I first speak with Dr. Levy late in 1969 after he has served twenty-six months of his sentence, the first six months at Fort Jackson, the next thirteen or so in the disciplinary barracks at Fort Leavenworth, Kansas, and the remainder at the U.S. Penitentiary at Lewisburg, Pennsylvania, from which he was released. A free man, and giving no evidence that he considers himself a martyr, he is in the middle of several activities. Slighter than I had expected from his pictures, vigorous and highly vocal, he is undeniably a product of New York. He agrees to respond to any questions or comments even though he says, quite correctly, that much of it must now be a matter of public record. But when he goes over material that interests him, or tells a story that he particularly relishes, his emotion charges them with immediate currency. I ask first about the formal charges that were brought against him.

LEVY: Well, there were three charges brought against me. The first was refusal to obey a direct order, the direct order being to train Special Forces so-called medics. The second charge was the uttering of statements whose intent it was to create disloyalty and disaffection among the troops. And the third charge was conduct unbecoming of an officer and gentleman.

FINN: You were judged guilty of all of these?

LEVY: I was judged guilty of all of those . . . and probably some more, which were not brought.

FINN: What was the sentence?

LEVY: Three years at hard labor, loss of all back pay and allowances, and dismissal from the service. And for an officer dismissal is equivalent to a dishonorable discharge.

FINN: Were there any things in your background which would have led you—or your friends—to have expected you to have been brought up on charges like this? Would they have expected you to have bucked the Army?

LEVY: You know, I don't know. It depends upon how far back you want to go. Certainly, before I went into the Army, I told my friends that I was going to be court-martialed. And I didn't know just why or how. Nobody at that point believed me. But by the time I went into the Army in 1965 I was so staunchly opposed to the war in Vietnam that I just anticipated that somewhere along the line I'd have trouble with the Army. Going back to my background as a child, there was a lot of very emotional testimony at the trial, the court-martial, mostly on the part of my father who talked about my heritage as a—God, I'm embarrassed to even talk about it—patriot, as a believer in the Constitution and the principles upon which the country was founded, the Founding Fathers, and so on and so forth. And he said that I had an American flag in the room— which was true, actually. You know, things like that. Now I don't really know; maybe that is important, but I don't really know.

FINN: What about high school and medical school? Were you interested in political groups and politics at that time?

LEVY: Very little, actually, and if I was interested at all it was from·a conservative point of view.

FINN: The opposition to the war in Vietnam was not at its height early in '65, and the number of people strongly opposed then was relatively small. How did you come to feel that . . . ?

LEVY: I became politicized somewhere at the time that I was at Bellevue Hospital, when I was doing my residency. As I say, up until that time, in college, medical school, internship, I was fairly apolitical, if not conservative. If you asked me about various questions, you'd get conservative answers for the most part. But when I was taking my residency at Bellevue, I gradually did become politicized because of the actually abominable conditions of that hospital —the kinds of facilities and treatment that were available for mostly poor people. And at that time I was also doing some reading about the civil rights movement. And I was emotionally very much tied in with the civil rights movement, although I wasn't doing anything actively, aside from offering financial support—mostly at that time to SNCC [Student Non-Violent Coordinating Committee]. I thought that SNCC was where it was at—this was about '63 and '64—and I was very much into SNCC activity. And before I went into the Army I wrote to SNCC, as a matter of fact, telling them that I was going to be stationed down in South Carolina and I'd like very much to work on some of their projects. But they didn't have any projects in South Carolina anyhow, and ultimately when I did go I did a lot of work with SCLC [Southern Christian Leadership Conference], Dr. King's group, which had the most going on in South Carolina and which was doing some very good work in voter registration.

So I became more and more political, and along with being politicized, I came more and more to oppose the war in Vietnam. And my position, oh, I don't know, back in late '64, was that we ought to pull all troops out immediately.

FINN: You say you were politicized, but how did you reach the decision that the war in Vietnam was a war we should not be involved in?

LEVY: Well, I was reading whatever books and materials were around at the time. I was, by that time, reading left-wing material mostly, as I recall, the then *National Guardian*, and I was reading *Liberation* magazine and things like *The Minority of One*. I read them sporadically; I didn't read them very consistently. But I was reading them. And there had been a few books, as I recall, published on Vietnam, even at that time. I think some of Bernard Fall's stuff was probably published by that time. And I was just convinced that the whole thing was absurd, and the United States ought not to be involved. And we were on the wrong side, anyhow. At that time I was at the stage of writing letters to Congressmen, urging immediate withdrawal.

FINN: When you told your friends you were going to get court-martialed, it's clear there was at least some emotional basis for it at that point.

LEVY: Oh sure. As a matter of fact, I thought very seriously, Jim, about not going into the Army.

FINN: That's what I was going to ask: Did it occur to you at the time to say you were an SCO, that you conscientiously objected to the war in Vietnam?

LEVY: Oh absolutely. It tore me up, it really did, before I went into the Army. One of my problems was that I really had no connection with anybody in the left wing. I had the views, but I just wasn't involved with anybody else who had similar views—or even anything close to similar views. Most of my friends were really very bourgeois doctors, who may have shared some of my feelings about Vietnam but weren't in any position to offer me advice as to what I ought to do with regard to the Army. And I thought very, very seriously about going to jail. Then I said to myself, "That's kind of a silly thing to do. Why would anyone want to go to jail? Anyhow, I can rationalize my going into the Army: G.I.'s need help, and it doesn't matter what their political views are." And so on and so forth. And in retrospect, with hindsight, I think that was a very good decision. I think it was a very political decision. Although at the time I made it, it was clearly not made on conscious political principles at all; it was made on the principle of being afraid to go to jail, which is quite different. I think in retrospect it was the right decision . . . but for the wrong reasons.

FINN: Did you know there was such a position as selective conscientious objection, people who worried about it, thought about it?

LEVY: There really wasn't much of that, I don't think, back in '65. That kinda came a little later.

FINN: This is really what you came to, once you got into the Army.

LEVY: Yes, except I never formally applied as a selective C.O., until *after* they brought charges against me.

FINN: How did you decide after you got into the Army not to cooperate in various ways? What led you to go in and then decide not to do what your superiors suggested was the proper thing to do?

LEVY: Well, the fact of the matter is that for the most part I did cooperate with the Army. I mean, my attitude was, "All right, I'll go into the Army." And, as I say, I rationalized it in part by saying that I'm a doctor and I have no right not caring for people who are sick, regardless of what their political views are. And the other part of that rationalization was to say, "In any event, I'll spend my spare time doing civil rights work." And I spent most of my time doing voter registration work in the black community. So that, in fact, I wasn't really relating to the Army except for six or seven hours a day that I was working. That work consisted of medicine for the most part, and I didn't really feel any great pangs of conscience about doing that.

Again, doctors in the Army, even though they're officers, don't really think the way officers do, for the most part. They have their own sense of elitism, which is professional, and in many senses it's very close to being an officer in the Army, but they don't think militaristically really, and they aren't very much hung up about military protocol. They may be hung up on professional protocol, but not military protocol. So I, like a lot of other doctors, was kind of a sloppy soldier. I mean, like my buttons were never buttoned . . . my brass was never polished. I could never understand why anybody would ever polish brass.

FINN: But your not having polished brass, and all that, did not make you stand out.

LEVY: I was a bit sloppier than even the average doctor, in truth. No, they never brought charges against any of that. It was never brought up at the court-martial, except jokingly by us. But there were a number of little incidents that upset them. For example, I had parked illegally. It was raining, and my nearest parking spot was like a mile away from my clinic. It was just pouring, drenching rain. So I parked alongside my clinic (which was clearly illegal) and then I forgot about the car. When an M.P. came about the car I was busy seeing patients. I was ready to pay the ticket, but he said, "Well, there's some information you've got to give me." And I'm speaking to the guy for about ten minutes, and I have a woman in the other room who happens to be in a very compromising position. And I say, "Hey, look, baby, I just don't have time to talk to you here. I'm going in to look at my patient. You can tow the car away. I don't care what you do with the car. If you think the car is so important, give me the ticket; I want to pay for the damn thing."

Fifteen minutes later I was called into the Provost Marshall General's office because I had insulted the M.P. So I walk into the Provost Marshall General's office, Colonel Wilson was his name I think, and I say, "My name is Howard Levy. I understand you want to speak to me." He says, "Is that the way to talk to a superior officer?" "Yeah, that's the way I talk to a superior officer." And he got furious. He said, "When you walk into this office you salute me." So finally I gave him a kind of crumpled salute or something like that. It was a really benign kind of interview. And I turned on my heels and left. And he says, "Wait a minute! You salute when you leave this office." And I didn't salute. And he was just screaming his head off as I was walking down the hallway.

The next day I was called in by the commanding officer of the hospital and he said, "Captain Levy," this was Colonel Fancy saying this, "you made a very, very poor impression on Colonel Wilson yesterday." And I said, "Well, Colonel Wilson didn't make much of an impression on me." He says, "You have to realize that when you go to visit other parts of the post, you are representing the hospital. It's important to make a good impression." And I said, "Colonel, maybe you'd better find somebody else to represent your hospital because maybe I'm not the one to do that. I'm not much interested in your hospital or making a good impression for you or anyone else in the Army. You're going to have to take it the way it is, because that's the way it is."

FINN: Was this the first thing that brought you into some kind of conflict?

LEVY: Oh no. There were a number of minor things. Every once in a while I'd be called in and they'd say, "Hey, Doc, your hair is too long." And I'd get a haircut. They were all such petty little instances that they didn't really amount to anything.

I had been investigated by the counterintelligence corps prior to all of this. And that's a long, very funny story. When I got to Fort Jackson, the first day I was there, there was a bill on my desk for $6.00. And I said to a sergeant in the clinic, "What the hell is this?" He says, "That's your bill for the Officers Club." "What do you mean, my bill for the Officers Club? I just got here today. I haven't been in the Officers Club." "Well, they bill you a month ahead of time."

"They ain't gonna be billing me, baby, I ain't gonna use your Officers Club." So I called the Officers Club and said, "Hey, look, there's a bill for $6.00 . . . I'm not going to pay it . . . why don't you stop billing me because I don't want to use the Officers Club . . . and I don't want to join." And they said, "You have to join." And I said, "What do you mean I have to join? Send me your constitution." So they sent me the constitution and it said very clearly in the constitution that membership in the Officers Club is voluntary; that's exactly what it said. And I read it and I called them back and said, "Look, your constitution says *this*. I don't want to join. Stop billing me." All right, the bills kept coming. Every month I got a bill for $6.00. I never went anywhere near the Officers Club. Every month the bill would come for $6.00. And it went up—12, 18, 24, 30 dollars. Finally I was called into the hospital commander's office. And he said, "Dr. Levy, when are you going to pay your Officers Club bill?" And we went through this whole wrangle. I said, "I'm not joining the Officers Club." And he said, "Well, you really ought to join the Officers Club." At first he took a very paternalistic approach. He said, "Look, Howard, it's just like any other country club." And I said, "Baby, I despise country clubs and people who go to them. When I was a civilian I despised country clubs and I despise them even more here. I just don't like country clubs." He says, "Well, we have certain traditions here in the Army, and one of those traditions is for officers to belong to the Officers Club. And these traditions are very, very important to us. You'd better join the Officers Club." I said, "I'm not joining the Officers Club. I don't really give a damn about your traditions." Finally he said, "All right, if you don't want to join the Officers Club, you're going to have to put that down in writing and send it to the Commanding General of Fort Jackson"—Perez at that time. And I said, "Is that all he has to do, is worry about me joining the Officers Club? I'll write the damn letter. That seems kind of silly, but I'll write it."

I went out of his office, and the next day he calls up and says, "Have you sent that letter yet to the General?" I said, "No, goddam it, I haven't sent the letter. It was just yesterday. I'm gonna send it. Is it an emergency?" He says, "Well; you'd better get it in the mail right away." So I went home and I wrote the letter and sent it to him. The next day I got another phone call from the hospital commander and he said, "Captain Levy, when you send a letter to the General it's supposed to be a typewritten letter." And I said, "Colonel, as a matter of fact, I happen to type most of my letters, but you were in such a damn rush. I didn't have a typewriter. It would have been typewritten if you had let me do it in my own time. But, all right, I'll keep that in mind. Thanks for the information." The months passed: 36, 42, 48 dollars. And finally, about three months later, I was called in again to the Commanding Officer and he says, "Well, General Perez says you don't have to join the Officers Club." I said, "Fine. Groovy."

I'm ready to leave when he says, "By the way, what about the money you owe?" "What money do I owe? I don't owe any money. There was no contract; it wasn't a freely arrived at contract. I've, goddam it, been yelling and saying I don't want to join the damn thing since I got in; I'm not paying the goddam money. You crazy? I've still never used the damn thing." And then he says, "Well, Captain, I just want you to know that it is a very, very serious offense for an officer to accumulate debts." And I said something like, "Look, baby, I guess I'm just going to have to live with it. I've done a lot of bad things in my life, and that's one of them." So the next day I was called down to be interviewed by counterintelligence corps, and they wanted to know about my political affiliations. They didn't mention anything about the Officers Club, but that's what it was all about. For a while there many people felt that my whole case really had to do with my not joining the Officers Club. That's not true, I think.

All right, so I was interviewed by counterintelligence corps and they asked me questions such as: "What kind of left-wing publications do you read?" And I said, "Well, in South Carolina, a lot of folks think the *New York Times* is left-wing. I read that." "What other publications?" "Well, there's *Time, Life, Newsweek, U.S. News and World Report.*" "No, no, no, no. We don't mean those kind of magazines. I mean, you know, political magazines. Those aren't political." So he ran down a list of about twenty magazines, and then they wanted to know about some meetings I had attended of the Socialist Workers Party. They weren't meetings, they were lectures. You know, people like Malcolm X and Mark Lane. So we spoke about that for a while.

And then one of them asked me a very interesting question. He said, "Captain Levy, would you obey an order under all and any given circumstances?" And my answer to that was, "Of course not." And I was thinking about Vietnam; obviously I wouldn't obey all orders. After all, who knows what order I may be given. And they said, "Well, you know, we're not talking about Nazi Germany." And I said, "As a matter of fact, that's exactly what I'm talking about. I'm talking about you." They had it all tape recorded. The next day I went down—a few days later, rather—I went down and they had a transcript. I signed the transcript, and that was that. And I just figured, well, all right, fine, they're doing their investigation, and I just kind of forgot about it . . . until the time of the court-martial when this loomed in importance, you see, because the court-martial was based upon a G-2 dossier—which gets into why the Uniform Code

of Military Justice is absolutely irrelevant to any discussion
of civil liberties in the Army.

So, what ultimately happened was, when I disobeyed a
direct order, my commanding officer planned to give me—
and did, in fact, give me, or drew up the papers to give me
—what's called an Article 15. It's a non-judicial form of
punishment, a slap on the wrist, something less than a jail
sentence. You cannot go to jail on Article 15. You can be
fined, you can be restricted to post, have privileges taken
away from you, but you cannot go to jail. I had already
disobeyed a direct order to train the Special Forces medics.

So, at that point, Colonel Fancy, the Commanding Officer, was visited by G-2, Security, who threw this G-2 dossier, the security dossier, on his desk. It was 180 pages, of
which we've seen sixty or eighty pages. He read it and decided he wouldn't give me an Article 15, that he'd give me a
court-martial, based on what was in that G-2 dossier. It includes statements I had made to various enlisted personnel
—we know that because those are the only pages we've
seen. It includes a lot of other stuff which we've not been
permitted to see. The only people who have not been permitted to see this are myself and my attorneys, because
we're security risks . . . and we're security risks because
I'm being court-martialed. And I'm being court-martialed
because I'm a security risk. There're lots of *Catch-22* situations; that's a real *Catch-22* situation.

Subsequent to my court-martial, Chuck Morgan received
a security clearance to review material that has a higher
classification than material in a G-2 dossier, and therefore I
do not see any reason why he couldn't see the dossier now,
since he is no longer deemed a security risk. In any event,
we were kind of escalated from a possible twenty-day restriction to a possible eleven years in prison based upon that
G-2 dossier. Now that G-2 dossier was prepared by a fellow

name of West, Agent West, who lives in the same town where I was doing voter registration work, who was friendly with the chief of police, a racist chief of police, who was intimately associated with the Ku Klux Klan, who thinks that civil rights groups, from the Urban League to the Black Panthers, are Communist fronts. He began his investigation forty-eight hours after I arrived at Newberry County, South Carolina. And that's what the case is all about. Agent West. James B. West.

This is why it's irrelevant when we go into court and argue on the basis of the First Amendment that if I made certain statements I can't be charged because, number one, I'm allowed to make any statement I want and, number two, because the statements are true—like Special Forces men are murderers. That's kind of an irrelevant argument. It wasn't why I was court-martialed in the first place. It's irrelevant to argue about the ethics concerned with training the Special Forces so-called medics. That wasn't why I was court-martialed; it's an irrelevant point as far as the Army is concerned. And to argue, with regard to the conduct unbecoming an officer and a gentleman—and the charge is overly vague and therefore meaningless because it includes everything from murder to fornicating birds . . . Yeah, if you fornicate a bird, like a pigeon or a sparrow, that's conduct unbecoming an officer and a gentleman. So all those are very good arguments, they're very logical arguments, you can make a good case from a constitutional point of view, and we may win an appeal on these grounds because they are valid points, but it's entirely irrelevant to the court-martial.

FINN: You say, get the whole judicial process out of the Army and into civil courts if there's to be judicial process . . .

LEVY: Not that I have a whole lot of faith in federal courts these days, but I think you have a better chance there than you do in military courts, on *political* cases. And I think that's important, because it's not necessarily true for a guy who robs a bank. He may do just as well in a military court, for all I know. Maybe better. But on a political case, you just are not going to be acquitted very often in a court-martial. Whereas in a civilian court, on lots of these kinds of offenses, particularly the free speech, free press, freedom of religion type, there's no question that you'd be acquitted, even in the more conservative federal districts. I mean there are just certain rules that at this stage of the game they themselves can't ignore. But in the Army these are all irrelevant.

FINN: I presume you made *a* decision not to train these people in the Special Forces any more. How did you come to do that?

LEVY: I trained them for three or four months. I began to speak to the guys, got to know them fairly well. And as I got to know them and got a kind of a sense of what they were doing and to what uses they would put their medical training, it seemed to me that I ought not be involved in doing that, that it was just wrong for me to be training them. My first response of course, as a position, when I'm asked to train somebody, is to say, "Fine, we'll train 'em. I'll train anybody." I mean, if they can provide some medical care, why not? Which was kind of an unthinking response and not illogical . . . at first glance, anyway. But they were very candid, you see, about the fact that they were going to use their medicine politically.

FINN: How do you mean?

LEVY: Well, for example, they would sometimes send one man into a hamlet—the medic—and he would provide medical care for civilians. And if he did that for a few weeks or a few months, he would win over the confidence of the people, at which point the hamlet would be much more receptive to the rest of the Special Forces team with their military equipment. And they'd move in and militarize the village.

FINN: And the aid men themselves knew this.

LEVY: Sure they did. Sure. It's a policy thing. At first this was all first-hand information, from them mostly. But later on I read things published by Special Forces, and they're quite open about it; there's no secret about that. And I just said that I ought not be doing that because . . . I don't know whether you should *never* use medicine politically, but I know you shouldn't use medicine politically in *that* situation because it's the wrong political side, and if you're going to be involved in a political position then you have to have some say as to what that politics is.

FINN: Did you say this in words much like that to the Commanding Officer when you decided you weren't going to train Special Forces anymore?

LEVY: Yeah. Well, I tried to talk to Colonel Henry Franklin Fancy. His reaction was . . . I never got very far in explaining it to him. The one line I blurted out which he later admitted to on the witness stand was that, "Well, Levy said he wouldn't train them for ethical reasons." I think that was the line. And he, at that point, said, "Look, I don't care about your ethical reasons. I gave you an order. The question is: are you going to follow it or are you not going to follow it?" And I said, "Look, baby, I'm not going to follow it." And I walked out. Before I walked out he said, "Well, all right. You know what the consequence is going to be."

And he just didn't want to discuss it. Colonel Fancy is not the kind of man you hold discussions with. He's not very bright; he really isn't. Colonel Fancy . . . I'll tell you a story about the court-martial. This was at the Article 32 investigation, preliminary to the court-martial. Colonel Fancy was asked a question something like this: "Colonel Fancy, we heard from a previous witness that you read Captain Levy's G-2 dossier, and after you read it you exclaimed, quote, Levy is a pinko, unquote. What did you mean by that term?" And he said, "Well, pinko's a Communist or someone who follows the Communist line." "Fine, Colonel Fancy. What's that?" "Well, a Communist"—I'm making this very brief—"is someone who believes in atheism, someone who believes in world domination, someone who believes in agitating to create a state of unrest to make the country easy for an overthrow." "Fine, Colonel Fancy. You say the Communists believe in atheism. Do you have any idea what the religious convictions were of some of the founders of the country?" "Well, yes. They were very upright religious men." "Like Thomas Jefferson, for example?" "Yes, Mr. Jefferson was a very religious man." "Fine, Colonel Fancy. How about Benjamin Franklin?" "Who?" "Benjamin Franklin." "I'm sorry, I thought we were talking about the founders of the country. Didn't he come a little later?" "No, Colonel, he was one of the founders of the country." "I don't know his religious views." "All right. Fine. Colonel Fancy, you say that Communist agitators create a state of unrest. The civil rights movement has done a fair amount of agitating. Do you think they may be Communist inspired?" "I think that may very well be the case, yes." "Well, fine, Colonel Fancy. The anti-war movement does a fair amount of agitating. Do you think they may be Communist inspired?" "Yes, I think that may be the case." "Like Senator Fulbright, for example?" "Who?" "Senator William Fulbright, Democratic Senator from Arkansas."

"I've heard the name. But I don't know much about him." "How about Wayne Morse, Democratic Senator from Oregon?" "I'm not familiar with that name." "How about former Ambassador Reischauer, former ambassador to Japan?" "I'm not familiar with that name." "Colonel Fancy, have you read any books on Vietnam?" "Certainly." "Name one." "I retract that last answer."

Now, I mean, you're dealing with a man who really has never read a book in his life, aside from medical books; he's a man who has absolutely no understanding of social forces, of political forces in the world at large; who has lived a very isolated life—who's been in the Army for fifteen years; and who simply doesn't really know what intellect's all about, he just has no comprehension of what it is that makes some people disagree with other people. In his world nobody disagrees about anything . . . except maybe who might win the football game on Saturday, or what brand of bourbon is best. You just can't believe how isolated those military people really are from the rest of the world. And what's true of Fancy is true to a greater or lesser extent of all military officers, virtually all.

FINN: I presume when you say this that you believe most of the military officers, faced with someone like you, would give a reaction somewhat like Fancy's. Maybe not as uncomprehending, but at least they would think that you should be subject to military justice, you shouldn't exercise independent judgment.

LEVY: I think they might be opportunistically more pragmatic. I think they might say, "Look, Levy's a pinko, Levy's a Commie, he's a goddam nigger-loving Commie Jew"—I think that's what would run through their mind—"but the best thing I can do with Levy is to ignore him, because if I'm going to mess around with Levy I'm going to mess up my own future." That's the pragmatic thing for an Army man to say. And we suggested that to the Army.

FINN: You did?

LEVY: Oh, absolutely. Before there was any publicity, we had a long discussion, myself and Chuck Morgan. Chuck called me one day and said, "Howard, what do you want to do about the publicity?" And I said, "I don't know, Chuck. You're the expert in publicity. I've never had any publicity." And he says, "Well, I think what we ought to do is give the Army an alternative first and see if they take it, and then make up our mind. I mean, once we publicize it they're not going to listen to any alternatives." So before there was any publicity, before anyone ever heard of the case, Chuck spoke to the Judge Advocate's office and Colonel Fancy and to other high-ranking Army people at Fort Jackson, and his line essentially was, "Look, it really is not in the Army's interest to court-martial Dr. Levy, and it's certainly not in Dr. Levy's interest to be court-martialed, and there's lots of other alternatives if you all just want to use 'em. You can transfer him to another clinic, you can transfer him to another post where he doesn't have to train the Special Forces men, you can move in an outside consultant to train them for the few weeks that are remaining, or you can forget about the program for the one or two more cycles that you have to go. There are all kinds of alternatives to a court-martial, becasue if you do court-martial him, I can assure you you're going to be hurt, because we're going to see to it that you're hurt." And they said, "That's the way it is; there's going to be a court-martial."

So Chuck told me that and I said, "All right, baby, it's time to make a political case now. We go all the way now. There ain't no more caution any more, you just throw the

caution away." And that's when we had the first press statement. But the Army did have alternatives, and up to the last
minute we were kinda ready to cop out. But not completely.
If the alternative was either train them or be court-martialed,
the answer was still no, we're not going to train them. The
point was, I wasn't trying to make a public stand. A lot of
people think I really was. But this simply was not true. At
that point, you see, I was much closer—and you can understand this because of your experience with other people
taking moral stands, stands of solitary witness—at that
stage it really was a solitary witness, and it didn't make any
difference to me whether anybody knew about it. It was
really a very ego-centered thing, where I just thought it was
wrong and I just didn't want to lose my pristine innocence
. . . if I ever had it. My perspective is just miles and miles
away from that now. As a matter of fact, it was miles and
miles away from that the moment they said no.

FINN: If they had done this, this pragmatic thing . . .

LEVY: I probably would have gone back to New York and
just . . .

FINN: It's hard to know exactly, but you wouldn't have
been radicalized in the way that you were.

LEVY: Clearly not. That's right. And that was really kind
of a turning point, their adamancy in saying . . . Because
gradually, of course, I came to understand that my personal
feelings really were of no importance whatsoever. They
really aren't. And that myself, as an individual, is of no importance whatsoever, and that my life is of no importance
whatsoever, and it really doesn't make a whole lot of difference whether I live or die—in terms of history and in
terms of the kinds of things that I think human beings ought
to be concerned with; that, in fact, this whole obsession
with the individual is really derivative of almost a kind of a

Adam Smith laissez-faire idea; this "just do your own thing" is a very, very conservative idea, it's a very reactionary idea, it's a very capitalistic idea, which comes straight out of laissez-faire doctrine. Now, not everybody agrees with that. But what in fact is important in the alternative is mass movements of people.

FINN: If you have a group of individuals, none of whom is important, why does it add up to anything? Why does the collectivity mean something then?

LEVY: I'm not saying individuals aren't important. I'm saying that when they're doing battle with the Government of the United States, the individual's welfare cannot be taken into consideration; that no sacrifice is too big a sacrifice, in individual terms, if it means in fact abolishing monopoly capitalism; and that people must be willing to die to do that. If they're not willing to die, the chances are they're not going to do battle. This larger struggle is so terribly important, so much rides on that struggle in terms of literally hundreds and hundreds of millions of people whose fate really will be determined by the success or lack of success in confronting that problem here in the United States, that individuals here in the United States who argue that they want to do their own thing are politically immoral. They can't afford that luxury. Now if they could afford that luxury, I'd be happy to give it to them, but I don't think we can afford it.

Even with many political people there's a lot of self-indulgence, though. Much more than people realize. I began to see all that much clearer at about the time that we started to publicize the thing. And the argument that was used very often with me was, "Well, you know, Howard, if you'd just shut your mouth, even if you're court-martialed you won't get much of a sentence"—which may have been true, in fact. Certainly it was the kind of thing you think about—I did think about it. And my answer to it was, "Well, it doesn't much matter. I don't really care at this point. The object is to defeat the United States Army." And from that point on . . . that's when I really started saying to myself, "Well, maybe you just ought to return a favor with a favor and begin to organize the Army." Because up to then I had really accepted these petty little things, the uniform wearing and haircuts. I really had been ignoring the Army; I really had been. In part because there was no opposition within the Army at the time, there was no anti-war movement to speak of in Columbia, South Carolina—we tried it once and it flopped on its face, and that was my sole connection with the war in Vietnam while I was in the Army really. But then, when I was in jail after the court-martial, I said, "Well, Christ, I think you really can organize the Army." And I had all these guys visiting me. Every day I had G.I.'s visiting me. We had a lot of support on post.

FINN: Of the three things brought against you—conduct unbecoming an officer and gentlemen and refusing to train aid men—one was spreading disaffection among G.I.'s.

LEVY: No, that wasn't the charge. It's very important to get it straight; it was "intent to create disloyalty and disaffection by uttering certain statements"—and the key word was "intent." At one point in this whole discussion Chuck said, "By the way, I don't understand this business about intent. Do I have to show that Dr. Levy did not create disloyalty and disaffection to disprove that second charge?" The law officer said, "No, no, no, no, that's of no importance whatsoever. What's important is that if the statements which Levy made would have been *likely* to have created disloyalty and disaffection, then we can assume that that was in fact his intent." And Chuck says, "Well now, wait a second. If the statements would have been likely to produce disloyalty and disaffection, don't you think we would have had maybe one example of somebody who's been made disloyal or somebody who's disaffected?" "No, no, no, Mr. Morgan. It doesn't matter whether anybody was made disloyal or disaffected. It's just whether it was likely to happen if he used those words." "But if it didn't happen, how could it be likely to happen? I mean, you presented twenty-four witnesses here, something like twenty-four witnesses, you sent out eight hundred letters to Dr. Levy's patients and people who he's been in contact with, asking whether they were made disloyal or disaffected. We have not a single person who said he was made disloyal, not a single person was made disaffected, and how can you say it was likely to happen if it never happened?"

Isn't it absurd? Now had I been organizing from within the Army I would have felt ashamed of myself that nobody was made disloyal and nobody disaffected. I mean, that would have been a hell of a job of organizing. Hang my head in shame, all of these people coming up and saying, "No, Levy had no effect on me whatsoever. Just thought he was a kook." But, in fact, there was no testimony that anybody was made disloyal, that anybody disaffected. And yet it was supposedly my intent to do it. It's weird. Chuck later on argued in the brief, it was kind of a Kafkaesque kind of world. You know the great quote from *Alice in Wonderland* about words meaning what I say they mean. I read it about once a year—*Alice in Wonderland*. It's my political bible. It's a good book. As Chuck later said, "We're dealing with a case of words. There's just no rhyme or reason to any of it, and the deeper you get into it the less reasonable it seems."

You see, there was no standard of proof for that intent charge. And if there's no standard of proof, there's also no standard for unproving it or disproving it. I mean, how can you prove it wasn't my intent . . . if in fact it never happened? It's sort of like this whole conspiracy trial in Chicago. It was their intent to cause a riot crossing state lines. Wow! How the hell do you ever prove that? You know, unless you have people together in a room, there's an informer there, and so on and so forth. But that's not what the Government's trying to do.

FINN: It was on the basis of these three things together, though, that you were convicted? You said that the Uniform Code doesn't really enter into it here, but it was on the Uniform Code itself that the prosecution rested their case.

LEVY: Well, yeah. Sure. But the Uniform Code is really a fiction. It may be uniform but it has nothing to do with justice. So it really is a kind of a euphemism . . . at best. And there's no question in my mind, and I think Chuck's mind, or Alan Levine's mind—you have to begin with the proposition that you have to, number one, abolish the Uniform Code of Military Justice; number two, abolish the court-martial system; number three, this would mean, as a result, abolishing all military stockades and brigs. And that's the beginning point of any opposition to that system of so-called justice. And I'm not much interested in people who want to reform it, because I don't think it can be reformed within that context. And I'm not against revolutionary reformism in general; I think there are certain reforms which *do* help us and which we would certainly favor. But not those reforms. And the reason for that is it's inconceivable to me, on these political charges, that any Army's going to let itself be destroyed. And if you give G.I.'s, really give G.I.'s freedom of speech, freedom of press, freedom of religion, freedom of assembly, you're not going to have an army for very long. Most G.I.'s oppose the war in Vietnam.

FINN: But that might merely mean that instead of the Army being destroyed, that in this particular case it might mean that our policy about Vietnam would be changed. There are G.I.'s, for example, who support a lot of other ventures. I wanted to ask whether you think free speech and assembly can be compatible with an army?

LEVY: I think they're compatible with *an* army, but not this army . . . fighting these wars. I think if they're fighting for something they believe in it's absolutely compatible. Sure. I can visualize it happening, for better or worse, in Israel. But it is my understanding that their soldiers *do* support that army and that therefore they don't have any great problem with discontent. I don't think they have elections of officers, but they really don't have much of a differentiation between the officers and the enlisted men in the Israeli Army. I can visualize these freedoms existing, but not under these circumstances, where you're fighting an unpopular war that the soldier doesn't want to get ripped off in. But if you remove the threat of prosecution for a G.I. exerting his rights, believe me, eighty percent of the G.I.'s are going to organize against the war. And the only thing that stops them from doing that right now is this fear of punishment. And it's a very powerful weapon. That's why you've got a military stockade system. Who do you find in the military stockade? In *any* military stockade you want to look at in the United States, ninety percent of the men are there for the charge of AWOL. That's a political offense . . . even if the man isn't always conscious of the political nature of his act—and I'm perfectly willing to admit that he often is not. Nevertheless, the fact that he said he'd rather be someplace other than the Army, makes it a political act, albeit *sometimes* unconscious.

FINN: Well, let me backtrack. After you decided that since you were going to go through with this and the Army was too, you wanted a lot of publicity, what then did you do —including after you were sentenced and in prison? What followed from that?

LEVY: Well, what followed after that was trying to make political capital out of virtually every act and to think of what the political consequences would be of any given act before I did it. I'm much less impulsive now than I may have been five years ago, and I just don't do things impulsively anymore. And I don't do things out of acts of moral witness anymore. I think that I'm more moral now than I was before, but I'm not much interested in convincing people about it.

FINN: You're obviously more politically conscious now and more politically effective in doing what you're doing.

LEVY: Right. It seems to me that if you do something which you know, or have reason to believe, will not be effective politically, that's immoral. Some militant acts may be politically inappropriate because they're politically ineffective, but I'm not sure they're immoral . . . in an *absolute* sense. But I think it's wrong to be obsessed with this question of morality. I think it immobilizes you, I think it paralyzes people. So I don't worry about that very much now. What I worry about is political effectiveness.

FINN: Were most people you talked with—those you were in prison with—sympathetic to your views? Some of them would be, I presume, because they were in because of views similar to your own. What about the people who were not, who were indifferent or opposed?

LEVY: At the disciplinary barracks at Fort Leavenworth, lots of the G.I.'s were, of course, sympathetic—even if they were not there for overtly political reasons. They didn't like the Army, the Army put them in jail, and they were sympathetic . . . for the most part. When I got to Lewisburg Farm Camp and Penitentiary, you had the sort of play of differences of opinion that you have on the outside. You know. There are people who oppose the war in Vietnam, there are other people who don't oppose the war in Vietnam. Lots of people thought that we were courageous and they kind of respected us for that. A lot of the hostility which seems to have been true of World War I and II, maybe even the Korean War, in federal prisons against draft resisters—against some of the older draft resisters like Dave Dellinger—seems to be much less evident now. You don't have instances really where many of the draft resisters get beaten up in jail. You may have instances where they get raped, but that's not because of their political views; it's because they're young, they're attractive, they're a little naive, they don't know how to handle themselves, they're non-violent—that's the reason why they're kind of set-ups for a rape attempt, not because somebody thinks that they're Commies and wants to do them in.

There was some hostility in jail for some of the C.O.'s. Some of the men did not like C.O.'s. But they didn't like C.O.'s for some of the reasons I find C.O.'s difficult to deal with: they thought they were arrogant and they thought they were "holier than thou"—that was the term they used very often. You know, there was this punk telling me what I ought to believe in and telling me if I don't believe the way he believes that I'm like the devil or something. But that's, again, not so much a political problem as it is a kind of a way of presenting it. Certainly I said some things that lots of people didn't agree with in jail, very open left-wing political opinions, and I never had any problem in jail. They didn't always agree with me, but that's fair enough.

FINN: What has this whole politicalization, radicalization, done to the kind of career you might have seen five years ago, or six or seven?

LEVY: Well, five or six years ago I would have liked to have earned $50,000 a year practicing dermatology, probably in the middle of New York City. But now, I think that would be rather unrewarding. I want to practice dermatology, but I want to do it in a different setting. I want to do it in a setting which isn't going to pay me a lot of money. And I'm working now a little bit, once a week, with the Medical Committee for Human Rights mobile unit in the East Village. I just started doing it last week, but it seems like it's going to be fun. And I'll probably be doing more of that on the Lower East Side, maybe with Nena [Northeast Neighborhood Association], for example, one of the neighborhood clinics. But I want to do it part-time because I still want to have time to do some of the other things which I also think are rewarding.

FINN: Other things, meaning political things?

LEVY: Yeah. Opposition to the war in Vietnam and forming part of what, for want of another term, is the left of the health movement. I think it's a real movement that's being generated.

FINN: You seem to have survived the things you've gone through and seem to have options open to you. What about other people who've run into this form of military justice in the last several years? Could you even speculate about how most people get through that? How does it change them if it does?

LEVY: Well, it's hard to generalize. I think most of the kids who I knew who got through it are fine, actually. I think, in general—although, again, generalizations are really risky—I think in general they became more political. Many of the people who I met at the disciplinary barracks have done various things after they've gotten out: some have been involved with radical politics, like Jimmy Johnson and Dennis Mora; one fellow was involved with District 65 Union; Duane Ferré is now in charge of the UFO coffee house in Columbia, South Carolina; other people have gone back to the universities. They've done fairly well as far as I can tell.

I've been visiting G.I. posts, in particular those that have coffee houses, and what I generally do is go up for a night, or more often a weekend, go to the coffee house on a Friday or Saturday night, rap with the G.I.'s there—on any given night you can expect to have anywhere between one hundred and two hundred G.I.'s there—and I'll just maybe give a little speech or maybe just answer questions; it varies from place to place.

FINN: What kind of questions do you get?

LEVY: Well, how do you resist in the Army? Why do you oppose the war in Vietnam? I was up at Fort Dix a few months ago and I was rapping about the immorality of the war in Vietnam, and a G.I. interrupted me and he said, "Well, you know we've heard that shit for three years, Nuremburg and all that kind of crap. Why don't you talk about the cause of the war—like can't you rap about American imperialism and monopoly capitalism?" So we did. They're very political beings. A lot of people just don't believe that, but it's true.

When Howard Levy took the position he did, when he refused to be a complicit agent in a war he condemned, he had some supporters—but few. Today I believe he would have many more, for every day since he took that stand and was sentenced to years in prison, the terrible aspects of that war have become apparent. If one compares his situation with that of recent military cases, ironies abound. One has only to choose from the front pages of the daily paper to be struck by the incongruities. For example, the *New York Times* of April 1, 1970, reports the case of First Lieutenant James B. Duffy. Lieutenant Duffy admitted that he had given permission to one of his sergeants to shoot an unarmed Vietnamese prisoner. The military court first declared the Lieutenant guilty of premeditated murder, but when the court learned that a sentence of life imprisonment was mandatory for such a verdict, it rendered a verdict of involuntary manslaughter, which drew a sentence of six months. The court then inquired whether that sentence could be suspended. Furthermore, Lieutenant Duffy was not dismissed from the Army.

Is it really worse to refuse to train Special Forces medics for ethical and conscientious reasons than to have an unarmed prisoner killed? Or is the system which allows that judgment at fault? Or are there mitigating circumstances which account for a discrepancy so vast as to seem at first unbridgeable? The case of Dr. Levy—and Howard Levy himself—is there to press such questions now and for an indefinite time.

Roger L. Priest

S*ave the Priest* STP Slogans of Roger L. Priest, a young Journalist Seaman Apprentice in the United States Navy. And what Seaman Priest wants to be saved from when I first talk with him are the tender ministrations of justice as it is understood in the U.S. Navy. It is difficult, when speaking to this tall, rangy, soft-spoken man, to realize that in high echelons of the Navy he is the object of such deep concern. But *that* he is, there can be no doubt. He is, when I speak to him early in 1970, facing court-martial charges that could incur penalties of almost forty years in prison.

The charges against Seaman Priest? They stem from what Roger Priest printed in *OM,* an anti-war, military newsletter that he publishes on his own time, with his own money, off-post. In journalistic terms, *OM* has its valleys as well as its peaks. In its most recent numbers published in red, white and blue, it offers not only a generous portion of Priest's opinions about things military but a real variety of cartoons, drawings, poems, and quotations. The eclectic nature of *OM* is suggested by those it quotes. Among those from whom Priest has garnered pertinent, brief comments are Phil Ochs, Goethe, Benjamin Constant, Frederick Douglass,

Walter Bagehot, Konrad Lorenz, Hermann Goering, and Louis Pasteur.

However diverse the authors, in the pages of *OM* the thrust of their comments is directed against a single jugular. For example, Justice William O. Douglas in *O'Callahan* v. *Parker*: "None of the travesties of justice perpetuated under the UCMJ is really very surprising, for military law has always been and continues to be an instrument of discipline, not justice." And General William C. Westmoreland on Vietnam: "I bet that Russian Army is jealous as hell. Our troops are here getting all this experience, we're learning about guerrilla warfare, helicopters, vertical envelopment, close artillery support. Those Russians would love to be here . . . Any true professional wants to march to the sound of gunfire." And this blast from General David M. Shoup, former Commandant of the Marine Corps and member of the Joint Chiefs of Staff:

> Civilians can scarcely understand or even believe that many ambitious military professionals truly yearn for wars and the opportunity for glory and distinction afforded only in combat. Standing closely behind these leaders, and encouraging and prompting them, are rich and powerful defense industries. Standing in front, adorned with service caps, ribbons and lapel emblems, is a Nation of veterans—patriotic, belligerent . . . finding a certain sublimation and excitement in their country's latest military venture. Militarism in America is in full bloom . . . the blight of Vietnam reveals that militarism is more a poisonous weed than a glorious blossom.

Such things didn't please the Navy; they counterattacked. Here is how Nicholas von Hoffman, not wholly unsympathetic to the problem of the military, described that attack in the *Washington Post:*

> . . . he was hit with a court-martial charge sheet accusing him of everything that's happened to the Navy except perhaps stealing

the Pueblo or letting the air out of that atomic submarine that sank in San Francisco Bay last month. It takes more than four, single-spaced typewritten pages to enumerate all the bad things Roger has done, which include the charge that he "did wrongfully use contemptuous words against the Chairman of the Armed Services Committee of the House of Representatives, L. Mendel Rivers." How Roger managed to use contemptuous words against the Congressman wrongfully is not explained, but if he did, he's a very clever boy and they should make him an admiral.

But Von Hoffman added that, "If Roger Priest were a civilian, the only place in the country he could be arrested would be in Montgomery County, because he has some drawings in it of parts of the body which are illegal there."

This is also Roger Priest's opinion and the basis of his stand. The passage of Priest through the Navy is a remarkable but not unparalleled example of how apolitical or conservative young men are politicized and sometimes radicalized by that system. For when Roger Priest was a student in his hometown at the University of Houston, he didn't question the war. "I wasn't the one that was fixing to go, and when it was somebody else I could easier think about fraternity parties and things like that." I ask him if Vietnam wasn't a part of his conversation at college among his friends.

PRIEST: Well, let's see. I graduated high school in '62, got out of college in '67, and the major escalation started in '65, so my involvement probably really started in '66, probably in my last year. This was when the whole country was undergoing a big change, a big shift in attitudes. I was a part of that too. It's hard to remember, looking back, and seeing the days when I was a hawk: "Let's win over there." When I started getting involved, in other words when the draft was going to take me and put me in that situation, that's when I started reading the relevant documents.

FINN: You didn't come out of a radical background, prepared to criticize. It was on the basis of reading and judging what was available at that time.

PRIEST: That's right. In fact the background is very, very, very middle class. Not radical at all. In fact it's non-involved. The only politics my father has ever been involved in is running for the school board.

On the basis of his reading, thinking and talking, Priest became strongly opposed to the war in Vietnam. When I ask why, if he was strongly opposed, he entered the service at all, he replies that he did consider two other alternatives. He thought of claiming exemption as a conscientious objector but thought that he did not qualify on two grounds: first, he thought that he did not have the kind of religious training that would satisfy the courts, and second, he was not opposed to all wars—he was not a pacifist—but only to the war in Vietnam. So he acted on what he thought of as his second alternative and took off for Europe, for Germany, France, Denmark and Sweden. But problems with money, language, work and homesickness brought him back to the States.

FINN: Enlisting in the Navy was better than being drafted into the Army or going to jail.

PRIEST: Yes. Well, I must say, I was still trying to honor my conscience in some way. I was compromising, but I didn't want to compromise it to the extent that I would fight in the Army. Because I knew that if I went in the Army that I would be sent to Vietnam and put in a combatant role, because they needed so many people. I knew that by volunteering in the Navy there was a chance that I could probably be a journalist, which is the job they gave me. And I figured I'd be on a ship rather than on land, so I wouldn't directly participate in some of these things. At least this was part of the thing that was going on in my head. Because I couldn't see going to jail. I *knew* that if I refused, I'd go directly to jail. I didn't want to do that. And I couldn't leave it any other way. So it was really just being backed up against the wall. It was just the best alternative. And now I'm not even sure it was the best. See, I thought when I went in that I could keep relatively straight for four years, that I could serve out my time, get my honorable discharge, and come back into civilian life. And I found it's actually impossible.

FINN: How did you first find this out?

PRIEST: It started about after I had raised my hand. Just about that fast. It started in basic training in San Diego, arriving there . . . just the treatment of people, the dehumanization which you undergo going through basic training, the brutality. I was slugged a couple of times in basic training.

FINN: Because you were resisting?

PRIEST: No, I wasn't resisting. In fact, I would be standing there, just minding my own business, and someone would come up behind and give me a kidney punch.

FINN: What was that for? Just for supposed discipline?

PRIEST: Well, maybe it's lack of discipline on their part, because the guy who was brutalizing us was a drunkard. So it's not really that *we* were being punished, it was just that he was a sadist and was taking out his frustrations on us. And this happened in many cases. And I was also witnessing the treatment of Marines. They were in a recruit depot directly across from us in San Diego—a Marine depot. But anyway, we would watch these guys being marched—a company of about sixty or seventy of 'em—double-time, full field pack. They would have a gray Navy ambulance following them, and I thought this was rather strange, this ambulance following 'em. But then I found out. When some of the guys would lag behind and would fall, we watched 'em kick 'em and beat 'em. In many cases they ended up hospitalized. So this was the start of this radicalizing thing.

In spite of "this radicalizing thing" and of developing "an increasingly individual, independent outlook," Priest did well the job his college training had prepared him for. Along with older career people he worked on *Direction,* a public affairs magazine that went out to public affairs officers around the world. But the office was split down the middle, the civilians on one side and the military—except for Seaman Priest—on the other. And when Priest told a Navy WAVE officer, who had previously been friendly, how strongly he felt about Vietnam, tensions mounted. These tensions and divisions, Priest feels, were the real basis for his first court-martial.

PRIEST: That prepared it. There were certain little things that led up to it, but the actual incident itself took place one afternoon when I requested early in the day to leave the office at a certain time to pick up a change of linen for the weekend—this was a Friday afternoon—and I asked off. But the problem was, this WAVE officer who didn't like me anymore was very upset that myself and several civilians had went out for lunch and stayed for about 2½ or 3 hours . . . drinking, and eating, and having a good time, which we did quite often, you know, when there was nothing else to do. So when I came in about 3:30, I was ordered to go next door and stamp return addresses on some envelopes. And it was at that time that I told this officer that I'd asked off to go and pick up my linen. She just said "No," that there was no way that I could do this, that I'd wasted enough time and now I was going to do some work. So I started to argue and I went to the officer right above me, a non-commissioned officer who was directly in charge of my work, and asked him to intervene in my behalf. And he went to talk to her and she . . .

FINN: Wasn't having any?

PRIEST: She'd made up her mind. She was very angry at us. Well, a little time elapsed here and she gave me another order, said, "You *will* go over next door and you *will* do it." So I went above her head to the captain who was in command of our office, who allowed me to go over, pick up my linen and come back and do the work—which I did. But on Monday, when I came back into the office, I'd been placed on report. And a court-martial resulted from this. And at the court-martial I was tried for willfully disobeying a lawful order. And the maximum punishment during time of war is death . . . for willfully disobeying a lawful order. It's really out of sight. I had a summary court-martial in which you have one officer who hears the case, who prosecutes, who defends you, and does the whole thing. It turned out to be a WAVE officer, who was also close friends with this other WAVE officer. I was busted from an E-3 seaman in the Navy to an E-2 seaman apprentice and fined $75 . . . for something that just quickly escalated, because I'm not stupid enough to stand up and disobey any orders. But it was just something that happened. It was just one of the little goal posts, sign posts, in this attitudinal change that led me to where I am now.

FINN: Had you published at that point any issues of your magazine?

PRIEST: This was in October of '68 and the first issue of *OM* didn't come out till the last week in March of '69.

FINN: Did things go fairly easily between those times?

PRIEST: No, they were straight downhill. I mean just that way: straight downhill. Because my mind opened up for the first time as to what the military's all about. In other words, I was opposed to the war, but I had sublimated my opposition and was able to continue my duties in the Pentagon. After that court-martial I couldn't even put on the uniform anymore and just carry out my duties. In other words, not only was it the war but it was also the whole military system that was responsible for the war, and its policies, that I was opposed to. It just started me thinking and shocked me into another whole new realm of research that I got into. You know. And that was the whole military situation.

FINN: Did you find it hard to get help?

PRIEST: No. It was at this time that I first found out there was a budding G.I. opposition to the war and to the military. And I found two servicemen's newspapers around this time. And one of 'em was *The Bond,* put out by the American Servicemen's Union in New York, and the other one was the *Vietnam G.I.,* put out in Chicago. And that was the first information I ever had about G.I. opposition, internally, to the war. And so I wrote both papers to get subscriptions, and then later became a member of the ASU and I talked to Andy Stapp [founder of ASU] about organizing a newspaper here in Washington. He told me what would happen if I put out a paper—which didn't happen at all. He says, "They will either transfer you or give you an undesirable discharge." And what they come up with was a new way.

FINN: He said that on the basis of . . .

PRIEST: . . . what had happened to him, and what had happened to others in the past.

FINN: Why do you think this did not happen to you? Or do you have any ideas about it?

PRIEST: It's just theory right now, since I don't have access to the minds that created this whole situation, or their files. From the very beginning there was a press interest in this case; the *Washington Post* had written about it. Also I was in the Pentagon, also I was in the Navy, rather than being in the Army. And I think it was a combination of all of these things. In other words, the Navy hadn't had a chance of dealing with this as the Army had. And because there was some national interest in *OM,* I think they may have been a little scared.

FINN: The national press and media got in *after* you brought out the issues of the magazine.

PRIEST: Yes.

FINN: And after charges were brought against you?

PRIEST: Well, there was national interest in it before the charges were ever brought . . . so I think that may have had a deterrent effect on what they could have done.

FINN: How many issues did you bring out before the court-martial? The court-martial charges against you now are primarily based on three issues: April, May and June issues, number one, two and three.

PRIEST: Well, it's on the basis of *only* those, not primarily. Only statements that appeared in those three papers. Nothing else.

FINN: And it doesn't relate to your other activities of marching, or protesting?

PRIEST: No. Just that; just the papers. In other words, I've solicited servicemen to desert and commit sedition through disloyal statements in *OM.* That's what I'm charged with—charged with making disloyal statements in *OM* and causing *OM* to be distributed.

FINN: How did you find that your superiors of whatever rank were getting unhappy about *OM?*

PRIEST: Well, they never knew about *OM,* if you're talking about my superiors in the Pentagon. In other words, *OM* came out, and when it came out I left. That fast. In other words, they had no inkling that *OM* ever was going to come out; it just appeared. And when it appeared, I was no longer in the Pentagon.

FINN: You were shifted pretty rapidly.

PRIEST: I was shifted within an hour . . . after they saw the first issue. And then the results of the story in the *Washington Post.* You see the thing was, I was sending out these press releases letting servicemen know what they could do to change their G.I. insurance as a form of protest, that they could designate peace and resistance groups as beneficiaries to their $10,000 life insurance policy. And a reporter for the *Washington Post*—it was von Hoffman—wanted to do a story on that, and when he called me up I said, "Hey, you'd also be interested in my first issue of *OM* that I'm producing on my own." He says "Yes." So he interviewed me, wrote up the story, and I asked him when the thing would come out and he said it would be out on March the 24th. I says, "Fine. I'll make sure I get my first issue of *OM* out that weekend." 'Cause I was anticipating transfer, since this is what Andy had said. You know, "They're going to transfer you to another side of the world somewhere."

So Saturday and Sunday *OM* appeared throughout the Washington area. On Monday, when I walked into the office, nobody even looked up from their desk. And they says, "Priest, they want to see you in the Admin office." I went in there to the Administration office and they says, "Boy, you really got things upset here." They were talking about the story in the *Washington Post,* and they also had a copy of

OM on their desk, and they gave me orders to report to the Washington Navy Yard, to the Navy and Marine Corps Exhibit Center. And so about an hour after, there I was. I was at the Yard until they transferred me across the river to the Naval station where the charges were formally filed. It's kind of a transit station.

FINN: You have enough time to still do *OM?*

PRIEST: I don't know about enough time—it keeps me up late at night. I stay rather sleepy. That's a real pain. But I do it. Because . . . I found out what type of opposition I'm facing, what type of opposition wants *OM* to be silenced. And that's enough right there for me not to let it go down.

FINN: Why do you think it bugs the Navy as much as it must for them to bring these charges against you?

PRIEST: Well, the actual investigation on me began before *OM* was even put out, I understand. This came from the testimony of one of the Naval investigative agents, who testified at my pre-trial hearing, before *OM* came out. And the reason for that is because of the changing of my insurance. I had a real hassle with a Lieutenant Commander when I changed my insurance, because I wrote down the War Resisters League, 5 Beekman Street, New York [now 339 Lafayette St., N.Y., N.Y. 10012—*Ed.*] as my beneficiary for my $10,000 life insurance policy. Be a Viet Cong shoot me or a D.C. transit bus run over me, ten thousand dollars would go to the War Resisters League. So this guy who was a personnel officer asked me about this. His lead statement was, "You know, of course, this is a Communist organization." And that kinda surprised me. And I said, "No, it's not a Communist organization." And I said that it's not on the Attorney General's list or anything like that. So then he started to ask me why did I change my insurance? Did I know anybody with this group? Was I a member of it?

If I was a member of any type of subversive group I could get dishonorably discharged and five years in jail. I told him I wasn't a member of it. Did my parents know why I was doing this? "Why *are you* doing this? Are you unhappy?" Just all these crazy inane questions.

He wanted to find out why and possibly talk me out of it, or if he couldn't talk me out of it at least get some information. And so his closing thing was, "We'll let you know right now that your parents will hear about this. And don't you think it would be better if you told them yourself?" That really surprised me.

FINN: That's really being a big brother.

PRIEST: Well, he promised me. He said, "We'll write a note home to your parents, and Naval Intelligence will investigate this, find out about this organization that you have named."

FINN: Did he actually know anything about it, or was it just the title that set him off?

PRIEST: He had no idea, I'm sure. It could have been American Friends Service Committee or something. It could have been anything. You know, anybody who's resisting war is bound to be a Communist, or Communist-affiliated, to that man. So this, I think, is how the Naval Intelligence got involved in the case. In other words, they were called right after that to start probing in my background. I didn't have any type of high clearance in the Pentagon. I had a secret clearance which just clears you for secret material—which is nothing. I was never really working with secret material because all my work was just preparing press releases, xeroxing material, or monitoring the AP, UPI teletypes. Nothing classified. I didn't have any access to this type of material, so I wasn't any type of security threat

—at all. No way. I knew no combinations of any safes or anything like that. I couldn't lay hands on classified material even if I'd wanted to . . . which I wouldn't. But just my being opposed to the war was enough, in their minds, to bring in the Naval Intelligence Agency.

FINN: The Naval Intelligence Agency came in after your signing your life insurance to WRL.

PRIEST: Yes. They started an investigation then. I first became aware of them in a very flagrant fashion, when I noticed these people standing out in front of the apartment. (I'm living off-base here, near Dupont Circle.) And one of the people in the apartment said, "Hey, there's some strange people out there in the parking lot." And we looked out and there were about four cars and about eight people. And all were in white shirts and they had . . . this was during the summer so they had their sport coats off. And we saw one of them bend over and we saw a gun. I was a little apprehensive; I didn't know who and what these people were. Then for several weeks, everytime I left the apartment—in my car, or walking, no matter how or when—I had these people following me. I started looking in the rear-view mirror, and when a car would get behind me I would turn around, run red lights or something, and then another car would come. They were all in radio contact. It's really spooky. In fact, we counted six different cars one day following me, two people in each car.

FINN: *Six different cars* in one day?

PRIEST: Six different cars following me, just to go cross town. Amazing. And it was so obvious. This was when I didn't know who in the hell it was. I didn't think "Naval Intelligence." That name! There's no intelligence in Naval Intelligence, believe me. I didn't know if they could be FBI, if they could be Minutemen, if they were right wing or what. I didn't think it could be the FBI 'cause I'd been brought up on the bit that the FBI had more on the ball. I *knew* I was being followed and I believed that the FBI wouldn't let me know *that*. So I didn't know. I never knew until the pre-trial hearing in July as to the exact number—when they testified that they had sent twenty-five agents. That's sworn testimony on their part, that they'd assigned twenty-five agents . . . to follow me.

FINN: For what purpose?

PRIEST: Just to observe me, I guess; where I was going, what I was doing. They also testified . . .

FINN: Did this take place before *OM* was published?

PRIEST: The bulk of it was while *OM* was being published. That's when I first became aware of being followed. In fact, it was during the month of May that I really became aware of it. I mean, that's when they would stand out in front of the apartment and look up at the window. And they were wearing this hearing-aid-type device. They'd just be standing there. And so one day, in cooperation with my roommate, I got the camera and some flash bulbs and we went out and decided to start taking some pictures of them. And we took a whole roll of film . . . which later disappeared.

FINN: They knew you were taking pictures.

PRIEST: Sure they did. So when I left the apartment I brought the film up here and had one of the secretaries here take the film.

FINN: Here at LINK [Servicemen's LINK to Peace]?

PRIEST: Here at LINK, to take the film down to get it processed. And we lost the film. It's never been found. The film was taken. We had a receipt for it. But when we went back to pick it up, there was no record of it. They also swiped some mail out of our apartment.

FINN: You mean open mail that you had read?

PRIEST: No, I hadn't read it. In fact, it was mail that we'd received at the apartment, sent to me, that hadn't even been picked up by me yet. In other words, it was stolen mail.

FINN: How did you know it was there?

PRIEST: My roommate saw it when it came in; he didn't pick it up. We've got four floors in our apartment. The outer doors of the apartment are locked. Mail in the morning is thrown through a mail slot and it's picked up and put on the community table by one of the residents. And we've all lived there for a long period of time. There's been no change in residents, so I'm not worried about anybody being a thief among us. So the mail was put out on this community table. When my roommate left he saw two letters sent to me. When I arrived home that night, he called me and asked me about one of the letters, he said it was from the Navy. And I says, "Oh, it's my Navy check." And so I went downstairs and I looked for it. There wasn't any mail for me; it wasn't there; I checked all over the place. So that night I called the metropolitan police and made an official report on the thing, that the mail had been stolen, showed them the procedure as to how the mail was delivered. And the next day the mail was returned. It had been opened and resealed . . . because it was all frayed on the edges. Why, I don't know. This is still a mystery—as to why.

I've talked to another agent who's a good friend of mine, just got out of the Air Force, and he was working with the Air Force Intelligence. And he said he had never heard of an investigation being done in this way. In other words, we don't know to this day why they were doing this . . . because they didn't need to do it. The letters can be steamed open before they ever reach you; they don't have to steal 'em out of a locked building. Why? Why were they doing it? You can be followed without even knowing why you're being followed. Why do you stand out in front of somebody's apartment? Why do you follow them doggedly, unless you're trying to do something else? And what that something is is still a question in my mind.

The result of all this harassment—and harassment's all it may have been (this is just my theory; I've got no way of knowing this)—they may have tried to harass me, scare me into stopping *OM*. And with my make-up it had the opposite effect. Because I made up the most radical, rabid issue of all, which was the third issue. The first and second issues were comparatively tame. Really and truly. I mean, when you look at 'em you can see a change in approach . . . in bitterness. Because it was very, very . . . Well . . . anytime you get people going through your personal affairs like that it's . . . They were also doing some other things too. This was only part of it.

FINN: Like what?

PRIEST: Well, they testified that they went through the garbage of my apartment. This came out in testimony. They testified that they'd made a special pick-up of the garbage, in cooperation with the Department of Sanitation of the District of Columbia. They testified that they picked up the garbage only one time. I don't know if it's more or not. But they entered a letter taken out of this garbage, as evidence against me. In fact, it was the original copy of a letter sent by an agent to me from a post-office box that he had rented under an assumed name. A Naval Intelligence agent. He was a special resident agent here in Washington, and he was assigned this case.

FINN: And he sent you . . .

PRIEST: And he sent me a letter under an assumed name from a post-office box in Alexandria, Virginia, asking for a copy of *OM* and enclosing a dollar, and using the assumed name of . . . I think it was Humphries, Ralph V. Humphries, YN3, United States Navy Reserve.

FINN: What kind of evidence was this supposed to be when it was introduced?

PRIEST: All of this was to prove the link between myself and *OM*. In other words, that I have put out *OM*, that I have distributed *OM* to servicemen. And this is why they've been going through all of this elaborate procedure. So what they did was introduce the original copy of this letter as evidence against me. So the first question—and this is very, very curious because the question was not from my defense attorney, but from the prosecution—the prosecution asked this agent, "How did you obtain this original letter?" And he stuttered a few minutes and said, "Well, we had this special pick-up with the Sanitation Department." All this did was just create a big stink: the Mayor of Washington, Walter Washington, called for an investigation, there were big headlines in the papers about it, for using a special pick-up of garbage. And they went through not only my garbage but the garbage of all four floors of the apartment; took all that garbage in burlap bags, threw it out and went through it.

Then one of the questions was, "Can you say for sure that this garbage came from Priest's apartment?" And they can't, because here it's all out in the alley. It doesn't mean anything. It's very strange. It's been one helluva case . . . the way the investigation's been carried out, the amount of charges that've been dropped . . . just no evidence at all. In fact, they got such a weak, weak case. It's just amazing that it's even being tried. The only strong thing that they've got going for them is that it will be tried in front of a court of military officers. And that's *all* they've got going for them as far as I'm concerned.

Roger Priest was not to know until some weeks later, when the syndicated columnist Jack Anderson revealed the existence of correspondence between the Pentagon and Congressman L. Mendel Rivers, that they might have something else going for them. There was a profusion of things in Priest's journal that might have upset Mr. Rivers, but the following item, called "Bobby Seale's Parable," must have been high on the list:

BOBBY SEALE'S PARABLE

Once upon a time, there was a very poor man who was walking along the base of a tall mountain.

The man was extremely thirsty, so he was delighted when he came upon a stream.

But as he bent down to quench his thirst, he noticed that the stream was full of muck and filth. In desperate need of a cool, clean drink, the man tried to get the muck and filth out of the stream, but to no avail.

As he was about to give up, another man appeared and asked him what he was doing.

"I am very, very thirsty," the poor man said, "but I can't drink from this stream because it is filthy and I am unable to clean it."

The second man smiled and explained that the stream was full of muck and filth because a huge hog was standing in the middle of the stream at the top of the mountain.

"This hog," the man said, "is pissing and shitting in the stream and that is why it is so dirty."

"If you want a cool, clean drink, you must get that hog out of that stream."

And with that, the two men set out to climb the mountain and get the hog out of the stream.

L. MENDEL RIVERS. GET YOUR ASS OUT OF THAT STREAM. YOU HEAR, BOY?

Whether this little parable was in itself responsible for Rivers' reaction, soon after its publication there was an exchange of letters between the Congressman and Rear Admiral Means Johnston, USN, about "R. Priest, U.S. Navy." (See Appendix 1.) Of this correspondence Jack Anderson wrote that it "establishes clearly that the Navy was acting to appease Rivers when it ordered Priest court-martialed." And there is no doubt about Rivers' own opinion of Priest since he volunteered in an interview that "that boy ought to be put in prison, that's what."

When, in fact, the Navy did act, Priest's case received considerable publicity and many people viewed it as a constitutional question. For example, on September 5, 1969, New York Senator Charles E. Goodell said that he had urged Navy Secretary John Chafee to give the Priest case "very careful personal attention before embarrassment and discredit to the Navy result." And he then continued:

> My basic concern is the question of the constitutional rights of a man in the service of the United States.
>
> I wish to emphasize that I am not referring to a case involving the insubordination of an enlisted man to his superior officer. I am referring to the rights of free speech and free press guaranteed to to every citizen and certainly to a soldier in his activities off base, with his own funds and on his own time.
>
> Given the fact that free expression of opinion is basic to our system, it seems especially inappropriate that Seaman Priest should be facing such serious charges for acting in a way which is protected by the Constitution of the United States.
>
> To use technical infractions to quiet the views of those who disagree with military procedure or policy is, in my estimation, a disservice to military justice and civil rights.
>
> It is disturbing to me that individual commanders throughout the service continue to have the discretion to determine what the permissible limits of dissent may be.
>
> The Priest case is typical of other such cases occurring throughout the Armed Services. Daily it becomes increasingly important that uniform guidelines be established by the Department of the Navy, and indeed by all branches of the Armed Services. This question must be resolved at the highest level.

When Roger Priest enlisted in the Navy on October 19, 1967,

he accepted certain well-defined responsibilities as a soldier. He did not, however, forfeit his constitutional rights as a citizen of the United States.

There are few people who think that apart from the merits of the case, the New York Senator could expect from the Navy the degree of attention that L. Mendel Rivers commands. But Roger Priest and I were both innocent of the Rivers' correspondence as we continued our discussion.

FINN: I wanted to ask you about this particularly because in his article about you, Nicholas von Hoffman quotes you as saying your case is a constitutional one: "What I do with my own free time, outside of the Navy, in my own apartment with my friends is my right as an American citizen." He then says it's not fair to blame the Navy because, "No military organization is going to survive very long if the privates can publicly go about calling the generals pigs. To say, as the indictment does, that such language interferes with loyalty, morale and discipline is a bit of an understatement. The fault lies not with the Navy." Do you agree with that?

PRIEST: I don't. I don't at all. I would make a distinction he doesn't. I'm not standing up in front of an admiral or a general and, publicly, with all of his men present, calling the man a pig. I am challenging him, but indirectly, in a publication produced off-base when I'm off-duty. There's a world of difference there.

FINN: Do you think those statements in *OM* referring to officers as pigs are as damaging to morale and discipline as von Hoffman suggests?

PRIEST: I don't know. I personally couldn't care less. If they're upset with these terms maybe we could escalate and come up with others. I use these terms as political weapons anyway. Because the problem is with the way the military is set up right now. In other words, they're set up to fight certain types of wars, to protect certain interests abroad, and if we can ever reverse this—in getting a military that's set up to protect not certain economic interests, certain companies, but to really protect people (I mean people in the most general term; not the rich, not certain companies like G.E., United Fruit), then this wouldn't even become a problem.

FINN: You are then saying in one sense it's not the fault of the Navy, either, it's the fault of the people . . .

PRIEST: It's the fault of the system.

FINN: . . . who make the overall policy.

PRIEST: The military makes policy too; by having the capabilities of doing certain jobs, they in fact make policy. In other words, by having a technology that makes it possible. to make rapid assaults, you enable a foreign policy to do things like Santo Domingo. Things like that where, just quickly, you move in.

FINN: But the military still doesn't make the decisions.

PRIEST: They get some advice. The Joint Chiefs of Staff have plans for any type of emergency that would crop up in the world. But whether this plan will be acted upon or not . . . sure, a decision will be made in that regard, but they still participate formally.

FINN: You do not yourself see a time when the United States would not have an armed force?

PRIEST: I would like to see a world government; I'd like to see all the countries stripped of their armies. In fact, this is what we're going to have to do if we're going to have any type of world. We better start thinking in those terms or we are not even going to be able to survive. And that's why I can't accept it. But to get back to *OM*. If you do your job, and eight hours later you print a paper that's circulated around and you're saying, "The general's an ass, what he's doing is wrong, it's immoral, it's genocidal," I think you should be able to have that right. I'll even go another step: I think we should have the right to stand up in front of him and tell him "No." In other words, if you buy one of the other programs of the American Servicemen's Union— and also one of the things I believe—is the right of the servicemen to elect their own officers and formulate their own policies. In other words, if you're really talking about a people's army . . .

FINN: You really think it could be democratized, to a much greater extent?

PRIEST: Sure, and it's not now. We've got this authoritarian elite that passes down things. And in many cases the only reason you obey is because of the penalties that are set up, not because you want to. I hear people saying most of the G.I.'s in Vietnam are against the war; that the sentiment over there is tremendous; that the only thing that's keeping it intact, that's keeping this stuff repressed, is just the fear. And apparently this is why I'm being court-martialed: they're playing on these fears. Thirty-nine years and dishonorable discharge. They'd love to give it to me, too. It's why they come down very hard on dissident G.I.'s . . . because they're afraid of this whole thing blowing up —and I think it should blow up . . . right in their face.

FINN: You said you are getting some feedback from *OM,* that whatever it's leading G.I.'s to *do* it's causing them to re-think . . .

PRIEST: I'm just one person right now, but the publicity from this case will cause *thousands,* literally thousands, of people to think through their own position. In other words, there's so many people within the Service who are right on the borderline of participating in dissident activity. And the activity can be perfectly legal; it can be marching in a peace march, off-duty, out of uniform—which is legal; it can be signing a petition, signing a full-page ad, giving money; it can be many perfectly legal activities that one can be right on the borderline of doing. But still you've got that fear. And this case will cause thousands of people to think through what they're doing. You see, this is the thing: You get people isolated, no communication, and they don't know what's going on, and their feelings aren't really worked on. This is why this whole thing is really kind of a Stateside phenomenon.

FINN: The whole G.I. opposition?

PRIEST: The whole G.I. thing. I mean, some of it's reaching Vietnam. You get some soldiers doing some things, like a few companies have refused to move, some of 'em . . . some people go on patrol wearing black armbands, some of 'em wore buttons. But a lot of these people are new draftees that were in the peace movement in college, and they just take their feelings right on into Vietnam. I mean, it's possible just to maintain a kind of isolated existence and not know what's going on.

FINN: Well, this is one of the things that you, *OM* and the underground papers are . . .

PRIEST: . . . trying to combat.

In the first week of May, 1970—some time after I last spoke to Seaman Roger Priest, and after several postponements—he was brought to trial. Captain B. Raymond Perkins, the Navy judge, instructed the trial board that "criticism of Government policy may not be considered in and of itself disloyal." David Rein, Priest's lawyer, denied that Priest had directly encouraged sedition; his reports on those groups in Canada that counsel U.S. servicemen who have gone North were reports and nothing more. Rein also argued that Priest's views, as those of every citizen, were protected by the First Amendment.

The five members of the trial board—all officers—acquitted Priest of sedition and soliciting desertion. But they judged him to be guilty of "promoting disloyalty and disaffection." They ordered that he be demoted to the lowest Naval rank and be given a bad-conduct discharge.

Andrew Pulley

Aclassic case approaches a climax this week at Fort Jackson, S.C. By harassing, restricting and arresting on dubious charges the leaders of an interracial militant enlisted group there called the G.I.'s United Against the War in Vietnam, Fort Jackson's brass has produced a *cause célèbre* out of all proportion to the known facts. It has also brought about two court actions, directed by capable and contentious civilian legal counsel, which may give a merely fractious episode lasting effect.

The Fort Jackson lawsuits, if they are upheld, will give the courts a clear opening to declare that American enlisted men do, indeed, have the same right to oppose by all lawful, orderly means the course chosen by their Government and military leaders . . .

Thus Ben A. Franklin in the *New York Times* for April 20, 1969. The "known facts" he mentions include a meeting of over one hundred enlisted men at Fort Jackson on March 20, 1969, and an attempt by a lieutenant to get the group to break up, although he admits that he did not give them a direct order to do so. There was no further interference with the meeting, but the following day there began a roundup of members of G.I.'s United who were charged with breach of peace, disrespect to an officer, disobeying an officer, holding an illegal demonstration, and breaking restriction. Nine G.I.'s were finally put in the stockade or under barracks arrest and when, sometime later, one was released by the Army because he was acting as an informer, the others became known as the "Fort Jackson Eight." Andrew Pulley, to whom I talk some months after that event, is one of the Eight. I ask him what it was that prepared him to be, as he was, one of the organizers of G.I.'s United, what road led him to become one of the Fort Jackson Eight.

PULLEY: Well, first of all, I was born in Greenwood, Mississippi. I grew up in Cleveland, from the age of twelve until '68 when I enlisted into the Service. See, my record in high school was not really the most correct or disciplined record that you could find. Actually, I pushed dope for one thing when I was in high school; I was hustling, I was doing all these things at a very young age. I was fifteen when I started. This was my way of beating the system. I found it very hard to go to school and do this hustling job adequately and efficient, so I had to decide which one and I chose hustling. And I was put on probation for truancy. My probation was supposed to last for a year, so for some strange reason I get the notion to go back to school, to try to make it in the system. I ran into a difficult problem again. I was charged with inciting to riot, but since there was not really a riot, they could not charge me with inciting to riot, so they brought it down to assault. Anyway, my probation officer suggested that either I go into the Service or go to jail—the Service: fun, travel and adventure, education and so on—so I chose the Army; I enlisted for three years at the age of eighteen, or seventeen, I should say—I lied to get into the Army, first of all.

Anyway, I went to Fort Knox and then to Fort Gordon and Fort Jackson. My career in the Army, or the time that I spent there, was not really pleasant either. It only took me a few days to realize I had made a mistake by joining the Army. Well, first of all, the repression, the harassment, the bad treatment was nothing more or less than slavery itself. Under cover of it being patriotic or defending your country. It's supposed to be relevant to maintaining discipline in the combat zone, which is really, really stupid. I mean, what does my getting a haircut have to do with anything allied with Vietnam, for instance? I was not political at the time; I didn't have any political perspective. But at Fort Jackson I met a few people who had a perspective that was very close to mine. That is, they could lay out in ideology or in words what I felt should be done for changing the society. To me it was contradictory for us to go 10,000 miles away from home to fight for democracy, especially when we are wasting thousands of lives of innocent people, people that don't have any significant role or voice to be heard in the government. In our counterinsurgency classes at Fort Jackson not only was I thinking about these things but the majority of the G.I.'s who were in these classes were asking questions like, "How can we fight in Vietnam for democracy when we don't have it here?" It developed into a beautiful discussion. We related the poverty-stricken people and the black people, the liberation struggle, to be parallel to the Vietnamese revolution and the other revolutionary movements around the world.

And the good thing about this is not only were the blacks participating actually in these classes, but so were the whites. I was a black nationalist then—my perspective was nationalist to some extent but without any politics behind it, I was just conscious of my oppression—but when I saw white people taking part actually and disagreeing with the role of the officer, I was really impressed. I was convinced then that they were also opposed to the war in Vietnam, also opposed to dying for a cause that is not really in their best interest. So we'd dwell on these things in the discussion, everytime these classes came about, and our sergeant got somewhat frustrated because of this and he asked us how would we like to live in a country where they tell you what time to get up, what kind of clothes to wear, what kind of shoes to wear, what kind of haircut to get, and so on. Well, little did he know that we was already in that country, in the U.S. Army.

FINN: I take it the answers you got when you asked about these things in class weren't persuasive.

PULLEY: No, they weren't persuasive at all. It was the same old military-conservative line that America has done this for you, and so on; that the black people have made progress—which is true, but it's not enough progress; that the role of President is to look out for the mass of the people —this is not true at all. We feel that there's a very deep disagreement between the mass of the people and the Establishment.

Anyway, we called for a meeting and discussion in the barracks after duty, realizing that we were justified in doing this. Our policy at Fort Jackson was that we were going to obey all their regulations, regardless how stupid they sound, how unnecessary they were. Really, the way to build a movement that could even come close to bringing the war in Vietnam to an end, you had to stay out of jail for one thing. We feel that the G.I.'s are going to play a very important role in bringing an end to the war. At our first meeting we had five black G.I.'s discussing these issues. We listened to a Malcolm X tape called "The Ballad of the Bully." But we felt that the most common issue that was affecting the G.I.'s was the Vietnamese war, was the U.S. intervention in Vietnam. Even though racism and oppression hammer us constantly, just the idea that thousands and thousands of G.I.'s are dying in the war that is presently going on, that we might be there any moment for some really unjust cause, brought us to the conclusion that the best way to relieve ourselves of oppression and the war in Vietnam was to build a movement on that issue, a movement that was relevant not only to the black but to the majority of the G.I.'s—to everybody in the Army, as a matter of fact.

The following meeting we had about fifty G.I.'s, and they were all black again. And at about our third meeting we decided that the black people was not the only ones who had disagreement with the war and that since there was a common issue, a common denominator, that we could all agree on this issue of the immediate withdrawal of troops from Vietnam, that we could organize not only with the black and Puerto Rican but the white and also with anybody else who had our perspective about ending the war in Vietnam. So at our next meeting, the meeting was multinational or interracial, black, white, everybody. And the solidarity among the G.I.'s was really great. We really became G.I.'s United Against the War in Vietnam. We grew from five G.I.'s at our first meeting into 250 G.I.'s on March 20 when we was busted for preaching disrespect to an officer, and illegally demonstrating, and so on. But the time in between the arrest and the first meeting was very important. That is, we felt that the best way to be safe against the Army harassment and the Army oppression, even though they acknowledge the Constitution, that the best way to be safe, to give yourself insurance that you would not be harassed or victimized or framed-up, was to get as much publicity as possible and to be perfectly legal, to make it known to the American people that we are the real patriots, and not the officer who is violating our constitutional right.

So we did this fairly good. We had a mass petition drive to demand a place to hold a mass meeting on base. This meeting was really going to be somewhat in the form of a conference where we would invite the officers, the people who were pro-war, to debate with us why they support the war in Vietnam, to try to win us over to their perspective, because we knew that we would really be glad to have this opportunity. And we knew that we could win the G.I.'s over to our perspective in the open debate. Unfortunately, the Army didn't allow us to hold this meeting. In fact, they rejected the petition, on the ground that petition was an instrument of collective bargaining and the Army does not recognize collective bargaining.

They only attempted to use all type of measures to break up G.I.'s United, to harass them, the leaders and especially the black leaders—I myself was court-martialed for allegedly disobeying a direct order to go to bed, for instance, and convicted. This was before the big case. But despite the fact that this was a loss, so far as the court-martial was concerned, it was still a victory for G.I.'s United, because this exposed them for what they really were. And more and more G.I.'s got involved as a result of this. Joe Miles and myself—Joe Miles was the initial organizer, the one who called the meeting from the beginning—went up to the inspector general. The inspector general in the Army is the guy that you go to to render complaints about harassment or what not. Anyway, we was told by him that our only rights as soldiers were to obey orders and die proudly. So we went back to the G.I.'s, to our constituency, and informed them of this new regulation, of this martial law, of this—I don't know what you can call it—a military dictatorship one hundred percent. And of course this did not really get over too good with the G.I.'s; they would not accept this. In fact, more and more G.I.'s came. The Army attempted to put us on extra K.P. duty, extra various duty, and so on. Not only the leaders of the organization but the entire company. But instead of the company turning against us, it turned against the Army. And the Army means of trying to break up the organization just backfired.

Joe Miles was transferred to Fort Bragg when they moved to break up G.I.'s United at Fort Jackson. But in four weeks at Fort Bragg he organized another G.I.'s United, this time with mostly veterans. And of course the Army now sent Joe Miles to Alaska where he's now stationed. He's doing some fairly good work there. So the anti-war movement within the Army is really growing. The potential of the G.I. movement is really great, especially since the Army came out with guidance for dissent, where they actually admit we do have constitutional right—that freedom of speech is linked with the Constitution—and warned the officers from over-reacting to G.I.'s who dissent or disagree with the military policy.

The constitutional right of G.I.'s is one of the most important issues that we are pressed with today, one of the most important struggles that the G.I.'s and the mass of people in this country can build around. Because if you don't have the basic constitutional rights, it's very hard for you to do anything. If you don't have the right to freedom of speech, you cannot even begin to organize a movement of any sort. So we attempted to build a movement against the war based on our civil rights and our constitutional right to express our opposition to the war in Vietnam. We have gotten lots of support not only from the left, not only from the liberal, but from congressmen who have the intelligence or the honesty to recognize the fact that G.I.'s are citizens. And the only way that G.I.'s can really gain their constitutional right in the fullest content is by building a movement and *taking* these rights. The way the black got their rights is that they fought for them and still they're being denied today. The way the Puerto Ricans, the women and the poor whites got theirs, they had to build a struggle to demand these. And of course they're still being denied. And the way the G.I.'s will insure themselves that they do have these rights is to build a movement, build a mass movement, to demand these basic constitutional rights, to build a struggle that can bring an end to the war in Vietnam.

FINN: You said you built G.I.'s United from five to fifty and then up. When did the authorities, your superiors, your officers, first start getting concerned with Miles or you?

PULLEY: Well, they were concerned from the first meeting. In fact, they was concerned from the first discussion in the classes that we were given because we took an active role in attacking not only the military policy but the establishment itself, and they sent military intelligence majors and colonels into the room to listen to us. And of course the discussion continued. And of course they was concerned from the beginning; they placed an informer into the organization, John Huffman—alias John Huffman; I don't know whether that's his real name or not. Anyway, on March the 20th, we had a big, large meeting on the base, on the grass outside the barracks when the G.I.'s was really ready to go; in fact, they was ready to break windows and set barracks on fire and so on—but, of course, this was against our policy.

FINN: You were not recommending these things?

PULLEY: No, not at all. In fact, we one hundred percent disagreed with these tactics, and really we were the most disciplined soldiers in our company—not because we loved the military or loved their regulations but because we knew this was the best way to stay out of jail, especially if you were an open organizer, openly anti-war and against the military policy.

So the Army, at this meeting, sent the guy who was the security officer, I think, the C.Q., yes, the guy in charge of quarters, a lieutenant. But at no point, at no time, did they attempt to break up that meeting. The meeting was peaceful, it was orderly, it was about eight speakers, it was a beautiful discussion, explaining to the G.I.'s why in the world did we get into Vietnam, or why are we in Laos or in the rest of these countries, and what we can do to solve this problem. The officers at no point attempted to break up that meeting. They came and spoke to some of the speakers and complained about Jose Rudder needing a haircut—which was really not true; in fact, he had a bald head. And of course this exposed the Army; the G.I.'s laughed at this remark and could see for themselves that we was being harassed because of our political perspective. So the Army at no point really came out openly or used strong-arm tactics to break up any meeting or even to break up the organization, so far as that goes. There was no goon squad action, no physical disruption of the meeting, nothing of this sort.

FINN: Why do you think they were so uptight, since you were being orderly and disciplined and you weren't doing anything that disrupted their . . .?

PULLEY: First of all, and the Army realized this, you cannot really have a democratic army to fight an undemocratic war. And at that stage what we was trying to do was build democracy, you know, and end the war in Vietnam. And this was not only going to hurt the war or bring an end to the war in Vietnam but it was going to be a black mark, I should say, on the military itself. Well, the Army recognized this threat, that it was not just a temporary thing but it was a movement that was developing. Even though we were legal at this time, when we became a majority they felt we might resort to any means necessary, for instance, to change the situation there. Even though I'm a Socialist, and the guys who were in leadership in the organization were Socialists, we did not impose our ideas on the organization, on the G.I.'s. The common denominator, the common thing that brought us together is that we was anti-war; even though we had perspectives that was revolutionary, we did not impose our ideas on anybody else. At one point while we was in the stockade, General Hollingsworth even went so far as to say that the only problem at Fort Jackson is four Communists, you know.

FINN: Did he say that for publication?

PULLEY: Right, he said that when he was speaking to students and the press and everything else: the problem at Fort Jackson is that we have four Communist agitators.

But when people have a common agreement, regardless of whether they're Socialist or Communist or whatever, they can build a struggle around it and be successful. And the Army recognized this. And since G.I.'s United was organized at Fort Jackson, there's others at Fort Bragg, at Fort Lewis; there's G.I. movements all around the country and some even in Germany and Vietnam. So the Army recognized this not only as an isolated incident but the beginning of a new phenomenon, a movement that was not going to end until the war in Vietnam ends. And the only way to really solve that problem was to end the war in Vietnam or put us in jail. Of course they resorted to putting us in jail. But that still did not kill the movement.

FINN: You're a Socialist now. When you went into the Army you weren't. So what happened in the Army was part of your own political education?

PULLEY: Right. Also I spent sixty-one days in jail, which was really *committing* me to my revolutionary perspective.

FINN: That was for what? The court-martial?

PULLEY: That was when the charges were brought against us on March the 20th; I was in pre-trial confinement for sixty-one days. Before then I had other plans to go back in the street and hustle again, but that really committed me to the struggle. Even though I agreed at that point to the importance of changing the society, I was not really committed. But that did it then, when I could see that the only reason we was put in the stockade was because of our anti-war politics and building a movement. Even though we were doing it legally, even though the Constitution justifies it, we were being harassed.

FINN: Do you think the reporting on your case, your group, by the press was on the whole accurate?

PULLEY: I could not say really "accurate," but I was really impressed by a guy from the *New York Times,* a reporter by the name of Benjamin Franklin who really did a beautiful job in reporting the truth, in my opinion. And the papers was very favorable to our struggle. Even the *Wall Street Journal* reported actually what's going on. All in all, we got lots of sympathetic reporting and lots of publicity that really resulted in a defeat to the Army on that case. But in a case such as ours, without civilian attorneys, we would have been doomed for at least five years; we were facing eight and ten years, and so on. In fact, in the Army there's no such thing as a fair trial—unless you have a lot of publicity, unless you have lots of support from around the country and on the base.

As it turned out, we did not have a court-martial. We had an Article 32 investigation, which is equivalent to a grand jury investigation. There was no evidence on the part of the Army that we were guilty of disrespect to an officer, illegally demonstrating or breach of peace, and the other charge for demonstrating without a permit. There was no *evidence* to that effect, that we was guilty of any charge. But what really got us off *is* the publicity, the brilliant defense team that we had, not the lack of evidence.

FINN: And what was the final result of this?

PULLEY: The result of that is that they dropped the charges against us; they felt that we was not really the type of soldiers that the American Army wants. They came to the conclusion that we present a threat to the nation's security. I was given an undesirable discharge for the good of the Service. And the rest of the G.I.'s, that is, six out of the eight, was also given dishonorable discharges. The other two are still in the Service. They was not really that active, first of all. One guy was charged and he was not even at the meeting; and another G.I. was charged for looking out of the window. That was not the specific charge, but that was all he was doing, and the Army admitted it. So what they did was discharge six out of the eight, the ones they thought was the most agitator, or the ones that was most detrimental to the role of the Army.

FINN: Your experiences in the Army have helped shape what you've been doing since you got out?

PULLEY: Yes, very definitely, very definitely. I, of course, have intensified my activities into the anti-war movement, the revolutionary movement, also. I'm on the steering committee of the New Mobilization committee, and also an acting member of the Young Socialist Alliance. And so I've really been very active, trying to win people to our perspective, not only against the war but to our revolutionary perspective.

FINN: What is your estimate of the G.I. movement, the protests, the demand for civil liberties and constitutional rights?

PULLEY: I think it's really escalating, primarily as a result of the war in Vietnam; that's the real thing that's pushing it. Perhaps you heard about the 1,300 G.I.'s who signed the *New York Times* ad, who are under investigation now because of that. And this is going to continue to occur. This is really going to be intensifying in the next coming period, when the G.I.'s relate specifically to the question of their constitutional rights. At this moment the Army does not recognize or does not implement their recognition of their rights as citizens.

Andrew Pulley has no doubt that the Army wished to silence or dissipate the critical views that were being formulated by the G.I's United. But he is also aware that that case received national attention and he feels that the Army outmaneuvered itself. As he talks it is clear that he is more concerned with his future activities than with past injustices. But the *New York Times* ad that he mentions highlights the political aspects of his case. For the ad which the G.I.'s signed was a statement of support for the November, 1968, Vietnam Moratorium. Many American citizens have signed similar statements without having the even tenor of their ways disrupted. But G.I.'s have been questioned on whether they signed the statement, whether they did so voluntarily, and whether they knew the names of other signers. Even if such investigations lead to no formal charges, they can have a chilling effect on the freedom which G.I.'s should have to express their views. And this, according to Andrew Pulley, is what the Fort Jackson Eight is all about.

Thomas J. Roberts

Fort Carson, Colorado. It has been more years than I care to remember since I put in Army time at Carson, and both the town of Colorado Springs and the Army have changed remarkably. Only the Rockies seem not to have changed. But they have: one of them now houses Norad, a huge complex of the Air Force. The Air Force Academy is close by and Fort Carson, with almost 30,000 men, is on the edge of the town.

After several abortive attempts by different groups, there has been established one of those centers for dissidence that sets off tremors in the military—a G.I. coffee house. When I visit the Homefront, as it is called, it has not yet been visited with the attentions that have disrupted or halted activities at some of the other half-dozen G.I. coffee houses scattered across the country. The operators of the UFO in Atlanta, Georgia, for example, have brought federal suit that they were arrested and the coffee house padlocked as a result of unconstitutional harassment by local, state and Army authorities. The Shelter Half, a coffee house near Fort Lewis, Washington, is suffering similar troubles. In an action in December, 1969, the Armed Forces Disciplinary Control Board of the 13th Naval District in Seattle notified operators of the coffee house that it was proceeding to have the coffee house placed off-limits to military personnel.

In the letter to the Shelter Half the Board stated: "The Board took this action after receiving information which indicated that the Shelter Half Coffee House is a source of dissident counselling and literature and other activities inimical to good morale, order and discipline within the Armed Services."

The fact that the Homefront has not received comparable attention may be misleading. For Colorado Springs is not especially hospitable to liberal or radical movements. And since almost 70 percent of the soldiers at Fort Carson are Vietnam veterans forced to do duty formation until the date of their discharge, the equilibrium is uncertain. One of the many underground G.I. papers also issues from Fort Carson, or, more correctly was initiated by two young men when they were stationed together at the Fort—Tom Roberts and Curtis Stocker. I ask Tom Roberts about their original intention in establishing *Aboveground*.

ROBERTS: Well, we really have been asked this question many times, so we eventually had to come up with some reasons and we came up with three: First, we disagreed with what was going on in Vietnam and we wanted to tell the soldier why we thought it was wrong, tell the other soldiers at Fort Carson. Fort Carson didn't have a newspaper, so we thought we'd start one. The second reason was kind of a vendetta thing. The Army had done some things to us which we didn't especially like and we thought that in this way we would try to slow down the Army machine, the military machine. And, to be quite honest, the third thing was more or less of an adventure or a lark, something to keep our minds occupied while we were in the military, to keep our minds from rotting away.

FINN: You said a vendetta against the Army because of things they'd done to you. What kinds of things did they do to you?

ROBERTS: Well, for example, on Vietnam. I was rather apolitical before I went to Vietnam, but while I was there, quite innocently I started writing articles for the Lehigh University *Brown & White,* which is a college paper I used to work for when I was going to school, and I was describing just things that I saw, like the Tet offensive in 1968. Nothing in the article was really that anti-war. It was just merely narrative pieces. Anyway, the Army found out that I was doing this, after I had done about twelve of them, and within two days they sent me into a combat zone, into a combat unit, where I remained until I left Vietnam.

FINN: How do you know that those two things were related? I mean, how do you know they found out and *therefore* you went out to a combat zone?

ROBERTS: They made no qualms about it. They made it quite clear that this was the reason I was being sent out. I had too much free time on my hands was what my captain told me.

FINN: Where were you before you went into a combat zone? How were you functioning?

ROBERTS: Well, I was more or less of a clerk with the 10th Psychological Operations Battalion in the Delta. I wasn't transferred out of the unit, but I was attached to an advisory team, so I was one of three Americans with a team, with a squadron of 150 Vietnamese that were in the Armored Cavalry. In the four months that I was out there we got into some very heavy combat with the Viet Cong, in the four months that I was out there before I left Vietnam. I left Vietnam on July 26, 1967, because I pulled a little stunt to get out of Vietnam. So I only wound up spending about eight months in Vietnam altogether.

FINN: Well, how did you manage that? Most people aren't able to do that kind of thing.

ROBERTS: Well, when I was sent out to the combat zone, I realized why I was being sent out, and so I started pouring through the Army regulations, trying to find a way that I could leave Vietnam aside from being in a box or on a stretcher, and I found one Army regulation, AR-350-55, which allows enlisted people to apply to the United States Military Academy Preparatory School. In other words, for eventually entering West Point, and the class would start in August. So I applied and luckily I was accepted. I was kind of surprised myself that it worked.

FINN: And you came back then?

ROBERTS: Right, and I spent three weeks at the prep school, which was the minimum time that I had to spend, and then I left and they sent me to Fort Carson. I resigned.

FINN: You said you were apolitical when you went into the Army. Did you go through regular channels to be drafted?

ROBERTS: No, I enlisted, as a matter of fact. When I dropped out of college in October of 1966, I was almost immediately 1-A, and the only thing that hit me was that I did not want to become an infantryman, which many of the draftees were becoming. I did not want to be killed in the Vietnam war. I didn't know why I didn't want to be killed, just, you know, a self-protection thing. A chicken thing. So I enlisted and they gave me a choice, supposedly a choice of skills and what have you, for three years.

FINN: But at that time, apart from a disinclination to be killed, you didn't have any highly developed ideas about the war itself? Moral or legal?

ROBERTS: None whatsoever.

FINN: When did you begin to question the war? I presume that at some point along the way, you thought not only about yourself but about the action that you were involved in. This consideration involved other people besides yourself.

ROBERTS: Right, it was a gradual evolution of attitudes. The first things that started me wondering about what we were doing over there was the Tet offensive in Can Tho, especially after a very small number of Viet Cong came in and took over a section of the city and the South Vietnamese Air Force came in, destroyed an entire section of the city, and of course, created many civilian casualties and refugees. And I wondered why they just didn't go in there on foot and, you know, flush these people out if they wanted to get rid of them. That was the first thing, and then when I got into combat itself, not only did I see what to me seemed the stupidity of it all—for example, going back and fighting for the same piece of real estate four times in the same month—but I also saw things like false body counts. Never, never once did I see an accurate body count reported to higher headquarters, and I started wondering why is this happening? Why are all these little things going on? So that got me interested enough so that I started reading about the history of the conflict and eventually came around to the idea that what we were doing there was wrong.

FINN: Well, when you got back to the States what led you and Stocker to get together and decide to begin this paper? After all, to bring out something like that while you are in the Army—even if it does keep your mind a little more active—keeps you a little more active in a way that can't always be easy.

ROBERTS: Stocker and I met in Vietnam on June 20, 1967. I was just about ready to leave the country and he had just about gotten into the country, and he was also sent out to the field to work with a South Vietnamese infantry unit, and I guess our friendship or our trust was built up.

We were out looking for marijuana on the streets of the city of Sa Dec and we wound up in an opium den by chance, and we thought oh, it was just a fantastic adventure, you know, and at the end of the day we just said goodbye, but strangely enough, exactly a year later, on June 20th, 1968, he walked into the hospital here where I was stationed.

FINN: Here at . . .

ROBERTS: At Fort Carson, Colorado. And, that night we just both started talking about how we felt about the war, and we both came up with the idea that instead of talking about it, it might be better to do something about it. And, I think that our attitude was that we'd just put out a paper and see what the reaction was, and the reaction to the first one was that it was a little bit too—well, let me say academic or little bit too scholarly or something like that, for the average soldier at Fort Carson.

FINN: Had you looked at other underground papers?

ROBERTS: Not at that point. We knew that they existed. But right after that we started getting into contact with other papers through the G.I. Press Service and so forth, and we realized that it would probably be better if we did not have such an academic approach to our writing in the future. I think slowly it's been been changing, but still it's considered academic by some people, at least compared to other G.I. papers.

FINN: Did you run into any kind of problems with distribution or with getting a printer?

ROBERTS: Well, we didn't have any trouble getting a printer, but distribution was something else entirely. When we first printed our paper, on August 11th to be exact, we submitted a request to the Fort Carson commanders for permission to distribute *Aboveground* at Fort Carson, and even in the Guidance for Dissent, it says that they must give reasons for denial. They sent it back about a month later (after they claimed they lost the request) with one sentence, "Your request is denied," or words to that effect. It was only one sentence and there were no reasons offered. So we did have problems distributing it. We had to go downtown and stand outside the gates. Within ten or fifteen minutes after we were standing outside the gates, a group of police would come and always chase us away because the M.P.'s would call them. There were always problems with distribution.

FINN: Did your being editor—you or Stocker—cause any problems for you? In terms of your relationship with the Army? Either with the other G.I.'s or superior officers?

ROBERTS: I never had any conflict with any other soldier. I mean, with relatively equal rank. Sure, there are a lot of them that disagree with it, but for some reason or other none of the guys ever came up and threatened us. They sort of stayed away from us, but the Army on September 15th, which is about a month after we put out the first paper, transferred both Stocker and I. We did have problems with the Army. They sent him to Fitzsimons General Hospital, which is in Denver, and they sent me to the 46th Artillery Group, and it's my belief that they did this, number one, to split us apart, and number two, by putting me in that artillery unit, to cut down on my free time.

FINN: And you're really quite convinced that that was not an accidental transfer?

ROBERTS: Not at all! We were both transferred on the exact same day. We were given one day to complete our transfers, where with Stocker it was supposed to be four days, for him to leave post. The ink was still red on the orders when we got them. In fact, they smudged as if somebody threw them on my desk.

FINN: I did read in one of the issues that you had some problem about getting a printer—or keeping the printer you had, I guess.

ROBERTS: Right. Well, the first four papers were printed by a printer in Boulder. But we found a printer here in Colorado Springs who would do it for much less, so we went to him and for three weeks everything was fine, and he had completed all but the very final step in the printing process, and the day before he was make the press run, at about three o'clock in the afternoon, according to the printer, FBI agents or FBI military intelligence and local police, came in and paid him a visit.

They didn't tell him not to print the paper, but they said they wanted copies of it and they advised him about who we are and what we were doing. I really don't know exactly what they said, but at any rate he made the decision not to print our paper. This leads me to believe that he was at least intimidated by the mere presence of these agents, if nothing else. We asked him why he wouldn't print it, and he gave us lots of off-the-wall reasons about copyrights, and he had printers there who were Army veterans and they didn't like what we were doing and they wouldn't work on the paper and things like that. But he changed the story several times. He eventually said that the FBI never came in there, which is after the FBI director in Denver said that they never do things like that. So, we eventually found another printer. It delayed the paper for about two weeks.

FINN: Do you have any reason to think that *Above-ground* has led your superior officers to distinguish you and Stocker in terms of the kind of treatment you would get?

ROBERTS: Right. I don't know exactly what happened to Curt, but when I was transferred, everybody in my new unit was quite obviously aware of who I was. As a matter of fact, the Sergeant Major called me in the first day I got there and gave me some kind of a rap about "We don't care who you are, but don't talk to any of my men about politics. As long as you do your job for us you'll be okay." That was his main point. He didn't want me destroying the morale of his unit or something, but they quite obviously had been briefed, at least on me; I don't know about Stocker. I had to be very, very careful about signing out and being places at a specific time so I wouldn't be given an Article 15 or a court-martial. I was always very conscious of that, that people were sort of checking on me. I didn't receive any actual penalties. The actual transfer itself was harassment, the fact that on certain days when activities were going on downtown, anti-war activities, it always seemed that I was restricted one way or another, on duty or G.I. parties or just plain restricted. That to me is a form of harassment.

When I ask Roberts to give me an example of restrictions that seemed deliberate and planned, he did even better. On October 15, 1969, there was to be in Colorado Springs, as there were in different cities across the country, a Vietnam Moratorium. That Roberts, Stocker and others were under tight surveillance was evident from an official Army memorandum, a copy of which he was able to show me. (See Appendix 2.) The memorandum referred to these two plus Tipton, Rozier and Boyd, "5 of our potential problem children," and spelled out the desirability but also the difficulty of "profitably engaging them" during the Moratorium. And it was evident that at least the writer of the memorandum was worried about any adverse scrutiny to which restraining orders would be subjected in the pages of *Aboveground*. I ask Roberts if all five who were mentioned had planned to speak at the Moratorium.

ROBERTS: All except for Stocker, who was in Denver. But the other four were at Carson, and we were all planning to speak, and as it turned out only three of us got to speak. One had to go AWOL to do it. As a matter of fact, Tipton left for Canada that night and he's in Canada now. And Stocker and myself had to go through unbelievable hassles just to get out in time for the Moratorium.

FINN: Do you think that they overestimate your effectiveness? They've given you quite a bit of attention. Do you think that you are as effective as their concern would seem to indicate?

ROBERTS: Probably not, because it seems to me that what's happening out there as far as Military Intelligence is concerned, is that they have so many agents with probably nothing to do, that they spend all of this time on people like Stocker and myself. I know for a fact that they have twenty enlisted men alone that are agents there. This was told me by the Chief of Counterintelligence at Fort Carson, and they only consider eleven to fifteen people at Fort Carson to be "true dissidents."

FINN: It's a very select group then?

ROBERTS: Well, this is according to the General. So if they have twenty agents and fifteen "true dissidents," you know, it seems to me that they could just about watch you all day long if they wanted to.

FINN: You said Tipton is now in Canada. Do you think

this kind of harassment has anything to do with his cutting out?

ROBERTS: Well, I'd say definitely. Not only from Tipton's case, but from my own experiences on that day. I'll tell you what Tipton said first of all. I saw him, of course, when he was speaking at the college and I talked to him right afterward, and he said that in order to speak, he had to go AWOL. And, instead of going back to face charges on this AWOL—he knew quite obviously that according to the Army regulations he was AWOL—he was going to split. He was going to desert and go to Canada. So I don't think he ever would have gone AWOL unless the Army had done their little dirty work in restricting him.

I was very, very seriously considering going AWOL that whole day because I wanted to speak that night. I thought it was very important that I speak, and through the grapevine I had heard what was happening to these other people and what was happening to me as far as this G.I. party was concerned. It was quite obvious that there was something fishy going on. So, I was very seriously considering going AWOL and finally a colonel talked me out of it. I actually went up and told him that if he didn't let me go, I was going to go AWOL, and finally he sort of calmed me down. But I think there is definitely a relationship.

FINN: You are working at the Homefront now?

ROBERTS: Right.

FINN: And you are circulating *Aboveground* and other material that's critical of Vietnam and various Army policies? What kind of response do you get from the servicemen?

ROBERTS: Well, we do get quite a few letters from G.I.'s at Fort Carson—not a tremendous amount, but considering that G.I.'s are usually very apathetic about things like that, we feel that's good. The letters are usually pretty good. We've printed some of them in the *Aboveground*. The other indication is when I was out at Fort Carson and I was driving around, if anybody was hitchhiking I would pick them up, and I'd ask them, "Hey, have you seen *Aboveground?*" And at least ninety percent of them said that they had seen it.

FINN: Ninety percent?

ROBERTS: Right. I'd say about nine out of ten said that they had at least heard of it or seen it, and a good number of those liked what was in it. It's kind of notorious out at Fort Carson because, number one, even though the military is not supposed to take it away from a soldier, there are many, many cases of G.I.'s coming to the Homefront who say that their commanders or their sergeants have taken *Aboveground* away from them, even though it very clearly states on the top that they can't do this, if a soldier doesn't want it.

FINN: What has the whole experience that you've undergone in the last couple of years done to you in terms of your general political orientation, aside from being simply critical of the Army and how the Army operates in Vietnam?

ROBERTS: Well, it's hard to label them. I think when I started *Aboveground,* I could have been referred to as a liberal. But I would say I was more radical now. I think that basically what I could say about how I feel about the American Government, is that radical changes have to be made. I don't mean radical changes necessarily in the sense of violence, but radical in the sense of very, very different.

So I'd say that I've changed quite a bit from when I came in the Army. I wasn't able to vote in the '64 election, but I probably would have voted for Barry Goldwater. Well, my family was Republican, and where I lived everybody is Republican and where I went to college everybody was Republican, but I voted for Eugene McCarthy and Al Lowenstein in 1968. But I think that my interest now is on G.I. organizing, to get a very large group of G.I.'s together, just with like any other kind of union. An American Servicemen's Union is one way of doing this. So that, for example, if another Vietnam situation came along, there might be enough G.I.'s binding together who would just refuse, go on strike if you will, refuse to perform any duty, and that this might prevent something like another Vietnam from coming about. The only way to do this, of course, is through numbers, you know. One person can always sooner or later be given the shaft by the Army, but when you have a very strong organization, it's much harder. It's still possible, but it's much harder. And I think if you try to get the person to see, as I think that I have seen, some of the interrelationships between the military-industrial complex, that it's just not an unfortunate accident what happened in Vietnam, that a lot of it was due to the fact that industry in this country is so very closely tied to the military and the threat of communism. It's such a dominant theme in our American way of life that it does affect not only who we make war on but our economy and how we spend our money, even in times when we're not at war.

FINN: Well, you're really interested in, if I read that right, is some fairly wide-ranging political education.

ROBERTS: Exactly. And to go along with that, another thing that we're trying to get people to realize, and in our case it's soldiers, is that the word communism or the word socialism is not as evil as they thought it was. I think especially soldiers, because from the very day you get into the

Army your individuality is taken away, but the theme of fighting communism, defending the flag, is really drummed into your head, from almost the day that you enter basic training. And so, by the time you're in the Army for six months or a year, when somebody mentions the word Communist, you do sort of cringe and get this sort of a bad feeling toward the people, and I even noticed this with myself when I was at Washington. I saw people walking around with a Viet Cong flag, and without thinking, deep down inside of me it disturbed me.

FINN: Are there a number of G.I.'s who are developing this kind of political interest in some of the political sentiments that you expressed?

ROBERTS: I think so; probably more now than before. There's kind of an evolution here as far as the movement is concerned. I'd say that several years ago the G.I. was almost regarded as an enemy. There was kind of a disgust . . .

FINN: You mean by people in the peace movement?

ROBERTS: Right, by people in the peace movement especially, I would say. But then they came around to the idea that the G.I. was in fact being screwed himself, that he potentially was an ally, and as Tom Hayden expressed it, they realized that "You can't radicalize the individual cop if you lump them all together as pigs."

So that there was a great change in the movement toward the G.I. As a matter of fact, they tried to cultivate G.I.'s, but at first there was a kind of a hiding of what some of their true political beliefs were for fear that they were going to offend the G.I. But I think that now these kinds of beliefs are more up front and the G.I. asks a person who works on the staff of a coffee house, "Well, what exactly are your political beliefs?"

So I think it's very important to make the connection or

help soldiers make the connection between Vietnam and political beliefs, just as I think I've been helped by some people here at the Homefront in Colorado Springs. They've been involved with what they call "the movement" for a helluva lot longer than I have.

Roberts' efforts to distribute *Aboveground* continued after I spoke to him with consequences that were discomforting both to the Army and to Roberts. On February 15, 1970, Roberts was taken into custody by military police as he was distributing copies of *Aboveground* in front of the post exchange in Fort Carson and almost ninety copies of the paper were seized. Shortly afterward, according to Roberts, he received from Colonel Richard Buyer, the deputy post commander, a letter informing him that he was barred from the post.

On April 15, when Jane Fonda and all those with her were allowed on the fort during a "sick-call" strike, Tom Roberts was one of those who entered. He is now charged with being found unlawfully on the military reservation and will be tried by the United States District Court of Denver.

In the meantime *Aboveground* has been transformed into a Press Service with Roberts, Stocker and Ronald W. Pearson —the latter an anti-war G.I. stationed at Fort Carson—as co-editors. The purpose of the Press Service is explained in a news release which they put out early in June from Post Office Box 1314, Boulder, Colorado.

> The My Lai story took well over a year to break into headlines. Recent Associated Press censorship of Peter Arnett's GI looting story from Cambodia further demonstrates the need for an information service by, and for, GIs.

A service that could collect information, from the inside, on the Army's many illegal activities. Pictures, articles, and information would be distributed to both the underground and "establishment" press.

Aboveground Press Service, a non-profit organization, will function as this distributor—for stories, and photos from GIs. The underground press would receive the information free of charge, while the "establishment" press would be charged for the service. The money would be given to the GIs who took the risk of exposing the story.

Aboveground, the newspaper, has given way to Aboveground, the Press Service, filling a wide-open gap in the mass communications field—reports from within the military.

William Sherman Reynolds

Tom Roberts had introduced me to friends at the Homefront, and I accompany some of them, one sub-zero night in midwinter, to visit Private William Sherman Reynolds, who is in pre-trial confinement on a charge of AWOL. Bill Reynolds, who was born in California in 1947, had spent over a year in combat in Vietnam even though he was strongly opposed to the war and had planned to refuse induction. He tells me of how he was persuaded to enlist—and of the career that awaited him in the Army.

REYNOLDS: I completed my high school and one year of college, and I was on probation at the time when I was arrested. The judge gave me a choice of five years' imprisonment or three years in the Army.

FINN: You did, then, go into the Army rather than take these five years.

REYNOLDS: Yes. I was sworn in on June 6, 1967.

FINN: Did you go through without much trouble for a while?

REYNOLDS: No, it's basically been trouble for me all the way because it's held against you a lot of places when you're a forced entry. You're given a prefix—it's an RA6 number —and soon as a lifer or a sergeant finds out you're one of these numbers, you end up on every shit detail they can find for you, and you always get the worst end of the stick.

FINN: How long were you in combat in Nam?

REYNOLDS: Fifteen months, but three months of it were spent in the stockade.

FINN: What got you into the stockade?

REYNOLDS: They called it refusing to fire on a village. I spent three months at hard labor. Longbinh Jail.

FINN: You said they "called" it that. Tell me a little about what was involved.

REYNOLDS: It was in August of '68 and I was TDY at a place called Red Beach outside of Danang, about forty miles north of Danang. And we had a mortar attack that night; it was the night of the 16th we had a mortar attack. Here the village was just off the Gulf of Tonkin, and where the NVA were at was a good two miles away. And we started hitting them with gun ships—I was flying at the time. And we called in for assistance—we'd lost three ships and only had five—and our assistance was a 227 from the First Combat Aviation. They came in on the village and started firing on the village. Now the Marines had cut the village off, so the NVA couldn't get into the village. And my ship flew over and they told me to open fire on the village, and I just threw my M-60 out the door and I said, "I refuse to fire." 'Cause I didn't believe there was any NVA in the village, 'cause there had been no reports of a breakthrough. That's basically what it came down to.

FINN: Who was the superior who gave you that immediate order?

REYNOLDS: We were ordered by a lieutenant colonel who was in charge of Red Beach compound. And then he gave the order that we break from there and start to the village, then I was given an order by a platoon sergeant from another ship, and then I was given a direct order by my warrant officer to fire. And I refused all three.

FINN: You refused all three because you simply thought it was an unjustified order.

REYNOLDS: Yes, because there was no reports on radio. You see, I had a head-set on me all the time and there was no reports there had been a breakthrough into the village.

FINN: And when you got rid of your weapon, then what happened?

REYNOLDS: Well, we pulled back into base camp. They took me back and I was placed under arrest as soon as I hit the ground.

FINN: Was there any kind of investigation about the village afterwards?

REYNOLDS: Well, they went into it and they found two bodies that were supposed to be NVA. I never did see 'em myself, because I was taken to Camp Evans the next day and waited there until my court-martial.

FINN: Who did the identifying of these two bodies, do you know?

REYNOLDS: They were supposed to have been Alert Patrol from the Marines, Long Range Reconnaissance Patrol.

FINN: And there was no real way for you to check on that, I suppose; there wouldn't have been at the time.

REYNOLDS: No, there's no real way. You see, I didn't have any witnesses at my court-martial; they were all from different units, and the Marines were only stationed there temporarily—they're always on patrol—and I knew none of them personally.

I was court-martialed on the 2nd of September, I received a special court-martial. The prosecution brought in the Marines, the two Marines who had supposedly seen the bodies, and they said that they were NVA—which you can't really say if they were NVA or just ordinary civilians. So my sentence was ninety days hard labor . . . Longbinh Jail . . . South Vietnam.

FINN: And then what happened when you got out?

REYNOLDS: Well, when I got out of the stockade I was made an infantryman. I was grounded from the air and I was a Private E-1. I did make it back to Spec 4 before I came back to the States.

FINN: Were you in combat after you got out of the stockade?

REYNOLDS: Yeah, I was sent right back out to the field. On two different occasions I was threatened because I wouldn't walk point, and they said, "They can always send you back to where you came from." So I ended up walking point . . . rather than go back to LBJ.

FINN: And right now, as I'm talking to you, you're preparing for another court-martial without seeming very optimistic about the outcome. After you got back here you didn't have much time to serve, did you, before you were going to be discharged?

REYNOLDS: No, they put me in for a dishonorable discharge. Well I requested a discharge—I put in for one myself—and then they requested one for my previous convictions. I mean, I've had quite a few Article 15's, because I didn't get along with Stateside duty. And then when I started to go down to the Homefront, military intelligence kept picking up my name here and there, and they picked up when I talked to a reporter from the *Washington Post* on the base. And the Colonel didn't like the idea of me getting scot free, so I think he put out the word that anytime I . . . you know, "one little screw-up and I want him nailed." So they got two half-baked cases. One of 'em was a half-day AWOL, when I was in the day room, and I have four or five witnesses to the fact. And I refused a lawful order: I didn't have a haircut. But I told the first sergeant who gave the order to get a haircut that I didn't have a dollar to get a haircut. They were constantly screwing with me all of this time, and it was like thirty days before I even heard anything about these charges. They hadn't set up trial, named the day or anything. And I just got fed up with it. I took off and went AWOL again—which blew my case. And now they've dropped those first two charges and the charge against me now is seven days AWOL. I came back last Monday, a week ago Monday. I've been under constant guard since. I sleep at the guard house at night and stay in the company room during the day.

FINN: Why did you go AWOL that last time, since your discharge was coming along?

REYNOLDS: No, my discharge got kicked back and had to be re-done all over again. It got kicked back for a physical; I hadn't taken my physical—which was the Company's fault. I mean my First Sergeant was trying to hold it back because he wants to see me go to jail more than he wants to see me get out. They tried throwing pre-trial confinement at me too.

FINN: What does that mean exactly?

REYNOLDS: You go to the stockade until your court-martial comes up. Well, it leaves a bad mark on the batallion commander's record everytime somebody has to go to pre-trial confinement, and he kept me out. He says, "You can't go." And I was at a point now where I was getting so fed up with this that I was afraid I was going to leave again. So I asked for pre-trial confinement and it was denied. 'Cause I was really thinking about splitting.

FINN: As stockades go, what are the conditions in this stockade?

REYNOLDS: I don't really know a lot about this stockade; it's got to be a lot better than LBJ, though.

FINN: Your feelings were apparently very strong about Vietnam before you went in. Do you have any reason to change those in any way?

REYNOLDS: I have a stronger hatred, and I know more about Vietnam, being over there myself, than I did before I came in. There was a lot of things I was misinformed on, then I found out when I was over there.

FINN: How do other G.I.'s on post, and in Vietnam, feel about your attitudes? I presume you expressed them when you were in Vietnam.

REYNOLDS: A lot of them disagreed with them, I got in plenty of fights about 'em. A lot of guys believed in why they were over there and they couldn't even tell me why they were over there. There's plenty of guys that do agree with my attitude, do agree with my feelings towards Vietnam. There's quite a number that don't believe in them too.

FINN: You were wounded in Vietnam?

REYNOLDS: Yeah, five times. I have something in my right leg. I was shot with an AK-47. I used to play basketball before I came in, but it put a cease to that. Sitting in one position for a long time, I have to move my legs to keep them from hurting.

FINN: You said you were wounded part of the time. Didn't that keep you out of combat?

REYNOLDS: The only time I really got out of combat was when I was sent to Japan to get my leg operated on. And most of the other time I was under fire, when I was not in the stockade. And I even came under fire quite a few times when I was in the stockade itself. Mortar fire. But I just went to the bunkers. They weren't about to give us any guns to go out and look for 'em.

FINN: You mentioned the terrible conditions of LBJ without any of the details.

REYNOLDS: Well, basically, you know, I don't think you can find anyplace else worse in the world to spend than LBJ, because there's always harassment. They *never* leave you alone. I was in maximum confinement. I went to regular confinement one day; I told an officer to kiss my ass. Some punk lieutenant just came in with his starched fatigues and the whole bit, and told me he'd personally shave every bit of hair off my head (because I had pretty long hair from being out in the field all the time). I told him, "Kiss my ass," and I was put in maximum. Of course, when he found out the charges of why I was in there he was planning on putting me in maximum anyway.

FINN: What does maximum mean?

REYNOLDS: Maximum confinement means you're worse than anybody else in that stockade and you're separated from the rest of 'em. They give you a lot more harassment. You get beaten more often than anybody else does. I never really did see anyone beaten in regular confinement. There was quite a bit of it in maximum. I mean, you could look at a guard crosseyed and tell him what kind of a man he was and he might smack you on the side of your head with a shotgun—it depends on how he feels.

FINN: Did most of the people there get clubbed once in a while, or was that just people who . . .

REYNOLDS: Well, usually you get beat up once in a while —at least once while you're in there. And if you give them any shit at all, like I did—I was constantly throwing it back in their face—I got beat seven times when I was in there for three months.

FINN: Were you especially harassed because of the reason you were in there?

REYNOLDS: For a while, in the first of the month. A lot of name-calling went on. But none of the other prisoners really held it against me. There was a couple of other guys in for the same charge and they never said anything about it. Once in a while I'd get into a hassle with the other prisoners . . . when they found out what I was in for. Most of the guys in maximum were in there for assault and battery with attempt to kill officers or first sergeants. Because there's a lot of officers and first sergeants that get killed over there; it wasn't no Charlie that put a hole in them.

FINN: When you were in Vietnam did you get much information about what was going on in this country and how critical things were?

REYNOLDS: I didn't get that information—how critical they were against the war. Mostly what we got were . . . One thing that really got me was when I got back from Nam, and after spending time in the stockade because I didn't want to shoot innocent people, I came into L.A. Airport and I had a lady walk up to me and call me a fucking butcher . . . just after I spent three months in there for *not* shooting at innocent civilians. I think that was what hit me worse of the whole thing. Because I can truthfully say, unless somebody was actually shooting at me, I'd let 'em go by. Unless they were shooting at me, I wouldn't shoot at them, because I didn't believe in it. That was one of the things: I never thought I could bring myself to kill anybody. When it came to the point where one guy was pointing a rifle right at me, and I knew he was going to pull that trigger, I had to pull it first to save my own life. That's basically what I did all the way through. That's why I was kind of glad I *was* grounded out of Aviation, because you don't know who you're shootin' from the air. You shoot at bushes mostly . . .

FINN: From your own experience would you say that the Son My incident was unusual or typical or likely or there'd be other incidents like that that would be fairly frequent?

REYNOLDS: I've never seen anything like it or heard anything like it. I've seen innocent civilians shot by guys; they just turn around and shoot one. Of course there are people like that over there.

FINN: Not under any orders to do so.

REYNOLDS: Not under any to do so. But I've seen quite a few innocent people shot over there. One thirteen-year-old girl especially. A guy shot her because he just felt like it. And I asked him why he shot her and he said he didn't have nothing else to do, and I went up and she didn't have anything that even looked like a gun on her. And I literally beat him until he couldn't stand up anymore, because it just pissed me off that bad. And I got a field grade Article 15 for assault and battery for beating him. He was a buck sergeant and I was a private, and that's why I was given a field grade. I've seen a lot of civilians shot when it wasn't actually the guy's fault. You know. They'll make a quick move or something and the guy will think they're going for a gun of some kind and they'll turn and fire. Almost every infantryman's seen that. It's a guy's reactions. I've still got quick reactions. That's part of what gets drilled into you after you spend some time in the field. Maybe I should call it "survival."

FINN: You say you were picked up for AWOL after being away for seven days. You either weren't very successful or you weren't making a big attempt to get very far.

REYNOLDS: No, I wasn't trying to go very far. After I'd been gone two days it was a matter of facing up to go back, because I had a thing at the time, a fear of going back to the stockade again after LBJ. I mean that kept me away until Friday, and then I says, "Well, you're going to have to go back again sometime."

FINN: If the M.P.'s hadn't picked you up, what would you have done?

REYNOLDS: I was on my way back here. I was in my fatigue uniform. I was walking to the bus station to take the bus back when they picked me up.

Appendix 1

PRIEST, R.
NAVY HOLD (FS)
June 6, 1969

Rear Admiral Means Johnston, USN
Chief of Legislative Liaison
Department of the Navy
Washington, D. C. 20350

Dear Admiral Johnston:

Today I received a copy of a publication
identified as having been prepared and
published by "R. Priest, U. S. Navy." The
publication, which is enclosed herewith for
your information, reflects a gross abuse of
the constitutional right of free speech.

I would appreciate being advised as to whether or not the alleged author is a member of the U. S. Navy.

In the event it is established that "R. Priest" is a member of the U. S. Navy, it is requested that the Judge Advocate General of the Navy provide me with an opinion as to whether or not this activity by the individual identified as "R. Priest" constitutes a violation of Navy regulations and/or a violation of Title 18, United States Code.

Finally, I would appreciate being informed as to what action you contemplate taking in this instance.

Sincerely,

L. Mendel Rivers
Chairman

Enclosure
LMR:fsk

COPY*COPY*COPY*COPY*COPY*COPY*COPY*COPY*COPY*

DEPARTMENT OF THE NAVY
OFFICE OF LEGISLATIVE AFFAIRS
WASHINGTON, D. C. 20350

IN REPLY REFER TO
LA-13:dn
6-1015:6-20
June 12, 1969

Dear Mr. Chairman:

   This is to acknowledge your recent letter
concerning a publication identified as having
been prepared and published by "R. Priest,
U. S. Navy."
   This matter is being investigated and I
will provide you with a complete report
shortly.

Sincerely yours,

J. M. HINGSON
Captain, U. S. Navy
Deputy Chief

Honorable L. Mendel Rivers, Chairman
Committee on Armed Services
2120 Rayburn Office Building
House of Representatives
Washington, D. C. 20515

DEPARTMENT OF THE NAVY
OFFICE OF LEGISLATIVE AFFAIRS
WASHINGTON, D. C. 20350

IN REPLY REFER TO
LA-13:dn
6-1015
June 20, 1969

Dear Mr. Chairman:

This is in reply to your recent correspondence concerning a publication identified as having been prepared and published by Seaman Apprentice Roger L. Priest, United States Navy.

The Judge Advocate General has informed me that a preliminary inquiry indicates the probability that offenses have been committed by Seaman Priest arising out of his publication and dissemination of a publication primarily for the consumption of military personnel. He is assigned to the U. S. Naval Station, Washington, D. C. pending investigation and further disposition.

It has been determined that Seaman Priest will be processed for a pretrial investigation on appropriate charges resulting from a preliminary inquiry. Although not final, such charges include about twenty or more specifications under several articles of the Uniform Code of Military Justice. Included therein are the following:

Article 82 - Soliciting others to desert in violation of Article 85

Soliciting others to commit
sedition in violation of
Article 94

Article 92 - Violation of U. S. Navy
Regulations, 1948 (Article
1252 - Disclosure and
Publication of Information)

Article 134 - Conduct to the prejudice of
good order and discipline
(disloyal statements)

Violation of Title 18, section
2387 (activities affecting
armed forces generally)
LA-13:dn
6-1015

I trust that the foregoing will be of
assistance to you.

Sincerely yours,

MEANS JOHNSTON, JR.
Rear Admiral, U. S. Navy
Chief of Legislative Affairs

Honorable L. Mendel Rivers, Chairman
Committee on Armed Services
2120 Rayburn Office Building
House of Representatives
Washington, D. C. 20515

Appendix 2

FOR OFFICIAL USE ONLY

ALCDGB   14 October 1969
SUBJECT: Preparations for Vietnam Moratorium -
15 Oct 69

.

   (1) Roberts: 46th Arty cannot come up with
any sound, above criticism type reason to
keep Roberts on post. The best they have to
offer so far is that Roberts may accompany
LTC Munson (XO) on an evening Army Aircraft
flight and be forced into an RON. This is
pretty flimsy at best.

   (2) Stocker: 47th Hosp cannot devise any
logical, reasonable action to be taken which
would not be highly suspicious (Comment: I

believe there is good reason to expect
Stocker's appearance in Acacia Park during the
evening of 15 Oct, since this area is his old
"stomping ground").

(3) Tipton (169th Engr Co): EM is a POL man
in unit which is preparing for CMMI. May be
employed thusly on evening of 15 Oct or may be
engaged in a platoon "GI Party" as a result of
a poor showing during Co Cmdr's inspection
(This is a normal activity during the week).

(4) Rozier (115th Petrol Co): EM will be on
guard. He was due either today or tomorrow.
This situation helped make the decision.

(5) Boyd (5th Med Bn): Acting as a clerk in
the company. With the influx of new officers
and NCO's, Boyd will be engaged in cutting
new unit orders (eg, CBR Off/NCO etc) which
will occupy him until approximately 2200 hrs.

c. It is obvious from the above that the two
most sensitive personnel (Roberts and Stocker)
are also the ones for which it is the most
difficult to justify detention. Certainly
any reason for detaining from going downtown
will be liable for scrutiny in <u>Aboveground.</u>
Rather than detain or deter these two from
the rally, another approach might be to let
them go. They are within their "legal rights"
to decry the Vietnam War. However, if they
overstep their bounds and counsel
insubordination or disloyalty they are then
liable for punitive action.

7. In summary:
   a. A "Huey" with bull-horn is laid on.
   b. The Garden Plot company is alerted.

c. Coverage of the rally in Acacia Park is planned.

d. There is some difficulty in "profitably engaging" all 5 of our potential problem children.

FOR OFFICIAL USE ONLY

Appendix 3

COPY   COPY   COPY

May 6, 1969
NUMBER 5210.56
GC, DoD

DEPARTMENT OF DEFENSE DIRECTIVE

SUBJECT   Use of Force by Personnel Engaged in
Law Enforcement and Security Duties

I. <u>PURPOSE</u>

This Directive establishes uniform policy
guidance concerning the use of force by
all military and civilian personnel of

the Department of Defense engaged in law
enforcement or security duties.

II. APPLICABILITY

The provisions of this Directive apply to
all personnel of all components of the
Department of Defense engaged in law
enforcement or security duties wherever
located throughout the world but not to
personnel assigned to duty in the
following areas or situations, as defined
by executive order or DoD directive:

1. Combat zone in time of war.
2. Designated hostile fire area not in
time of war.
3. Service with the U. S. Secret
Service.
4. Civil disturbance objective area.

III. POLICY

A. The responsibility of personnel
engaged in law enforcement or
security duties normally extends to
the protection of persons and
property, to the apprehension of
individuals reasonably believed to
have committed offences, and to the
guarding of prisoners. Personnel
engaged in law enforcement or
security activities will avoid the
use of force when the assigned
responsibilities can be discharged
without resort to its use. If
security and law enforcement

responsibilities cannot be discharged
without resort to the use of force,
personnel shall use the minimum amount
of force necessary to discharge their
assigned responsibilities. Deadly
force (defined below) may be used
only under the circumstances
discussed in section IV. and subject
to the restrictions set forth in
section V.

B. Commanders are encouraged to
substitute nonlethal devices such as
night sticks for firearms when use of
the latter is not necessary for the
proper performance of law enforcement
or security duties.

C. It shall not be permissible to
conceive an offense against the law
and then, with a view to subsequent
prosecution of a particular
individual, induce that individual
to commit the offense. Such
provocation on the part of law
enforcement or security personnel by
entrapment will not be authorized
or permitted under any circumstances.

IV. <u>DEADLY</u> <u>FORCE</u>

A. Deadly force is that force which
a person uses with the purpose
of causing-or which he knows, or
should know, would create a
substantial risk of causing-death or
serious bodily harm. Its use is
justified only under conditions of

extreme necessity as a last resort,
when all lesser means have failed
or cannot reasonably be employed, and
only under one or more of the
following circumstances:

1. Self-defense. When deadly force
   reasonably appears to be necessary
   to protect law enforcement or
   security personnel who reasonably
   believe themselves to be in
   imminent danger of death or serious
   bodily harm.

2. Property involving national
   security. When deadly force
   reasonably appears to be necessary
   (a) to prevent the threatened
   theft of, damage to, or espionage
   aimed at property or information
   specifically designated by a
   commander or other competent
   authority as vital to the national
   security; (b) to prevent the
   actual theft of, damage to or
   espionage aimed at property or
   information which-though not vital
   to the national security-is of
   substantial importance to the
   national security; or (c) to
   apprehend or prevent the
   escape of an individual whose
   unauthorized presence in the
   vicinity of property or information
   vital to the national security
   reasonably appears to present a

threat of theft, sabotage or
espionage. Property shall be
specifically designated as vital
to the national security only
when its loss, damage or
compromise would seriously
prejudice national security or
jeopardize the fulfillment of an
essential national defense mission.

3. Serious offenses against persons.
   When deadly force reasonably
   appears to be necessary to
   prevent the commission of a serious
   offense involving violence and
   threatening death or serious
   bodily harm (such as arson, armed
   robbery, aggravated assault or
   rape).

4. Apprehension. When deadly
   force reasonably appears to be
   necessary to apprehend or prevent
   the escape of a person
   reasonably believed to have
   committed an offense of the nature
   specified in subsections IV.A.2.
   and IV.A.3.

5. Escapes. When deadly force has
   been specifically authorized
   by competent authority and
   reasonably appears to be necessary
   to prevent the escape of a
   prisoner.

6. Lawful order. When directed
   by the lawful order of a superior

authority who shall be governed
by the provisions of this
Directive.

B. In order to comply with local
law a commander may impose further
restrictions on the use of
deadly force if in his judgment
such restrictions would not
unduly compromise important security
interests of the United States.

V. ADDITIONAL CONSIDERATIONS INVOLVING
FIREARMS

If in any of the circumstances set
forth in section IV. it becomes
necessary to use a firearm, the following
precautions shall be observed,
provided it is possible to do so
consistent with the prevention of
death or serious bodily harm:

A. An order to halt shall be given
before a shot is fired.

B. Shots shall not be fired if they
are likely to endanger the
safety of innocent bystanders.

C. Shots shall be aimed to disable.
However, if circumstances render it
difficult to direct fire
with sufficient precision to
assure that the person will be
disabled rather than killed, such

circumstances will not preclude
the use of a firearm, provided such
use is otherwise authorized by
this Directive.

VI. <u>INSTRUCTION</u>

A. No individual will be permitted
   to perform law enforcement or
   security duties until he has received
   instruction on applicable
   regulations relating to the use
   of force in the performance of such
   duties. In addition, instruction
   will be given periodically to
   all personnel assigned to these
   duties to insure that they
   continue to be thoroughly familiar
   with all restrictions on the
   use of force.

B. All personnel shall be instructed
   that it is not permissible to
   induce an individual to commit
   an offense against the law for the
   purpose of providing a basis for
   subsequent prosecution. Such
   provocation by way of entrapment
   will not be authorized or permitted
   under any circumstances.

VII. <u>IMPLEMENTATION AND EFFECTIVE DATE</u>

The provisions of this Directive
will be effective ninety days
from the date of issuance. All military
departments and all affected

DoD agencies will issue
implementing regulations and will revise
existing regulations to conform with
the provisions of this Directive,
as necessary. Regulations which
implement this Directive in overseas
areas should be framed, if appropriate,
in the light of applicable provisions
of international agreements or
arrangements relating to law enforcement
and security matters. Implementing
regulations will be forwarded to
the General Counsel, Department of
Defense, within 90 days of the issuance
date of this Directive.

Deputy Secretary of Defense

COPY   COPY   COPY   COPY   COPY   COPY   COPY

ANNEX C

DEPARTMENT OF THE ARMY
OFFICE OF THE ADJUTANT GENERAL
WASHINGTON, D.C. 20310

(Department of
Defense Seal)

                in reply refer to
AGAM-P (M) (27 May 69) DCSPER-SARD
SUBJECT: Guidance on Dissent

SEE DISTRIBUTION

1. In the past few weeks there have been press
reports suggesting a growth in dissent
among military personnel. Questions have
been raised concerning the proper treatment
of manifestations of soldier dissent
when they occur. The purpose of this letter
is to provide general guidance on this
matter. Specific dissent problems can, of
course, be resolved only on the basis
of the particular facts of the situation and
in accordance with provisions of
applicable Army regulations.

2. It is important to recognize that the
question of "soldier dissent" is linked with
the Constitutional right of free speech
and that the Army's reaction to such
dissent will--quite properly--continue

to receive much attention in the news media.
Any action taken at any level may
therefore reflect--either favorably or
adversely--on the image and standing of the
Army with the American public. Many
cases involve difficult legal questions,
requiring careful development of the
factual situation and application of various
constitutional, statutory, and regulatory
provisions (See Appendix A). Consequently,
commanders should consult with their Staff
Judge Advocates and may in appropriate cases
confer with higher authority before
initiating any disciplinary or administrative
action in response to manifestations of
dissent. The maintenance of good
order and discipline and the performance
of military missions remains, of course, the
responsibility of commanders.

3. "Dissent," in the literal sense of
disagreement with policies of the
Government, is a right of every citizen.
In our system of Government, we do not ask
that every citizen or every soldier agree
with every policy of the Government.
Indeed, the First Amendment to the
Constitution requires that one be permitted
to believe what he will. Nevertheless,
the Government and our citizens are entitled
to expect that, regardless of disagreement,
every citizen and every soldier will
obey the law of the land.

4. The right to express opinions on matters
of public and personal concern is
secured to soldier and civilian alike by

the Constitution and laws of the United
States. This right, however, is not absolute
for either soldier or civilian. Other
functions and interests of the Government
and the public, which are also sanctioned
and protected by the Constitution, and
are also important to a free, democratic and
lawful society, may require reasonable
limitations on the exercise of the right
of expression in certain circumstances.
In particular, the interest of the
Government and the public in the maintenance
of an effective and disciplined Army for
the purpose of National defense justifies
certain restraints upon the activities
of military personnel which need not be
imposed on similiar activities by civilians.

5. The following general guidelines are
provided to cover some of the manifestations
of dissent which the Army has encountered.

   a. Possession and distribution of
      political materials.

     (1) In the case of publications
distributed through official outlets such
as Post Exchanges and Post Libraries, a
commander is authorized to delay distribution
of a specific issue of a publication in
accordance with the provisions of para. 5-5,
of AR 210-10. Concurrent with the delay,
a commander must submit a report to the
Department of the Army, ATTN: CINFO.
A commander may delay distribution only if
he determines that the specific publication
presents a clear danger to the loyalty,
discipline, or morale of his troops.

(2) In the case of distribution of
publications through other than official
outlets, a commander may require that prior
approval be obtained for any distribution on
post. Distribution without prior approval may
be prohibited. A commander's denial of
authority to distribute a publication on post
is subject to the procedures of para. 5-5,
AR 210-10, discussed above.

(3) A commander may not prevent distribution
of a publication simply because he does not
like its contents. All denials of permission
for distribution must be in accordance with
the provisions of para. 5-5, AR 210-10. For
example, a commander may prohibit distribution
of publications which are obscene or otherwise
unlawful (e.g., counselling disloyalty,
mutiny, or refusal of duty). A commander may
also prohibit distribution if the manner of
accomplishing the distribution materially
interferes with the accomplishment of a
military mission (e.g., interference with
training or troop formation). In any event,
a commander must have cogent reasons, with
supporting evidence, for any denial of
distribution privileges. The fact that a
publication is critical -- even unfairly
critical -- of government policies or
officials is not in itself, a grounds for
denial.

(4) Mere possession of a publication may not
be prohibited; however, possession of an
unauthorized publication coupled with an
attempt to distribute in violation of post
regulations may constitute an offense.
Accordingly, cases involving the possession

of several copies of an unauthorized
publication or other circumstances (sic)
indicating an intent to distribute should
be investigated.

b. Coffee Houses.

The Army should not use its off-limits
power to restrict soldiers in the exercise of
their Constitutional rights of freedom of
speech and freedom of association by barring
attendance at coffee houses, unless it can
be shown, for example, that activities taking
place in the coffee houses include counselling
soldiers to refuse to perform duty or to
desert, or otherwise involve illegal acts with
a significant adverse effect on soldier
health, morale or welfare. In such
curcumstances (sic), commanders have the
authority to place such establishments "off
limits" in accordance with the standards and
procedures of AR 15-3. As indicated, such
action should be taken only on the basis of
cogent reasons, supported by evidence.

c. "Servicemen's Union."

Commanders are not authorized to
recognize or to bargain with a "servicemen's
union." In view of the constitutional right
to freedom of association, it is unlikely
that mere membership in a "servicemen's union"
can constitutionally be prohibited, and
current regulations do not prohibit such
membership. However, specific actions by
individual members of a "servicemen's union"
which in themselves constitute offenses under
the Uniform Code of Military Justice or Army

Regulations may be dealt with appropriately.
Collective or individual refusals to obey
orders are one example of conduct which may
constitute an offense under the Uniform Code.

d. Publication of "Underground Newspapers."

Army regulations provide that personal
literary efforts may not be pursued during
duty hours or accomplished by the use of Army
property. However, the publication of
"underground newspapers" by soldiers off-post,
on their own time, and with their own money
and equipment is generally protected under
the First Amendment's guarantees of freedom
of speech and freedom of the press. Unless
such a newspaper contains language, the
utterance of which is punishable under Federal
law (e.g. 10 U.S.C. Sec. 2837 of the Uniform
Code of Military Justice), authors of an
"underground newspaper" may not be disciplined
for mere publication. Distribution of such
newspapers on post is governed by para. 5-5,
AR 210-10, discussed in para. 5a above.

e. On-Post Demonstrations by Civilians.

A commander may legally bar individuals
from entry on a military reservation for any
purpose prohibited by law or lawful
regulation, and it is a crime for any person
who has been removed and barred from a post
by order of the commander to re-enter.
However, a specific request for a permit to
conduct an on-post demonstration in an area
to which the public has generally been granted
access should not be denied on an arbitrary
basis. Such a permit may be denied on a

reasonable basis such as a showing that the
demonstration may result in a clear
interference with or prevention of orderly
accomplishment of the mission of the post, or
present a clear danger to loyalty,
discipline, and morale of the troops.

f. <u>On-Post Demonstrations by Soldiers</u>.

AR 600-20 and 600-21 prohibit all on-post
demonstrations by members of the Army. The
validity of these provisions is currently
being litigated. Commanders will be advised
of the results of this litigation.

g. <u>Off-Post Demonstrations by Soldiers</u>.

AR 600-20 and 600-21 prohibit members of
the Army from participating in off-post
demonstrations when they are in uniform, or
on duty, or in a foreign country, or when
their activities constitute a breach of law
and order, or when violence is likely to
result.

h. <u>Grievances</u>.

The right of members to complain and
request redress of grievance against actions
of their superiors is protect by the Inspector
General system (AR 20-1) and Article 138,
UCMJ. In addition, a soldier may petition or
present any grievance to any member of
Congress (19 USC, Sec. 1034). An open door
policy for complaints is a basic principle of
good leadership, and commanders should
personally assure themselves that adequate
procedures exist for identifying valid

complaints and taking corrective action.
Complaining personnel must not be treated as
"enemies of the system." Even when complaints
are unfounded, the fact that one was made
may signal a misunderstanding, or a lack of
communication, which should be corrected. In
any system as large as the Army, it is
inevitable that situations will occur giving
rise to valid complaints, and over the years
such complaints have helped to make the Army
stronger while assuring compliance with proper
policies and procedures.

6. It is the policy of the Department of the
Army to safeguard the service member's right of
expression to the maximum extent possible, and
to impose only such minimum restraints as are
necessary to enable the Army to perform its
mission, in the interest of National defense.
The statutes and regulations referred to above
(as well as other provisions of law and
regulations) are concerned with these
permissible restraints and authorize a
commander to impose restrictions on the
military members's (sic) right of expression
and dissent, under certain circumstances.
However, in applying any such statutes and
regulation in particular situations, it is
important to remember that freedom of
expression is a fundamental right secured by
the Constitution. Furthermore, it is important
to remember that the Commander's
responsibility is for the good order, loyalty
and discipline of all his men. Severe
disciplinary action in response to a
relatively insignificant manifestation of
dissent can have a counter productive effect
on other members of the Command, because the

reaction appears out of proportion to the
threat which the dissent represents. Thus,
rather than serving as a deterrent, such
disproportionate actions may stimulate
further breaches of discipline. On the other
hand, no Commander should be indifferent to
conduct which, if allowed to proceed
unchecked, would destroy the effectiveness of
his unit. In the final analysis no
regulations or guidelines are an adequate
substitute for the calm and prudent judgment
of the responsible commander.

7. The mission of the Army is to execute
faithfully, as ordered, policies and programs
established in accordance with law by duly
elected and appointed Government officials.
Unquestionably, the vast majority of service
members are prepared to do what is required
of them to perform that mission, whether or
not they agree in every instance with the
policies the mission reflects.

BY ORDER OF THE SECRETARY OF THE ARMY:

(signed)
KENNETH G. WICKHAM
Major General, USA
The Adjutant General

1 Incl
App A

DISTRIBUTION:
Commanders in Chief
U.S. Army, Europe
U.S. Army, Pacific

Commanding Generals
    U.S. Continental Army Command
    U.S. Army Materiel Command
    U.S. Army, Alaska
Commander, U.S. Army Forces Southern Command

Copies furnished:
Commanding Generals
    CONUS Armies
    Military District of Washington, U.S. Army

COPY   COPY   COPY   COPY   COPY   COPY   COPY

COPY-COPY-COPY-COPY-COPY-COPY-COPY-COPY-COPY

September 12, 1969
NUMBER 1325.6
ASD(M&RA)

(Department of
Defense seal)

DEPARTMENT OF DEFENSE DIRECTIVE

SUBJECT Guidelines for Handling Dissent and
Protest Activities Among Members of
the Armed Forces

References: (a) U. S. Constitution, First
Amendment
(b) Title 50, U. S. Code Appendix,
Section 462
(c) Title 18, U. S. Code, Sections
1381, 2387, 2385, 2388
(d) Title 10, U. S. Code, Chapter
47 (Uniform Code of Military
Justice)
(e) DoD Directive 1334.1, "Wearing
of the Uniform," August 11,
1969

I. PURPOSE AND APPLICABILITY

This Directive provides general guidance
governing the handling of dissident
activities by members on active duty of
the Army, Navy, Air Force, and Marine
Corps. Specific problems can, of course,
be resolved only on the basis of the
particular facts of the situation and in
accordance with the provisions of

applicable Department regulations and the
Uniform Code of Military Justice.

II. <u>POLICY</u>

It is the mission of the Department of
Defense to safeguard the security of the
United States. The service member's
right of expression should be preserved
to the maximum extent possible,
consistent with good order and discipline
and the national security. On the other
hand, no Commander should be indifferent
to conduct which, if allowed to proceed
unchecked, would destroy the
effectiveness of his unit. The proper
balancing of these interests will depend
largely upon the calm and prudent
judgment of the responsible Commander.

III. <u>SPECIFIC GUIDELINES</u>

The following guidelines relate to
principal activities in this area which
the Armed Forces have encountered:

A. <u>Possession and Distribution of Printed</u>
   <u>Materials</u>

   1. A Commander is not authorized to
      prohibit the distribution of a
      specific issue of a publication
      distributed through official
      outlets such as post exchanges and
      military libraries. In the case of
      distribution of publications
      through other than official
      outlets, a Commander may require

that prior approval be obtained for
any distribution on a military
installation in order that he may
determine whether there is a clear
danger to the loyalty, discipline,
or morale of military personnel, or
if the distribution of the
publication would materially
interfere with accomplishment of a
military mission. When he makes
such a determination, the
distribution will be prohibited.

2. While the mere possession of
unauthorized printed material may
not be prohibited, printed material
which is prohibited from
distribution shall be impounded
if the Commander determines that
an attempt will be made to
distribute.

3. The fact that a publication is
critical of Government policies or
officials is not, in itself, a
ground upon which distribution may
be prohibited.

B. Off-Post Gathering Places. Commanders
have the authority to place
establishments "Off-limits," in
accordance with established
procedures, when for example, the
activities taking place there,
including counselling members to
refuse to perform duty or to desert,
involve acts with a significant

adverse effect on member's health,
morale, or welfare.

C. <u>Servicemen's Organizations.</u>
Commanders are not authorized to
recognize or to bargain with so-called
"servicemen's unions."

D. <u>Publication of "Underground
Newspapers."</u> Personal writing for
publication may not be pursued during
duty hours, or accomplished by use of
Government or non-appropriated fund
property. While publication of
"underground newspapers" by military
personnel off-post, on their own time
and with their own money and
equipment, is not prohibited, if such
a publication contains language the
utterance of which is punishable under
Federal law, those involved in the
printing, publication, or distribution
may be disciplined for such
infractions.

E. <u>On-Post Demonstrations and Similar
Activities.</u> The Commander of a
military installation shall prohibit
any demonstration or activity on the
installation which could result in
interference with or prevention of
orderly accomplishment of the mission
of the installation, or present a
clear danger to loyalty, discipline,
or morale of the troops. It is a
crime for any person to enter a
military reservation for any purpose
prohibited by law or lawful

regulations, or for any person to
enter or re-enter an installation
after having been barred by order of
the Commander (18 U.S.C. 1382).

F. Off-Post Demonstrations by Members.
Members of the Armed Forces are
prohibited from participating in
off-post demonstrations when they are
on duty, or in a foreign country, or
when their activities constitute a
breach of law and order, or when
violence is likely to result, or when
they are in uniform in violation of
DoD Directive 1334.1 (reference (e)).

G. Grievances. The right of members to
complain and request redress of
grievances against actions of their
commanders is protected by Article 138
of the Uniform Code of Military
Justice. In addition, a member may
petition or present any grievance to
any member of Congress (10 U.S.C.
1034). An open door policy for
complaints is a basic principle of
good leadership, and Commanders should
personally assure themselves that
adequate procedures exist for
identifying valid complaints and
taking corrective action.

IV. EFFECTIVE DATE AND IMPLEMENTATION

This Directive is effective immediately.
Two (2) copies of implementing
regulations shall be forwarded to the
Assistant Secretary of Defense (Manpower

and Reserve Affairs) within ninety (90)
days.

                              (signed)
                         MELVIN H. LAIRD
                         Secretary of Defense
Enclosure - 1
  Constitutional and Statutory Provisions

                    Sept 12, 69
                    1325.6
   COPY   COPY   COPY   COPY   COPY   COPY

Sept 12, 69
1325.6 (Encl 1)

CONSTITUTIONAL AND STATUTORY PROVISIONS
RELEVANT TO HANDLING OF DISSIDENT AND
PROTEST ACTIVITIES IN THE ARMED FORCES

A. Constitution: The First Amendment, U.S.
   Constitution provides as follows:
      "Congress shall make no law . . .
      abridging the freedom of speech, or of
      the press; or the right of the people
      peaceably to assemble, and to petition
      the Government for a redress of
      grievances."

B. Statutory Provisions:

   1. Applicable to All Persons

      a. 18 U.S.C. 1381 -- Enticing desertion.
      b. 18 U.S.C. 2385 -- Advocating
         overthrow of the Government.
      c. 18 U.S.C. 2387 -- Counselling
         insubordination, disloyalty, mutiny,
         or refusal of duty.
      d. 18 U.S.C. 2388 -- Causing or
         attempting to cause insubordination.
      e. 50 U.S.C. App. 462 -- Counselling
         evasion of the draft.

2. Applicable to Members of the Armed Forces

    a. 10 U.S.C. 917 (Article 117, UCMJ) -- Provoking speech or gestures.

    b. 10 U.S.C. 882 (Article 82, UCMJ) -- Soliciting desertion, mutiny, sedition, or misbehavior before the enemy.

    c. 10 U.S.C. 904 (Article 104, UCMJ) -- Communication or corresponding with the enemy.

    d. 10 U.S.C. 901 (Article 101, UCMJ) -- Betraying a countersign.

    e. 10 U.S.C. 888 (Article 88, UCMJ) -- Contemptuous words by commissioned officers against certain officials.

    f. 10 U.S.C. 889 (Article 89, UCMJ) -- Disrespect toward his superior commissioned officer.

    g. 10 U.S.C. 891 (Article 91, UCMJ) -- Disrespect toward a warrant officer or noncommissioned officer in the execution of his office.

    h. 10 U.S.C. 892 (Article 92, UCMJ) -- Failure to obey a lawful order or regulation.

    i. 10 U.S.C. 934 (Article 134, UCMJ) -- Uttering disloyal statement, criminal libel, communicating a threat, and soliciting another to commit an offense.

Appendix 4

G.I. Anti-war Papers
(as of August 1970)

A Four Year Bummer
  (Chanute AFB)
Box 2325, Sta. A
Champaign, Ill. 61820

About Face (Camp Pendleton)
Box 54099
Los Angeles, Cal. 94709

Aerospaced (Grisson AFB)
Box 1015
Kokomo, Ind. 46801

Ally (San Francisco)
Box 9276
Berkeley, Cal. 94709

As You Were (Ft. Ord)
Box 1062
Monterey, Cal. 93930

Attitude Check
  (Camp Pendleton)
Box 1356
Vista, Cal. 92083

AWOL Press (Ft. Riley)
Box 425
Manhattan, Kansas 66502

Bayonet (Presidio)
Box 31387
San Francisco, Cal. 94131

The Bond
156 5th Ave., Rm 633
New York, N.Y. 10010

Bragg Briefs (Ft. Bragg)
Box 437
Spring Lake, N.C. 28309

Broken Arrow (Selfridge AFB)
Box 471
Ft. Clemens, Mich. 48043

Chessman
Box 187
Frogmore, S.C. 29920

Counter Attack (Ft. Carson)
Box 1594
Colorado Springs, Colo. 80903

Counterpoint (McChord AFB)
515 20th East
Seattle, Wash. 98102

Drum (Ft. Hamilton)
649 Fulton St.
Brooklyn, N.Y. 11217

Duck Power (San Diego)
751 Turquoise
San Diego, Cal. 92109

Dull Brass (Ft. Sheridan)
9 S. Clinton Rm. 225
Chicago, Ill. 60606

Eyes Left (Travis AFB)
Box 31387
San Francisco, Cal. 94131

Fatigue Press (Ft. Hood)
101 Ave. D
Killeen, Texas 76541

Fed Up (Ft. Lewis)
Box 414
Tacoma, Wash. 98409

Final Flight (Hamilton AFB)
Box 31387
San Francisco, Cal. 94131

Forward March (Annapolis)
38 Maryland Ave.
Annapolis, Md. 21401

FTA (Ft. Knox)
Box 336
Louisville, Ky. 40201

GAF (Barksdale AFB)
525 Wichita
Shreveport, La. 71101

GI Voice
Box 825
New York, N.Y. 10009

Gigline (Ft. Bliss)
Box 31094
Summit Hts. Station
#1 Paso, Texas 79931

Good Times
1550 Howard St.
San Francisco, Cal. 94103

The Green Machine
   (Ft. Greely, Alaska)
Box 2697
Fairbanks, Alas. 99701

Head On
Box 822
Havelock, N.C. 28532

Last Harass (Ft. Gordon)
Box 2994 Hill Station
Augusta, Ga. 30904

Left Face (McClellan)
Box 1595
Anniston, Ala. 36201

The Looper (NG)
Box 31387
San Francisco, Cal. 94131

Navy Times Are Changin'
Box 164
North Chicago, Ill. 60064

Napalmed (Ft. Campbell)
Box 44
Clarksville, Tenn.

Oak
Box 31387
San Francisco, Cal. 94131

The Obligore (Nas N.U.)
Box 732
New York, N.Y. 10022

The O.D.D.
1434 Makaloa St., Rm. 9
Honolulu, Hawaii 96814

OM (D.C. area)
1029 Vermont Ave., N.W.
Washington, D.C. 20005

Open Ranks
315 E 25th St.
Baltimore, Md. 21218

Open Sights (D.C. area)
1029 Vermont Ave., N.W.
Washington, D.C. 20005

The Pawn
Box 481
Frederick, Md. 21701

Rap (Ft. Benning)
Box 894 Main Post Office
Columbus, Ga. 31902

Rough Draft
(Norfolk Naval Sta.)
Box 1205
Norfolk, Va. 23501

Shakedown (Ft. Dix)
Box 68
Wrightstown, N.J. 08640

Short Times (Ft. Jackson)
Box 543
Columbia, S.C. 29202

Top Secret (Ft. Devens)
19 Brookline St.
Cambridge, Mass. 02139

Truth Instead (Treasure Is.)
Box 31387
San Francisco, Cal. 94131

Task Force B
Box 31387
San Francisco, Cal. 94131

Twin Cities Protester
(Ft. Snelling)
529 Cedar Ave.
Minneapolis, Minn. 55409

Up Front
Box 60329 Terminal Annex
Los Angeles, Cal. 90060

USAF
221 Xenia
Yellow Springs, Ohio 45387

Vets Stars & Stripes for Peace
Box 4598
Chicago, Ill. 60680

Vietnam GI
Box 9237
Chicago, Ill. 60690

Your Military Left
(Ft. Sam Houston)
Box 561
San Antonio, Texas 78206

OVERSEAS:

We got the brASS
c/o Socialist Club
6 Frankfurt 1 Postfach 2441
Germany

Where It's At
1 Berlin 12
Postfach 65 Germany

We got the brASS
c/o Beheiren
Ishii Bldg 6-44 Kagurazaka
Shinjuku-ku, Tokto, Japan

COFFEEHOUSES:

Shelter Half (Ft. Lewis)
5437 S. Tacoma Way
Tacoma, Wash.

Oleo Strut (Ft. Hood)
101 Ave. D
Killeen, Texas 76541

Green Machine
  (Camp Pendleton)
Oceanside, Cal.

Home Front (Ft. Carson)
Colorado Springs, Colo.

Ft. Ord Coffee House
Box 359
Seaside, Cal.

Long Beach MDM
523 W. 6th St.
Long Beach, Cal.

Index

About the Editor

JAMES FINN is editor of *worldview* and director of publications for the Council on Religion and International Affairs, and was previously an editor of *Commonweal.* He has taught at a number of universities, including the University of Nebraska, the University of Chicago and New York University. Mr. Finn, who was educated at the University of Chicago, saw combat as a private in the infantry in World War II. His widely praised *Protest: Pacifism and Politics* was published in 1968, and was followed by *A Conflict of Loyalties: The Case for Selective Conscientious Objection,* which he edited; his articles have appeared in the *New York Times, Christianity and Crisis,* the *New Republic,* and the *National Catholic Reporter.*

Mr. Finn was born in Gary, Indiana; he now lives in New York City with his wife and five children.

About the Contributors

Edward F. Sherman, who received an LL.B. from the Harvard Law School and is presently a member of the Law School faculty at Indiana University, has completed a study of military justice entitled *The Civilianization of Military Law.* For two years he served as Army captain in the Judge Advocate General's Corps, and has filed briefs on behalf of military defendants in some of the most significant cases of recent years.

Luther C. West served as an enlisted man in the Navy during World War II, received his law degree from George Washington Law School. After becoming a member of the Maryland Bar and serving as attorney for the Federal Power Commission he was, for seventeen years, a member of the regular Army, where he served in the Judge Advocate General's Corps and from which he retired with the rank of lieutenant colonel. After completing a book on the trial of Lieutenant William Calley, he will become an active partner of Grant, Harris, Huddles and Rosenblatt.

Leonard B. Boudin is a member of the New York and federal bars, specializing in constitutional law. In addition to serving as general counsel for the National Emergency Civil Liberties Committee he is Visiting Professor From Practice, Harvard Law School, for 1970–71.

Dr. Peter G. Bourne, who served as a captain in the Army, received a Bronze Star and Air Medal during Vietnam service as chief of a Walter Reed Army Medical Center research team studying stress. Now a member of the Department of Psychiatry at Emory University Medical School, he is the author of several books, the most recent being *Men, Stress and Viet Nam,* and many scholarly articles.

DATE DUE

MAR 0 5 2001

10. 15. 81

BRODART, INC.

Cat. No. 23-221